CW01024887

DOGS
OF THE SHEPHERDS

A Review of the Pastoral Breeds

DOGS
OF THE SHEPHERDS

A Review of the Pastoral Breeds

DAVID HANCOCK

THE CROWOOD PRESS

Previous Books by the Author
Dogs As Companions – 1981
Old Working Dogs – 1984 (reprinted 1998 and 2011)
The Heritage of the Dog – 1990
The Bullmastiff – A Breeder's Guide Vol 1 – 1996
The Bullmastiff – A Breeder's Guide Vol 2 – 1997
Old Farm Dogs – 1999
The Mastiffs – The Big Game Hunters – 2006 (six editions)
The Bullmastiff – A Breeder's Guide – 2006 (one volume hardback edition)
The World of the Lurcher – 2010
Sporting Terriers – Their Form, Their Function & Their Future – 2011
Sighthounds – Their Form, Their Function & Their Future – 2012
Gundogs – Their Past, Their Performance and Their Prospects – 2013
Hounds – Hunting by Scent – 2014

First published in 2014 by
The Crowood Press Ltd
Ramsbury, Marlborough
Wiltshire SN8 2HR

www.crowood.com

© David Hancock 2014

British Library Cataloguing-in-Publication Data
A catalogue record for this book is available from the British Library.

ISBN 978 1 84797 808 0

Page 1: Highland shepherd's boy with Collies, c.1870.
Page 2: *The Good Shepherd* by Richard Ansdell, 1870.
Page 3: The dog of the flock – working Collie of 1858.
Page 4: The shepherd's dog.

Typeset and designed by D & N Publishing, Baydon, Wiltshire

Printed and bound in Singapore by Craft Print International

CONTENTS

White-headed, white-fronted prize-winning trials working sheepdog.

DEDICATION

This book is dedicated to the shepherds of the world. For centuries, in every type of terrain and climate, they have devotedly not only tended their flocks and herds but bred and developed a whole range of quite remarkable dogs, able to fend off all manner of wild beasts and human threats, then herd or drive vulnerable livestock from old pasture to new pasture and often to distant markets. From the high-altitude grazing grounds of the Himalayas and the windswept steppes of Eurasia, to the hot dry pastures of East and South Africa northwards to the wet hill farms of Wales, Scotland and the Lake District and the flat, sometimes recently drained fields of the Low Countries, shepherds have used talented dogs to aid them. These dogs have varied from the giant flock guardians to the diminutive heelers, but have one thing in common: the management of livestock for man. Compared to sporting dogs, little has been written of such dogs and even less about their masters. Shepherds have sometimes been philosophical but rarely literate; there is comparatively very little on record about them or their dogs. This book is a tribute to the shepherds who used, bred and developed the quite admirable breeds of dog that still remain with us. We have a duty to perpetuate their impressive work by breeding the pastoral dogs of today to their criteria: sound, robust, functional and yet so often extremely handsome. It is worth remembering that on just one day, 24 January 1794, nineteen shepherds and forty-five sheepdogs perished in a severe storm in the south of Scotland. We owe the shepherds of our islands and the world a deep debt of gratitude – for their work and, especially, for their dogs.

Shepherd of 1875.
COL. JOSEPH GALE, MUSEUM OF RURAL LIFE.

ABOVE LEFT: *Shepherd of the Transylvanian Alps with his Romanian Sheepdog.*

ABOVE RIGHT: *Portuguese Shepherd with his Rafeiro do Alentejo.*

The Highland Flock *by Thomas Sidney Cooper, 1887.*

PREFACE

The group in which the sheepdogs are included is characterised by a high order of intelligence. In order that their duties may be performed creditably they must be sensible, tractable and hardy. Besides learning readily the lessons that are taught them at an early age, they must acquire certain powers of initiative that are shown sometimes in a form so remarkable as to make one wonder if psychologists are justified in denying the faculty of reasoning to dogs.

Arthur Croxton Smith, *About our Dogs*

The value of shepherds to the human race over many centuries is indisputable. The value of their dogs to the shepherds has long been accepted as immense and unmatchable. In remote areas where sheep are grazed the worth of such dogs is still immeasurable. In western urbanised countries, the types of dogs that once were known only to shepherds have become developed as distinct breeds and have earned widespread popularity away from the pastures as companion dogs. The competitive exhibiting of these dogs has predictably changed their appearance, as cosmetic appeal inevitably outscored working skills no longer exercised. The challenge today is to protect such admirable dogs from human excess, think much

more of *their* best interests and respect their heritage. Shepherds have used dogs for well over two thousand years. Man has conducted dog shows for less than two hundred. We would be very foolish to ignore the hard lessons learned by shepherds over many centuries and think we know better. The dogs of the shepherds deserve to be perpetuated in their own mould, *not* to a transient template produced by the all too often self-indulgent breeders of today. These are precious and important breeds of dog.

In 1908 there were just six pastoral breeds on the Kennel Club's list of recognized pedigree dog breeds: Collies Rough and Smooth, Old English Sheepdogs, Shetland Sheepdogs and Welsh Corgis, plus the 'Alsatian Wolf Dog'. In 2013, there were thirty-one – the biggest number of breeds in any of the KC's Groups – although perversely the KC places pastoral breeds like the Hovawart, the Beauceron, the Bouvier des Flandres and the Swiss mountain dogs in their Working Group. It is worth a glance at these 'dogs of the shepherds' to see their widespread use across the globe, showing the immense value of such dogs to man: the Anatolian Shepherd Dog and the Kangal Dog (from Turkey); the two Australian breeds – their Cattle Dog and their Shepherd Dog; the Bearded,

Early show Collie.

Early show Bobtail.

BELOW: *Shepherd and his Sheepdog on Salisbury Plain, 1864.*

Border, Rough and Smooth Collies, the Old English and Shetland Sheepdogs, the Lancashire Heeler and the two Welsh Corgi breeds, all from Britain; the four breeds of Belgian Shepherd Dog; the Briard from France and the Catalan Sheepdog from Spain, with the two Pyrenean breeds – Mountain Dog and Sheepdog – and the Maremma Sheepdog of Italy coming from adjacent countries; the three Hungarian breeds: Kuvasz, Komondor and Puli; the Estrela Mountain Dog from Portugal; and finally those from much further north, the Polish Lowland Sheepdog, the Norwegian Buhund, the Finnish Lapphund, the Samoyed, and the Swedish Vallhund.

Most of these originated overseas, but, because of its wide-ranging capabilities, our native breed – the Border Collie – for long never even considered as a pedigree dog, attracted over 2,000 new registrations, making it our most favoured native pastoral breed. The German Shepherd Dog, however, totalled over 8,000, as our love affair with breeds from overseas showed itself again. Far too many of our native pastoral breeds are under threat of extinction in this century, with breeds like the Smooth Collie, the Cardigan Corgi and the Lancashire Heeler each only attracting around 100 new annual registrations each year.

Never listed by the KC were the Smithfield Sheepdog (a leggy, shaggy-coated drover's dog), the Blue

Shag of Dorset (a mainly blue-grey bobtailed sheep-dog), the Cotswold Beardie (often black and white and possibly a variant of the Bobtail), the rough-haired Lakeland Sheepdog, the Welsh Hillman (the longer-legged uplands sheepdog of Wales), the Old Welsh Grey (the bearded sheepdog of Wales), the Welsh Black and Tan Sheepdog (the shorter-coated 'valleys' sheepdog of South Wales), the Galway Sheepdog of Southern Ireland (a big tricolour dog resembling the Bernese Mountain Dog) and the Glenwherry Collie of Antrim (a mainly merle or marbled type, often wall-eyed), each one a distinct type, however little known outside their favoured areas. Every year, the use of pastoral dogs declines a little further, as modern pressures alter our agricultural methods and the urban sprawl continues. But every year it seems a new use is found for that talented breed the Border Collie, as its sheer versatility and wide range of skills find employment. It is now the case that many pastoral breeds are, more often than not, unlikely to be utilized in the pastures and far more likely to be employed as service dogs, with the military, the police and search and rescue organizations. They are still valued; they can still do things that humans cannot.

The lost pastoral breeds of the British Isles are illustrated here and on pages 12 and 13.

TOP RIGHT: *Smithfield Sheepdog with shepherd.*

ABOVE: *The Welsh Hillman.*

LEFT: *Blue Shag with shepherd.*

TOP LEFT: *Cotswold Shepherd with local Beardie.*

TOP RIGHT: *Welsh Grey Sheepdog with Welsh Drover.*

ABOVE: *The old Welsh Black and Tan Sheepdog.*

RIGHT: *Lakeland Shepherd with rough-haired Collies, c.1890.*

Glenwherry Collie of Antrim with distinctive 'wall-eyes'.

Unrecognized Foreign Breeds

The international kennel club, the Federation Cynologique Internationale (FCI) lists quite a number of pastoral breeds in their Group 1 that are not recognized by our KC: the Picardy Sheepdog, the South Russian Sheepdog, the Croatian Sheepdog, the Dutch Shepherd, the Mallorquin Sheepdog, the Portuguese Sheepdog, the Kelpie, the Schapendoes, the Hungarian Mudi and Pumi but puts the flock-guarding breeds like the Anatolian Shepherd Dog, the Pyrenean Mountain Dog, the Caucasian Sheepdog, the Estrela Mountain Dog and the Hovawart into a separate Group, 2. This does not help the allocation of judges from England to their shows or the reverse; judges need to appreciate role, the function that led to the design of the breed. Herding dogs need a very different anatomy from the mountain dogs or flock protectors and the rating of such physical points deserves specialist knowledge and judgement.

The FCI also recognizes foreign breeds in this Group quite unknown in Britain: the Cao de Castro Laboreiro and Rafeiro do Alentejo from Portugal, the Karst and Sar Planinac from the former Yugoslavia and the Central Asian Sheepdog. As, especially in countries that emerged from behind the Iron Curtain, more native pastoral breeds are ratified, this process will continue. Breeds such as Romania's Mioritic Shepherd, the Bucovina Shepherd, the Carpathian Shepherd and the jet black, appropriately named Raven Dog have been presented at the country's shows for the first time. In Western Europe too, native breeds are becoming recognized as the canine heritage of each nation is at last being valued by the show fraternity; in Spain, for example, at the 2013 Madrid show, the Garafiano Sheepdog (from the Canary Islands) was paraded, then three other native breeds, the Carea Leones, the Carea Manchego and the Euskal Artzain Txakurra were introduced to the curious onlookers in the main ring programme. In this book, I aim to

their physical form is remarkably similar to the bet-ter-known herders and flock guardians.

Unlikely to survive a lack of recognition and fail-ing interest in the pastures are the brindle Cypro Kukur or Kumaon Mastiff of northern India, the Cane Garouf or Italian Alpine Mastiff or Patua, and the Corsican native livestock protection dog, the Cursinu, resembling the Karst. The little Croatian heeler the Medi is now being promoted, the Portu-guese (Azores) version of our Old English Sheepdog: the Barbado da Terceira, the huge Cao de Gado Transmontano of North Portugal, quite similar to the registered Rafeiro da Alentejo, and the Chodsky Pes, a Czech herding dog rather like a smaller Tervueren, are all attracting interest at long last. Meanwhile, as ever, zealous individuals are at work, promoting newly developed breeds like the Panda Shepherd in Canada, a GSD with a very specific coat colour; the King Shepherd and Shiloh Shepherd in America – 'improved' GSDs; the Swiss Shepherd – an all-white GSD that is gaining support in Switzerland; with the Welsh Mountain Dog being promoted in the Prin-cipality. It is noticeable that in several countries the GSD is being 'improved' by dissatisfied fanciers of the show GSD in the 1990s style of that dog. The recently developed Eastern European Shepherd, an attractive, more traditional GSD-variant, soon became Russia's most popular breed.

In this book, I aim to make a case for the origin and function of all pastoral types, ancient and mod-ern, to be respected, not in the pursuit of historical accuracy, important as that is, but because they can only be bred both soundly and honestly if their past development *and traditional form* is honoured. Their original lowly rural breeders have left these magnifi-cent canine servants to us and we have a duty of care towards these impressive and quite admirable breeds of dog. There is less research material on the dogs of the shepherds than, say, on sporting dogs such as gundogs and hounds. Both the latter types were owned and patronized by the wealthy and better-educated, the former usually by illiterate agricultural workers. This increases my resolve to do them jus-tice after centuries of neglect. My personal affection for this type of dog rests on the thirty-odd years of loyal yet stimulating companionship that I was given by my own working sheepdogs, perhaps better de-scribed as unregistered Border Collies; they taught

Galway Sheepdog – quite similar to Bernese Mountain Dog.

cover many of these, but because their function was the same as the pastoral breeds already recognized,

me an enormous amount about dogs – and quite a lot about myself.

The sheepdog is so completely absorbed in what seems the sole business and employment of his life, that he does not bestow a look, or indulge a wish beyond the constant protection of the trust reposed in him, and to execute the commands of his master; which he is always anxious to receive, and in fact is invariably looking for by every solicitous attention it is possible to conceive. Inured to all weathers, fatigue and hunger, he is the least voracious of the species, subsists on little…the sagacity, fidelity, and comprehensive penetration of this kind of dog is equal to any other, but that there is a thoughtful or expressive gravity annexed to this particular race, as if they were absolutely conscious of their own utility in business of importance, and of the value of the stock so confidently committed to their care.

The Sportsman's Cabinet, 1803

ABOVE: *The Eastern European Shepherd Dog.*

Working Sheepdog intent on stalk.

ACKNOWLEDGEMENTS

The author is grateful to the staff at Sotheby's Picture Library, Christie's Images Ltd., Bonhams, Getty Images, Arthur Ackermann Ltd, David Messum Galleries, Richard Green & Co., Rountree Fine Art, The Bridgeman Art Library, The Nature Picture Library, The National Art Library, The Wallace Collection, R. Cox & Co., Lane Fine Art, The Mary Evans Picture Library, The Lady Lever Art Gallery – Port Sunlight, The Kennel Club, The American Kennel Club, The National Trust, The Royal Collection – Photographic Services, the Art Director/ Graphics Department of *Dogs in Canada* magazine and private collectors (especially the late Mevr AH (Ploon) de Raad of Zijderveld, Holland, who gave free use of her extensive photographic archive of sporting paintings), for their gracious and generous permissions to reproduce some of the illustrations used in this book.

AUTHOR'S NOTE

A number of the illustrations in this book lack pictorial quality but are included because uniquely they either contribute historically to or best exemplify the meaning of the text. Old depictions do not always lend themselves to reproduction in today's higher quality print and publishing format. Those that are included have significance beyond their graphic limitations and I ask for the reader's understanding over this.

Where quotes are used, they are used verbatim, despite any vagaries in spelling, irregular use of capital letters or departures from contemporary grammar. For me, it is important that their exact form, as presented by the author originally, is displayed, as this can help to capture the mood of those times.

Old English Sheepdogs of 1812.

INTRODUCTION

The Emergence of the Pastoral Dogs

In his informative *A History of Domesticated Animals* (1963), the distinguished zoologist Frederick Zeuner wrote:

> In the Bronze Age a moderately large dog is frequently found which, in many respects, is like some of the primitive breeds of sheepdog still to be found in parts of Europe. The modern collies, Alsatians and others with elongated skulls are products of very recent systematic breeding... In view of the palaeontological material now available, this means that the sheepdog group can be traced back to the Bronze Age... Its frequent occurrence in Bronze Age sites may be connected with the increasing importance of sheep-breeding in the economy of Bronze Age Europe. Thus the forerunners of the modern sheepdogs can so far be traced back to the Bronze Age only.

Evidence of far earlier use of pastoral dogs, not surprisingly, can be found in the artefacts of Ancient Egypt, as these two images demonstrate.

No Breed Identity

It is unwise for enthusiastic breed historians to link contemporary *breeds* with depictions of dogs on ancient artefacts. As Juliet Clutton-Brock wrote in her *Domesticated Animals from Early Times* (1981):

> The majority of the remains of the earliest domestic dogs have been retrieved from archaeological sites in western Asia, although small numbers have also been found in North and South America, northwest Europe (England and Denmark), Russia and Japan. They are nowhere very common until the Neolithic period when livestock animals are of course also represented... The dogs of these early periods, before the invention or widespread use of agriculture, were already quite variable in size and they probably also varied in their pelage, length of ears and tail, and shape of facial region ... it is not acceptable to divide these dog remains into separate categories or subspecies, let alone into breeds.

Statue of 18th Dynasty shepherd dog from Egypt (Louvre Museum).

Early Egyptian knife handle depicting two huge livestock protection dogs (second row down).

Function ensures physical resemblances but pure-breeding for appearance is a modern phenomenon.

Usefulness to Man

If man is the most successful mammal on the planet, then, dog, man's closest animal companion, is arguably the second most successful and certainly man's most *valuable* animal companion. Dogs have changed history, allowing for example early farmers to protect their livestock from predators, primitive hunters to obtain meat for the table

and facilitate travel in Arctic conditions. In his *Dogs: A Historical Journey* (1996), Lloyd Wendt writes: 'The earliest evident pattern of human and dog migrations and partnership activity began in south-eastern Africa, extending to Lakes Turkana and Omo in Ethiopia and the Nile tributaries, the Nile itself, and may have reached past the deserts of Sudan...' In his *Dogs through History* (1987), Maxwell Riddle writes: 'Asia is a huge land mass, with high mountains separating fertile valleys. Such valleys were ideal for developing dog breeds. Their comparative isolation and highland stock grazing areas challenged the people within to produce dogs for specialized purposes.'

In *The Lost History of the Canine Race* (1996), Mary Thurston writes:

> At its height, Rome was a veritable melting pot of both domesticated animals and people... At the same time, 'exotic' dogs continued to arrive from Northern Europe, Africa, and the Middle East. Outcrossed with one another as well as with the more primitive, Neolithic canines still residing in rural parts of Southern Europe, they gave rise to a plethora of new varieties...

These three quotes provide background to the timeless development of dogs with people, the movement of people with their dogs and the trading in dogs once their value was known.

The Farmers' Needs

It was during the eighth and seventh millennia BC that man first began to domesticate sheep and goats in western Asia. Unlike nomadic animals such as gazelles, antelope and bison, humans, sheep, goats and dogs were all part of a social system based on a single dominant leader and tended to settle on what became known as a *home range*. They therefore became inter-dependent, with the herdsman as leader and the dog as his agent. Dogs also protected humans and their livestock against wild predators such as lynxes, lions, wolves, tigers, jackals, leopards, cheetahs, foxes, civets and, in some places, huge eagles. The protection of flock-guarding dogs was vital; such dogs had to be brave and determined, alert and resolute, vigilant and reactive – but above all, protective.

The Spread of Agriculture

In *Farmers in Prehistoric Britain* (2011), Francis Pryor gives the view that:

> The spread of farming across Europe has been well documented by excavation and radiocarbon dating. At present it would appear that farming reached the north and west extremities of the continent by two distinct routes, or groups of routes: overland by way of the Danube and Rhine valleys to modern Germany, northern France and the Low Countries; or via the Mediterranean to the Alps, or up the Rhone into central and northern France or, finally, across south-western France via the Carcasonne-Narbonne 'gap'.

Pryor estimates that there may well have been as many as 5,000 sheep in just one fen basin, Flag Fen basin, in the Bronze Age in Britain. If such sheep farming here involved sheepdogs and the routes above were followed by farmers with dogs, it is easy to see how their pastoral dogs ended up in the nations of today covered by these routes and perhaps why, in time, such dogs ended up resembling each other.

Roles for Pastoral Dogs

Not surprisingly, the dogs that *protected* flocks of sheep from wild predators, human rustlers or other dogs were large and fierce. Those that *controlled* the flock or herd were smaller, more biddable, and, although less fierce, were still very resolute, such as the German Shepherd Dog – used as a 'living fence'. The *driving* dogs combined stamina and robustness with an instinctive desire to keep the flock or herd together as a group. The *herding* or *penning* dogs were required to be highly responsive to the human voice or whistle and yet still be very strong-willed. British breeds have long excelled in this role. The *heeling* dogs were used to turn or drive cattle and had to be small, quick and extremely agile, as the Corgi breeds demonstrate to this day. The *pinning* or *gripping* dogs, once hunting dogs and utilized extensively by butchers, were needed to seize and hold one individual animal, for example a powerful sow, to facilitate handling, loading on to transport or even slaughter. Broad-mouthed breeds like the old type of Bulldog, the Cane Corso of Italy and the Rottweiler of Germany were used for this type of work, valued for their fierce determination and widely traded.

Dog-traders have earned themselves a questionable reputation in modern times, but trading in dogs in past times allowed the widespread movement of dogs and a wider appreciation of their usefulness. Dogs accompanied wandering tribes, campaigning armies and migrating peoples, provided they had some use. The game-catchers, like the sighthound breeds, the game-finders, like the modern gundog breeds, and

Pyrenean Mountain Dog with charges – protection dog.
PATRICIA LORE

ABOVE: *Beauceron of 1899 – flock controller and driving dog.*

Working Sheepdog – herding dog.

Kelpie – a penning dog.

BELOW LEFT: The author's dogs heeling cattle.

BELOW RIGHT: A pinning or gripping dog at work.

the flock-guarding breeds each had a distinct value to man. The need to control vermin led to the development of the terrier breeds. The need to control sheep gave us the herding breeds. Dogs that excelled in their specialist function have long been extensively traded. In due course, dogs that worked with livestock went with that livestock, even across national boundaries and on ships sailing to the colonies. That is how many pastoral breeds developed eventually as separate distinct breeds once modified by local conditions overseas. But wherever they went they had to *function*.

Needs of the Role

Whatever their role, their work, the climate and the terrain demanded excellent feet, tough frames, weatherproof coats, enormous stamina, really good eyesight and hearing and quite remarkable robustness. These dogs operated in harsh conditions, ranging from the hottest to the coldest, the stoniest, thorniest, windiest, most mountainous and most arid areas of Europe and western Asia. Farmers and shepherds had to have entirely functional dogs; physical exaggeration does not occur in any of the flock-guarding breeds, unlike the ornamental ones. Hunting ability was not desired although the physical power and bravery of such dogs did lead to their use in bear hunts in Russia and boar hunts in Central Europe, where they were used at the kill, not in the hunt itself. The demands of climate have led to both the flock guardians and the shepherd dogs featuring

The Bergamasco from Italy.

BELOW: The Komondor from Hungary.

ABOVE LEFT: *The Schapendoes from Holland.*

ABOVE RIGHT: *A Dorset drover, Nat Seal, who died in 1898, with his working sheepdog.*

Belgian Shepherd Dog – the Laekenois variety.

The Drover by T.G. Audlay, c.1860, with the symbols of his trade.

A Drover with an English working bobtailed sheepdog, c.1820.

appropriate coats for their region. The Hungarian Komondor and the Italian Bergamasco display the thick corded or felted coats required to survive in their working environment. The Swiss Entlebucher and Appenzeller and the New Zealand Huntaway exhibit the smooth sleek coats best suited to their working conditions.

If we then look at the shorter legs of the heeling breeds, like the Corgis, and the longer legs of the herding dogs, like the Belgian, Dutch and German Shepherd Dogs, we can see how not only climate but also terrain and function determined type. In some areas the harsh-haired or goat-haired breeds, like the Bearded Collie and the Schapendoes of Holland, were favoured, because of the local conditions and their instinctive skills. The breeds were shaped by the farmers' needs. Wherever they worked or farmed, farmers needed dogs with the innate characteristics, the appropriate physique and the suitable length and texture of coat to protect, drive or herd their stock, hunt down vermin and guard their farmsteads and pastures. Their

demanding requirements have left us with some of the most popular breeds of companion dog today, although, sadly, these are so often bred more with cosmetic than functional considerations in today's society. In order to appreciate the extraordinary value of the pastoral dogs of the recent past, it is worth a study of the drovers and their dogs – transhumance in Britain.

The Drovers and Their Dogs

… for centuries, at least from the time of the Norman conquest to the establishment of the railways, the most important long-distance travellers were the drovers… they formed great cavalcades that blocked the way for other travellers for hours at a time… if farmers did not want their cattle to join the drove they had to make sure they were safely enclosed… Some parts of the drove-ways were also used to transport pigs, sheep, geese and turkeys, and these animals also had to travel great distances.

Those words from Shirley Toulson's *The Drovers* (1980) provide an immediate concept of the significance of historic markets and the total reliance on dogs to get the livestock to market. It's difficult to visualize nowadays 6,000 sheep being moved on foot in more or less one huge flock from east of the Pennines to the markets of Norfolk and Smithfield. It's not easy to think of thousands of cattle, sheep and even geese being shepherded by a small number of dogs from remote rural pastures along established drove-roads to city markets – and the dogs either accompanying the mounted drover homewards or then being left to find their own way home. These were very remarkable dogs.

In his *Cynographia Britannica* of 1800, Sydenham Edwards wrote, of the drover's dog:

> … he appears peculiar to England, being rarely found even in Scotland. He is useful to the farmer or grazier, for watching or driving their cattle, and to the drover and butcher for driving cattle and sheep to slaughter; he is sagacious, fond of employment, and active; if a drove is huddled together so as to retard their progress, he dashes amongst and separates them till they form a line and travel more commodiously; if a sheep is refractory and runs wild, he soon overtakes and seizes him by the foreleg or ear, pulls him to the ground. The bull or ox he forces into obedience by keen bites on the heels or tail, and most dexterously avoids their kicks. He knows his master's grounds, and is a rigid sentinel on duty, never suffering them to break their bounds, or strangers to enter. He shakes the intruding hog by the ear, and obliges him to quit the territories. He bears blows and kicks with much philosophy…

Those picturesque words are a concise summary of the dogs' purpose, as well as showing their prowess as heelers too.

In *The Dog* (1854), Youatt wrote, on the drover's dog: 'He bears considerable resemblance to the Sheepdog, and has usually the same prevailing black or brown colour. He possesses all the docility of the Sheepdog, with more courage, and sometimes ferocity.' The drover's dog would have needed ferocity to keep an endless stream of village curs from attacking the flock, great courage in facing every kind of obstacle and threat en route to the 'fattening fields' and the docility to obey every command

from the accompanying drover while ignoring rustlers, thieves or the wrath of inconvenienced citizens finding their path blocked. Such dogs had to think for themselves – in the modern idiom, 'think on their feet'. From that background come the gifted sheepdogs of today.

In his *British Dogs* (1888), Hugh Dalziel wrote:

> In all parts of England and Scotland I have seen drovers, and narrowly scanned their dogs, and I have come to the conclusion that no distinct breed can be justly described as the Drover's Dog, but that the latter, like the poacher's dog, the Lurcher, may be compounded of many varieties, the drover utilising for his purpose the kind of dog that comes most readily to hand.

These few words on such important dogs indicate the wide gulf between the educated classes and the peasant-shepherd over dogs; the better-off, especially the landed gentry, sought style and followed fashion in their gundogs and hounds. The peasant-shepherds

Working collies in Westmorland, c.1895.

needed performance and were content with utility in their dogs. In books on dogs in the nineteenth century the pastoral dogs were rarely covered in any detail or indeed accuracy.

In his three-volume work, Dalziel also wrote:

> The English Sheepdog, as I recognize him, and as he is seen with the shepherd on the South Downs, on the Salisbury Plains, and on the Welsh, Cumbrian, and Scotch hills and dales, is usually, but not invariably, bob-tailed – either born so, or made so by docking. I have in vain consulted past writers on dogs for any minute description of this animal's size, build, general appearance, and, in show language, his 'points'.

Against this background, with its lack of familiarity with its subject, it is never easy to research the pastoral breeds, either here or abroad.

Changed World

The advent of the pedigree dog show in the middle of the nineteenth century changed the world of the domestic dog forever. For the very first time, the working, pastoral and sporting breeds were to be judged on what they looked like rather than what they could do. A handsome but brainless, unmotivated dog could be rated as more valuable than a skilful, hard-working sheepdog serving its master in all winds and weather in harsh unforgiving terrain. A determination to 'stamp out the drover's dog', as William Weager put it in *The Kennel Gazette* in 1889, eventually affected every pastoral breed:

OLD ENGLISH SHEEPDOGS

> The increased interest now taken in this, one of the most useful and picturesque of English dogs, was apparent at the Kennel Club show, where more purchases were effected and higher prices realized than in any other class. Farmers and others will do well to look about them and send dogs to shows, where they will find a ready market for good specimens. The quality of the dogs shown on this occasion has greatly improved on the corresponding exhibition of last year. The club's determination to stamp out the

drover's dog has been most effectual, and here on this event was only one wrong specimen shown.

The 'wrong specimen', as Weager termed it, might well have been highly effective herding or driving dogs but were not as handsome as the ringside viewing expected. Judging dogs entirely on their appearance is not exactly a rational act but sadly so often a wallet-led human choice. The exhibiting of dogs too has led to some pastoral breeds being seen much more often in towns than was once the case. It is noteworthy that the pastoral breeds of Britain were very much the dogs of working people. Early photographs of rural communities illustrate this fact. If you read Victorian dog books, packed with chapters on hounds and gundogs, you quickly detect a lack of real knowledge from the monied, educated classes of these humbler but certainly more valuable canine workers.

A number of pastoral breed types never reached the show ring, perhaps lacking the glamour that the public seek in their canine pets. As mentioned in the Preface, most of the old Welsh breeds were lost to us, and the Smithfield Sheepdog is only kept going by the lurcher fraternity – and in Tasmania (*see* Chapter 2)! The small heeler types of England vanished too, although eventually the Ormskirk Heeler was reclaimed for us and named the Lancashire Heeler. Undoubtedly, the show ring saved some pastoral breeds, even if many were changed morphologically and not to their benefit. Depictions of the pastoral breeds of a century ago show very different creatures from their counterparts today.

Breed Titles

I do wish the kennel clubs of the world would get their act together over the nomenclature used for pastoral breed titles. The flock-guarding breeds, like the Anatolian Shepherd Dog, should not be called 'shepherd dogs'; the herding breeds like the Belgian and Dutch Shepherd Dog breeds are best described by this title. But when is a sheepdog not a shepherd dog? Is there a difference in role here? The Pyrenean pastoral breeds make a point for me: the biggest, the Pyrenean Mountain Dog, is the flock guardian, with the size and role of the Hungarian Kuvasz; the next down in size, and on the Spanish side of the range, but more fiercely protective, is the Pyrenean Mastiff,

a shepherd's mastiff, with the size and role of the Tibetan Mastiff; then comes the Pyrenean Sheepdog, a much smaller, much more active herding breed, but appreciably smaller and with a different role from our Old English Sheepdog. Breed titles should reflect breed purpose. Their role gave them their phenotype, their temperament and their nature. These are breed points as, if not more, important than showring breed points, such as skull shape and ear and tail carriage. Breed type originated in function not appearance.

A further complication is the breed titles imposed on the pastoral breeds from outside. The Tibetans do not call their flock protector a 'Tibetan Mastiff', the Polish do not call their Tatra Mountain Dog by that label, the Romanians do not call their Carpathian Sheepdog a Mountain Dog despite its mountain pastures, the St Bernard of today was the Alpine Mastiff of yesterday and the Sar Planinac works in the mountains of that name but is not called a mountain dog here, unlike the Pyrenean equivalent. I suspect that the noun 'mastiff' has become shorthand for big, strapping dogs out of the long-held view, especially in North America, that mastiffs are today's molossers. They are not; the Mollossi, of Epirus in Ancient Greece, had two sorts of big dog – one was a flock protector, the other a hound. The mastiffs of their

ABOVE LEFT: Pyrenean pastoral dogs: Mountain Dog (left), Labrit sheepdog (right).
PATRICIA LORE, COURTESY OF BRYAN CUMMINS

Pyrenean Mastiff.

time came from Hyrcania and were referred to as 'Indian Dogs'; scholars have since misused the term mastiff to cover every large dog in ancient writings. The Swiss use the word *'sennenhund'*, or dog of the high pastures, for their livestock-protection dogs. The FCI should really differentiate between mountain dogs, steppe dogs and plains dogs; their anatomies are different, as is their coat texture. Breed identity can help in its long-term survival, as the Lancashire Heeler demonstrated.

Vulnerable Native Breeds

I believe that our breeds of domestic dog are in unprecedented danger, not from one single distinct threat and not next year or the one after, but from a multiplicity of menaces over the next two decades. Some breeds, like the Smooth Collie, the Sealyham Terrier, the Sussex and Field Spaniels, the Cardiganshire Welsh Corgi and the Lancashire Heeler could simply fade away because of lack of numbers. Already there is concern over their immediate future. Their registrations in 2012 reveal the cause of this concern: eighty-eight Smooth Collies, seventy-six Sealyhams, seventy-four Sussex Spaniels, ninety-four Cardigan Corgis and forty-seven Field Spaniels; each is now an endangered species. Breeds we have imported, like the Maremma Sheepdog, with only twenty-five registrations in 2012, could also disappear from our breed list. There are quite a number of imported pastoral breeds just not making ground here, after the initial enthusiasm for them faded.

Unlike some countries, Denmark, Portugal and Japan for example, we lack a society devoted to the perpetuation of our threatened native breeds of dog. We have already lost the English White Terrier, the Smithfield Sheepdog, the Glenwherry Collie, the Welsh Hillman and the Llanidloes Setter and only just saved the Irish Wolfhound, the Mastiff, the Field Spaniel and the Lancashire Heeler. Only in the late twentieth century did the best working collie breed in the world gain interest from the show fraternity, with the Border Collie going from 700 registrations in 1980 to over 2,000 twenty years later. Many less gifted foreign herding breeds were registered with our KC before this important national breed. But it is worth noting that in 1970 there were no registrations here of Anatolian Shepherd Dogs, Belgian Shepherd Dogs, Bernese Mountain Dogs, Briards, Hungarian Pulis or Maremma Sheepdogs. Another half dozen pastoral breeds that are in favour now were not even recognized by our KC then. Human fickleness does not assist breed stability.

Perils of Over-Popularity

Paradoxically, another serious threat comes from the unwise over-breeding of certain over-popular breeds: German Shepherd Dogs (over 8,000 registered annually), Rough Collie (8,462 in 1979), Shetland Sheepdogs (5,872 in 1969) and Pembroke Welsh Corgis (4,165 in 1969). (The last three breeds had very different figures in 2012: 943, 1,085 and 333 respectively, indicating the sheer fickleness of the show dog world.) I don't recall seeing as many badly bred specimens in these breeds as I did in the 1990s. Too many under-standard bitches are being bred from; too many faulty or weedy pups are being retained. Glamorous pastoral breeds like the Rough Collie, the Shetland Sheepdog and the Bearded Collie have become victims of the show ring – being prized for coat. The Shetland Sheepdog attracted over 5,000 registrations a year throughout the 1970s. The Bearded Collie went from three registrations in 1951 to nearly 2,000 in 1989. Fine working breeds like the German Shepherd Dog have suffered from over-popularity (over 21,500 in 1985), with the faddists altering the breed from its prototypal phenotype. The specimens I used to admire when working in Germany in the 1960s lost their level toplines and effortless movement based on powerful hindquarters. The 'banana-backs' became favoured and crippled dogs actually became desirable as misguided 'gaiting' or racing around the show ring with all the power in the front legs (that is, being pulled along instead of being pushed by the hindquarters, as nature intended), developed into the only acceptable form of movement – just for this breed! They deserved better. The best GSD I have seen in recent years was a variation developed as the East European Shepherd, Russia's most popular breed. The brace I saw at the World Dog Show in Budapest was truly impressive.

Employment as Service Dogs

Evidence of the remarkable merit of the pastoral breeds is shown daily in the way in which they are used as service dogs – all over the world, by the military, by police forces and as support dogs for the disabled or handicapped humans. Over the years, breeds used as service dogs have lost their role through being bred away from their function and into the world of the fancier. The Border Collie is widely used across many needs, based on its quickness to absorb training and

willingness to work – two basic requirements in a dog of the shepherds. I do not know, however, of a Rough or Smooth Collie or of an Old English Sheep-dog being used as a service dog. Is this a reflection of their lost capabilities, sheer human fickleness or, in two cases, the demands of their coat care? This is discussed later in the book. Throughout this book, I argue for the pastoral breeds to be bred true to type and fit for function; these may now be clichés but both expressions really do matter for the breeds concerned. They will, in my view, either survive because they retain traditional physical form and character or be lost to us through simply having no independent breed in-dividuality and, more importantly, no purpose – and that, when their remarkable past is taken into account, would be *our* loss too.

TOP LEFT: German Shepherd Dog of 1922.

TOP RIGHT: German Shepherd Dog of today.

The type of farm collie that graduated to the show bench, c.1890.

Working Bobtail, c.1850. Livestock by the River Thames by E. Bristow.

BELOW LEFT: Anatolian Shepherd Dog.

Turkmen Watch-dog. This is a large, rugged, and fierce race, equalling the wolf in stature, shaped like the Irish Greyhound, and with equally powerful jaws; the ears are erect, the tail rather hairy, their colour a deep yellowish-red, and so like a Natolian wolf, that a friend being present, in Asia Minor, at a wolf-hunt, allowed one to pass out of a brake, because he mistook him for one of the Turkmen dogs, and his Greek guide called out Lyke! when it was too late to fire. There are among them a few white and black, evidently crossed-dogs from another origin. This race extends wherever the Turkmen, or Toorkee people reside, from central high Asia to the Bosphorus, and is everywhere employed to guard their tents and cattle. We believe it is also in similar use among the Kurds; and, it appeared that in the mountains north of the Mekran, and west of the Indus, dogs of this description were likewise the guardians of the peasantry.

Charles Hamilton Smith, *The Naturalist's Library*, Vol. X (1840)

…such are the dogs used in Persia to guard the flocks of sheep, such the shepherd's dog of Natolia; but we must not suppose that they perform the duties of our shepherd's dog, which render it so interesting – on the contrary, they are to be regarded simply as watch-dogs, defending the flocks from wild beasts and strangers, and consequently are more remarkable for other qualities than sagacity and intelligence. In the East, be it remembered, the sheep are not driven – they follow the shepherd – at least in Western Asia, Greece, etc.; but in our country the shepherd's dog acts as drover and gatherer of the sheep together, and takes no little labour from the shepherd, to whom his dog is of the utmost importance.

W.C.L. Martin, *The History of the Dog* (1845)

CHAPTER 1

THE PASTORAL PROTECTORS

The Flock Guardians

From Portugal in the west, right across to the Lebanon and then on to the Caucasus mountains in the east, from southern Greece, north through Hungary to most parts of Russia, there are powerful pastoral dogs to be found, developed over thousands of years to protect man's domesticated animals from the attacks of wild animals. Some are called shepherd dogs, others mountain dogs and a few dubbed 'mastiffs', despite the conformation of their skulls. Their coat colours vary from pure white to wolf-grey and from a rich red to black and tan. Some are no longer used as herd-protectors and their numbers in north-west Europe dramatically decreased when the use of draught dogs lapsed. A number of common

The Greek Sheepdog (Ellinikos Poimenikos).

Cane Garouf – Italian Flock Guardian.

The Tornjak.

characteristics link these widely separated breeds: a thick weatherproof coat, a powerful build, an independence of mind, a certain majesty and a strong instinct to protect. As a group, they would be most accurately described as the flock guardians. In North America they are usually referred to as Livestock Protection Dogs or LPDs.

In southwest Europe these dogs became known in time as breeds such as the Estrela Mountain Dog, the Cao de Castro Laboreiro and the Rafeiro do Alentejo of Portugal and the Spanish or Extremadura 'Mastiff'. To the northeast of the Iberian peninsula, such dogs became known as the Pyrenean Mountain Dog or Patou, on the French side, and, separately, on the Spanish side, as the Pyrenean 'Mastiff'. In the Swiss Alps they divided, as different regions favoured different coat colours and textures into the *'sennenhund'* or mountain pasture breeds we know today as the Bernese, Appenzell, Entlebuch and Greater Swiss Mountain Dogs and the Alpine Mastiff, which is behind the St Bernard, a breed once much more like the flock-guardian phenotype. In Italy, local shepherds favoured the pale colours now found in the Maremma Sheepdog and the very heavy coat of the Bergamasco. In the northwest of Italy, the Patua or Cane Garouf, the Italian Alpine Mastiff, may soon be lost to us. In Corsica, their flock protector, the Cursinu, is also under threat as numbers fall. In the Balkans, similarly differing preferences led to the emergence of the all- or mainly white Greek sheepdog and the wolf-grey flock guardians of the former Yugoslavia, the Karst

of Slovenia, the Sar Planinac of Macedonia and the parti-coloured Tornjak or Croatian Guard Dog.

Emergence of Breeds
Further east, other breed types were stabilized into the Barachesto and the Karakatchan of Bulgaria, the Kuvasz and Komondor of Hungary, the Romanian Bucovina, Carpathian Shepherd and Mioritic Shepherd Dogs, the Tatra Mountain Dog or Goral of Poland, the Slovakian Kuvasz or Liptok, the Mendelan (widely used in bear-hunting) of north Russia and the Owtcharkas of south Russia and in the Caucasus – with varieties in Dagestan, Armenia, Azerbaijan and Georgia. In Kyrgyzstan there was the Kyrgysian Shepherd Dog; in Tajikistan the Dahmarda or Tajikistan Mastiff; in Mongolia the Mongolian Livestock Guarding Dog; in Turkmenistan the Turkmenian Shepherd and in Uzbekistan the Torkuz and the Sarkangik. In the Himalayan regions appeared the so-called Tibetan 'Mastiff' or Do-Kyi (Gate or Guard Dog), the Bhotia or Himalayan Mastiff, the Bisben,

the Bangara 'Mastiff', the Sage Koochi or Aryan Flock Guardian of Afghanistan and the closely related Powendah dog of northwest Pakistan. In Iran there is the Sage Mazandarani.

In central Europe, protective breeds like the Beauceron, the Briard, the Bouvier (meaning drovers' dog) des Flandres, Bouvier des Ardennes, Bouvier de Roulers, Bouvier de Paret, Bouvier de Moerman (with only the Flanders and Ardennes dogs surviving), the Giant Schnauzer and the Hovawart emerged. Kennel club breed names have blurred the

herding dogs and the flock guardians; the latter treat their livestock as siblings, the former regard them as prey, with the prey-pursuit instinct subdued then modified into protection. In Scandinavia the long-extinct Dahlbo-hound, the size of an English Mastiff, was used to guard the cattle of the Dahlbo people in forest pastures. Where Europe and Asia meet, types now referred to, perhaps mistakenly, as breeds – the Anatolian Shepherd Dog (a western title), the Kangal Dog, Karabash (black-headed), Akbash (white-headed), Kars Dog, near the border

TOP: *The Bucovina Shepherd Dogs from Romania.*

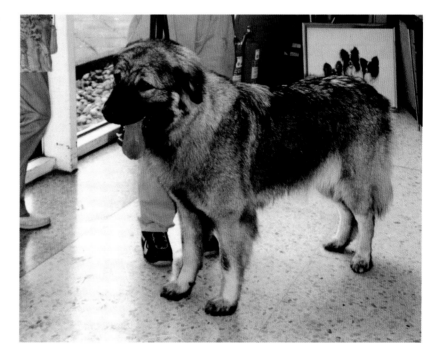

Karst.

Anatolian Shepherd Dog.

The Transmontano Mastiff of Portugal.

with Georgia, and the Kurd Steppe Dog – developed in separate areas, with a very attractive shepherd dog coming from the Kastamonou area, near the Black Sea. The Slavic dogs are named 'owcharkas' (or sheepdog, coming from their word 'ovtsa') but often written as 'ovcarka' too. In their *Dogs: A Startling New Understanding of Canine Origin, Behavior & Evolution* (2001), a must-read for researchers of these dogs, the Coppingers mention a recent study by KORA, a Swiss conservation programme, that identified twenty-six countries from western Europe across to Tibet, with around fifty versions of flock guardian dogs; these cannot truly be called breeds because they moved from country to country, were inter-bred and could only be differentiated by location not type.

I believe that these pastoral dogs originated with the dogs of the Indo-European peoples (hunters then nomadic shepherds) who migrated south 3,000 years before Christ. The East Indo-Europeans moved from just north of the Caucasus Mountains around the northern shores of the Black Sea to settle in Greece and Anatolia and southwest of the Black Sea into Turkey. Over the next 2,000 years this migration continued, to produce the settlements of the Slavs, Illyrians and Thracians in the west and similar civilizations east of the Caspian Sea, southeast to the Tibetan plateau and south to the Indus valley.

Just look at the resultant distribution of such big herd-protectors: the Maremma of Italy, the Estrela Mountain Dog, the Transmontano Mastiff or Cao de Gado Transmontano and Cao Rafeiro do Alentejo of Portugal, the Kuvasz of Hungary, the Anatolian Shepherd Dog, the Pyrenean Mountain Dog, the Bulgarian Sheepdogs, the Tatra Mountain Dog of Poland, the Romanian Shepherd Dog, the Sar Planinac of Yugoslavia, the Transcaucasian Owtcharka and the Himalayan dogs. Some of these modern types may have developed separately *as breeds* over the last thousand years but the similarities are all too

Flock guardian of the high pastures.

Mobile Pastoralists

Where did these flock guardian breeds originate? The history of dog is the history of man; when tribes migrated, their valuable flock-guarding dogs went with them. The flock-guarding breeds have three principal elements in common: their general appearance, their protective instincts and the fact that they are found wherever the Indo-Europeans settled. This latter area stretches from northern India through Iran into northwest Asia, eastern Europe, the northern Mediterranean countries, northern and western Europe to the British Isles as well as the southern hemisphere. As a type they are the most widely spread of all canine varieties.

Three thousand or so years ago, the people from the area north of and between the Black and Caspian seas, using their mastery of the horse and their invention of the wheeled chariot, migrated to the west, southwest, southeast and due south. These mobile pastoralists, over the next thousand years or so, were to reach the Tibetan plateau and the river Indus in the east, the Taurus mountains in Anatolia and the rivers Tigris and Euphrates in the south and then beyond the rivers Rhine, Danube and Po in the west and southwest to form what eventually became the Celtic, Italic, German, Baltic, Illyrian, Thracian, Slav and Greek settlements.

Extensive trade was conducted between western Anatolia and the Mediterranean littoral, from southern Portugal and Spain to southern Italy and Greece. Valuable hunting and flock-guarding dogs would have been coveted and then traded.

obvious. Local preferences have manifested themselves, with black and tan dogs being favoured in northern Switzerland (rather as with the Beauceron in nearby France and the Rottweiler in neighbouring southern Germany) and the red and white of the St Bernard in the south, more like the big dogs of the Pyrenees, the Abruzzi and the Greek and Yugoslavian mountain areas.

Hungarian shepherd with his sheepdog – the Kuvasz.

Tatra Mountain Dog – the Polish Owtcharka.

Rafeiro do Alentejo of Portugal.

BELOW: *Caucasian Owtcharka.*

Agricultural and social change both affected the way the flock-guarding dogs developed, and so too did climate and terrain. In Poland, for example, the Tatra Mountain Dog is a large, thick-coated breed whereas the Portuguese breed of Rafeiro do Alentejo is lighter-coated but still sizeable. Man's dependence on huge dogs to guard his livestock is not however as dramatic as using dogs for war and hunting, and because shepherds were not usually literate, they rarely featured in art or literature. Yet sheep migration alone has historic significance, both over the movement of people and their culture. The Foundation for Transhumance and Nature in Switzerland has estimated that there are 77,000 miles of sheep trails in the world, with each migration averaging from 370 to 620 miles. International boundaries had no importance.

It is forgivable to believe that such breeds are sizeable because they need to be able to see off wild animals that prey on sheep. But much more important are the bigger stride afforded by size, the ability to carry more fat reserves and store more heat than a small dog and to survive disease, severe weather and the odd accident – big bones break less easily than tiny ones. This is why such breeds possess

St Bernard – originally much more of a mountain dog/flock protector.

Bernese Mountain Dogs in 1950.

a similar phenotype; the Estrela Mountain Dog is easily confused with a Slovenian Karst or Caucasian Owtcharka, or a Maremma with a Tatra Mountain Dog. The Caucasian Owtcharka can resemble the early St Bernards, the Alpine flock guardian, too. The shepherds, drovers, stockmen and traders in such dogs knew what made a dog effective and therefore more valuable. It is wrong, however, to breed for great size alone in such breeds: dogs on long migrations were 60lb in weight not the 100lb-plus often desired in breeds like the St Bernard and the Newfoundland, which suffer badly in extreme heat. The warmer the migration route the lighter the dogs had to be to cope with the temperature. The more substantial dogs – with heftier frames, able to conserve heat – were used further north or purely in mountainous regions.

The Mountain Dogs – Swiss Breeds

With 60 per cent of its land surface made up of mountains, it is not surprising to find that Switzerland has more breeds of mountain dog than any other nation. We have known of the Mount St Bernard dog for many centuries and the Bernese Mountain Dog increasingly over the last decade. But the other three 'sennenhund' breeds: the Appenzeller, the Entlebucher and the Greater Swiss Mountain Dog are not yet established in the United Kingdom, although the Entlebucher and the Greater Swiss are making ground here and have an interim breed standard authorized by the KC. The Greater Swiss, however, is making better headway in the United States, where it was introduced in 1968. Now there are around 200 of them there, a slow but sensibly paced increase based on a careful selection of imports and well-planned breeding to maintain the breed's sustained high level of physical soundness and excellent temperament.

The four Swiss breeds of *sennenhund* (strictly speaking, 'a dog of the Alpine dairy pasture' rather

Greater Swiss Mountain Dog.

than '*Gebirgshund*' or mountain dog) have been utilized in any variety of ways: herd-protector, drover's dog, butcher's dog and draught dog, and their physical strength, willingness to work and equable temperament reflect man's requirements of them. Professor Heim first proposed the generic name, *sennenhund*, for the four tricolour Swiss breeds but it was opposed by the early breed devotees of the Bernese dog. The name is of course misleading, for the Senn, the cattle herdsmen of the Alps, kept either small, fast, nimble dogs or none at all. The big dogs were employed in the valleys, where the farmers wanted dogs that would not hunt or wander but instinctively guard the homestead. They wanted dogs impressive enough to deter ill-intentioned strangers yet be well-disposed towards the family.

It is simply absurd to claim that these breeds were known as such by the Romans or descended from Molossian dogs. The Roman armies would have found (rather than introduced) big guard dogs, and very ferocious ones too, in all the mountain areas they invaded. Such big dogs were found all over the mountainous areas of Europe at the time the Molossian dogs were being extolled by Greek and Roman intellectuals. Why pick out the big dogs found in Epirus so specifically? It is also incorrect to claim centuries of pure-breeding behind each of these big Swiss breeds of dog. Researchers quoting from the German author Strebel (*Die Deutschen Hunde*,1904) and Professor Heim, a geologist not a historian, need to exercise great care. Newfoundland fanciers are

Entlebucher.

aware of some of Professor Heim's rather unusual theories on their breed.

The other Swiss breeds show no signs of exaggeration. The Entlebucher, 16–19in, tricolour and short-tailed, has survived bad times through the dedicated interest of people like Franz Schertenleib and the veterinary surgeon Dr Kobler. Coming from the Entlebuch region in the Lucerne canton, mainly between the valleys of the Little Emme and the Enteln, they are alert, agile, sure-footed dogs, eager to work and make themselves useful, sharper and nimbler than their sister breeds. Now recognized by our KC and backed by an enterprising and lively breed club, the Entlebucher Mountain Dog Club of Great Britain has worked closely with its Swiss counterpart in running comprehensive breeding tests, spanning health tests, conformation checks and character examinations. There are now six bitches qualified to breed in the UK, with Norfolkfields Benji accepted as the first UK stud dog for the breed.

The Appenzeller, resembling the Rottweiler from further north, is a bigger, 19–23in and 48–55lb dog, also tricolour, with a short, thick, glossy coat and a full tail, curling over the back. Coming from the Toggenburg valley around St Gall, it was once known as the Toggenburger or Toggenburg Triebhund (drover). Watchful, vigilant, full of vitality and more boisterous than the look-alike Entlebucher, it was used with sheep and cattle and as a draught dog. The bigger (25–28in) Grosser Schweizer Sennenhund (or Greater Swiss Dog of the Alpine high pastures, once called the Bouvier Suisse) is more

Appenzeller.

like a taller, lighter-boned, shorter-coated Bernese Mountain Dog and it surprises me that this breed has only recently been favoured in England, although it now possesses an Interim Standard, having become recognized by our KC. In America it is an outstanding obedience trialler and is considered an ideal family dog – sturdy, robust, friendly by nature but instinctively protective, gentle with children and easily managed.

The big Bernese farm dogs came in different colours, tricolour, red, yellow and red with white. The old records show all these colours and they were not bred separately. From the middle of the nineteenth century, the cheeseries were built in the valleys and on the lower slopes and farmers began to use big draught dogs to bring milk there by dog-cart. When the St Bernards became fashionable after 1850, some of the bigger red and yellow dogs were actually sold as St Bernards. The tricolour dogs fell out of favour except in a few isolated places like Schwarzenburg in the south of Berne canton. Here the people were less well off and had poor roads. They found big draught-dogs extremely useful to dairymen, butchers, basket-weavers, tool-makers and traders in garden produce. These dogs were bought and sold at an inn called Durrbach-Gasthaus and became known as Durrbach-dogs.

The St Bernard
The breed histories of the Swiss tricolour breeds compare most favourably with the sheer nonsense written about the St Bernard down the years. And what a pity that is, for the St Bernard is a truly magnificent breed, full of virtue and worthy of our admiration. The St Bernard really doesn't need wildly exaggerated stories about its prowess in the snow-rescue field. The facts indicate that the role of the hospice-dog was to *prevent* travellers from getting lost in deep snow, rather than rescue them with brandy and blankets. The monks had no fixed ideas on breeding, resorting to outside blood of other breeds and never having success in rearing puppies at the hospice, needing to send whelping bitches down to the valley.

The monks sold or gave away the very large pups and those with long coats. Yet the short-coated variety has never had the acclaim of the longer-coated version. Wynn, in his *History of the Mastiff* (1886), states that at one stage the monks obtained dogs that

were probably identical with those that defended flocks in the Abruzzi mountains. The legendary Barry was a medium-sized short-coated dog. Herr Schumacher has written that around 1830 the monks had to resort to Newfoundland and Great Dane bitches to produce more robust offspring. From 1835 to 1845, huge 'Alpine mastiffs' were often recorded and even drawn by Landseer. A dog called L'Ami was exhibited in 1829 as the largest dog in England and as an Alpine mastiff but was probably a cropped-eared Great Dane. Many of the St Bernards imported into Britain from 1860 were described as 'coming from the Monastery of St Bernard' but most of them were merely descendents of dogs that had been bred there years before. 'Idstone' refers to an outcross to a Pyrenean 'wolfhound' when the hospice kennels were stricken with distemper.

Looking at contemporary St Bernards, I suspect that the master breeders who developed the breed in Britain towards the end of the nineteenth century resorted to mastiff blood to produce the desired massiveness and powerful head and obtain extra stature in the breed. This is perhaps now coming through in excess and the St Bernard has become very different from every other breed of dog from the mountainous areas of the Western world. But whether true to their ancestor breeds or not, the big dogs from Switzerland have captured our hearts with their massive grandeur, considerable handsomeness and long-acknowledged qualities as companion-dogs. We are indebted to the Swiss for giving us such widely admired breeds. The quite remarkable feature of these big dogs is their character, remarkable for its tolerance, urbanity, restraint and self-discipline – an ideal model for any hefty young human; as Shakespeare once wrote:

> O! It is excellent
> To have a giant's strength, but it is tyrannous
> To use it like a giant.

The Iberian Dogs
I have been impressed by the Portuguese and Spanish livestock protection breeds and seen some of them at work. I was surprised to learn of a Portuguese judge, when judging his Estrela Mountain Dog entry at Bath Dog Show in 1978, refusing to judge a short-haired exhibit in the same class as the long-haired variety.

Smooth-haired Estrela Mountain Dog.

BELOW LEFT: *The look-alike Rafeiro do Alentejo – also from Portugal.*

Shortly after this incident, I was in Lisbon and called on the Clube Portugues de Canicultura, based there, for clarification. I was briefed that both the long- and short-haired varieties are within their breed standard, but not inter-bred. This is to me a needless reducing of the gene pool and can only be yet another manifestation of the dreaded 'purebreeding' mantra. The shepherds I talked to about this matter just shrugged dismissively and expressed scorn at such a foolish distinction, never respected by them. Their dogs were smaller than the show entry here and those paraded

at the World Dog Show held in Oporto and Lisbon in 2001. I asked the shepherds about the other Portuguese breed of this type, the Rafeiro do Alentejo; they pointed to a tawny-yellow solid-coloured dog lying nearby, saying that it was one and their favoured sire! (The others I saw elsewhere of this breed were bicoloured, several were dappled.) They mentioned, with admiration, a breed further north, the Cao de Gado Transmontana, often 30in at the shoulder and used to get the cattle between summer and winter pastures. The Portuguese shepherds, like all shepherds before them, bred good dog to good dog; breed identity didn't matter for them.

The Spanish Mastiff is, for me, unwisely named. In time, the exaggerators will doubtless aim to make them increasingly mastiff-like, using our Mastiff as a mistaken model. The Spanish Mastiff should be modelled on a companion breed like the Portuguese and Pyrenean livestock-protection dogs. Again, the specimens in the field were appreciably smaller (and noticeably fiercer!) than the exhibits at World Dog Shows, and there were plenty at both the Oporto and Lisbon shows. The working dogs I encountered in the high pastures of upland Spain were not all happy to catch the scent of my own dog, secured in my car. They were wolf-grey, around 28in at the shoulder and

Heavily boned Spanish Mastiff.

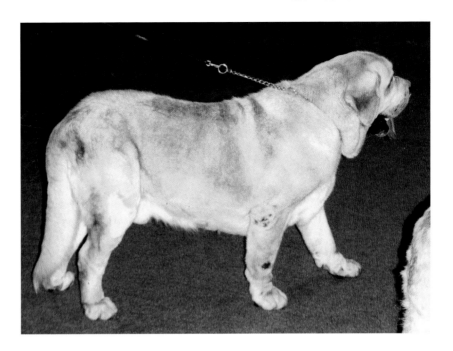

BELOW: *Uruguayan Sheepdog.*

completely at ease with the shepherds' young children. They were highly suspicious of a stranger like me. They had a much more powerful gait than the show dogs but were lighter in bone and substance. The show exhibits I have seen at several world shows were dangerously over-boned and quite clumsy-looking; this is not a good sign for their long-term future. In Uruguay, developed initially as a Spanish colony

and whose main income comes from agriculture, there is a large flock-guardian breed, quite similar to the working type of Spanish Mastiff; perhaps a useful source for an outcross should Spanish lines become too close. Here, again, the classic flock guardian physique is seen, as function decided form.

The Balkan Dogs

The countries of the former Yugoslavia are only now revealing the range of breeds, especially in the pastures, developed and valued there. Slovenia has long been proud of its Karst Shepherd or Krasevec, once known abroad as the Istrian Shepherd and worked in the Slovene Karst area around Pivka. Two feet tall at the shoulder and around 90 pounds, silver-grey or dark grey, there are well over a thousand of them, mainly around Ljubljana, where the breed is widely used as a service dog and guard dog. From the mountain of that name, in Macedonia, comes the Sar Planinac, a very similar breed to the Karst, in size and coat, with a bigger variety called the Sar Tip. The Tornjak of Bosnia/Croatia is of similar size, but carries its tail high and comes in piebald or white with black patches; in 1997 there were only 200 registered dogs but in the last decade national pride has ensured their survival. The Greek Sheepdog is in the mould of the Maremma, the Kuvasz types and the Tatra dog of

Spike-collared Greek Sheepdog.

Poland – a strapping white, or mainly white, thick-coated dog, purely a working dog.

In Romania, their old Romanian Shepherd Dog is now known as the Carpathian Shepherd Dog, in a wide range of coat colours, with the mainly white or piebald Mioritic Shepherd becoming the better-regarded breed by the urban community seeking larger more handsome guard-dogs. Less favoured but equally distinctive is the Karakachan Dog of

Romanian Sheepdog.

Bulgaria, now being specially bred by a conservation organization called Semperviva to deter wolves from pastures rather than face a more drastic culling by organized shoots. Similar breeds in nearby countries such as the Kuvasz and Komondor of Hungary, the Tatra Mountain Dog of Poland and the Slovakian Shepherd or Cuvac show how the white coat in flock-guarding dogs has been preferred. This is covered later in the book.

Transhumance Studies

In their book, referred to earlier, the Coppingers recorded how they sat by the roadside in Macedonia near the Albanian border for over a fortnight studying the thousands and thousands of sheep, with shepherds and dogs, moving from the lowland winter pastures of Greece over to the summer pastures along the border, the annual spring migration to the Sarplanina Mountains. They point out that claims of a separate identity for the Italian flock-guarding breed, the Maremmano-Abruzzese, rested on the fact that the two were the same breed – with one much more visible, in Maremma, the pasture by the sea, and the other, the Abruzzese, less so in the more remote mountain pastures of the Abruzzi Mountains along the central Apennines – but seen in different coats at different times of the year. They found all over southern Europe and the Balkans that the dogs were named after the locality they worked in, not developed as distinct breeds, with separate breed 'points'. They hazarded a guess that well over a million adult sheepdogs are moving back and forth over three continents in a thousand-mile-wide band from the western Mediterranean to somewhere east of the Himalayas, pointing out that each year there is a mixing and remixing of endless populations of dogs. How could 'breed sanctity' be maintained in such circumstances?

The Coppingers, both biologists, have set up the Livestock Guarding Dog Project at Hampshire College in the USA, based on the Anatolian Shepherd Dogs imported there. The reintroduction of wolves in parts of America, backed by a change of public attitude towards them, led to sheep being lost to them at an unacceptable rate; in 1990 for example, one million sheep a year were lost to wolves at a cost of 22 million dollars. Research into the Coppingers' project showed that seventy-six producers, who had

Maremma Sheepdogs.

BELOW: *Pyrenean Mountain Dog in the pastures.* PATRICIA LORE, COURTESY OF BRYAN CUMMINS

suffered between one and 202 attacks in just one year, found that within a year, after the introduction of dogs, no further losses were experienced, and no predators had been killed because the dogs had so effectively deterred them. Here, the National Farmers Union has estimated that in 2012, dog attacks on livestock cost farmers in England and Wales an estimated £1 million; there could be a role for flock guardians here, although their role and type would need as much careful consideration as their training and location.

Essential Criteria

We have sadly but perhaps inevitably lost most of the flock-guarding dogs, including some distinct breed types, through economic change and the extinction of many wild predators. Working dogs that wore spiked collars, had their ears cropped, fought wolves, gave birth to their pups in a hole in the ground and slept out of doors in the snow and chill wind deserve a better fate than becoming victim to misguided modern breed enthusiasts and their fads. In preserving those breeds that have survived we must remember the *essential* criteria that led to these flock-guarding dogs developing as such magnificent examples of the canine race, such as robustness, a functional physique and size commensurate with soundness.

Big flock-guarding dogs have been vital for centuries in countries where sheep are pastured in remote mountain areas. Charles Darwin, on a South American tour, noted how such dogs were trained from puppyhood for their future role. His surprise at finding such dogs is in itself surprising; the mountain pastures of Spain, Portugal, Italy and the Balkans, much nearer home, had featured such dogs for centuries. The flock-master taught the pups how to be suckled by ewes, sleep in a nest of wool and then progress to expect meat at the end of the day at a set location, where the sheep would accompany it. Puppies of the sheep-guarding breeds slept with the lambs and sometimes adult bitches allowed lambs to

Kangal Dogs at work in Turkey.

BOTTOM LEFT: *Spike-collared Cantabrian flock guardian, northwest Spain, 1988.*

BOTTOM RIGHT: *Caucasian Owtcharka at a World Dog Show.*

suckle from them. Dog and sheep bonded from such activities, but it was absolutely vital that the whelps lived with the sheep even before their eyes opened. When flocks of sheep were sold it was common practice to sell the dogs that managed them as well. In this way many sheepdogs went from countries like Britain and Spain to their colonies. This has led to British herding dogs in particular becoming not only the

most valued in the world but adapted and developed into native breeds in their new countries. This is discussed in Chapter 2.

It was enlightening to see breeds from the Eastern European countries, ranging from the rather proud Black Russian or Tchiorny Terrier, the formidable mid-Asian Owtcharka, the charming Sarplaninac, the

highly individual Pumi from Hungary, a variety of Laika breeds, the Chart Polski (which I wrongly identified as the Chortaj or West Russian coursing hound) to the Karelian Bear Dog (which I thought was so much bigger). Other countries provided the very attractive Iceland Farm Dog, the impressive Greenland Dog, the magnificent Greater Swiss Mountain Dog, the rather nondescript Kromfohrlander, the distinctive Spanish Mastiff, the imposing Pyrenean Mastiff and the modest Pyrenean Sheepdog in two types of facial hair.

David Hancock, writing on the Brussels World Dog Show in *Dogs Monthly* (1995)

I was impressed by some of the Leonbergers and most of the Great Swiss Mountain Dogs, a strapping handsome breed with no exaggerations and a manageable coat. I was less impressed by the Spanish Mastiffs, a flock guarding breed rather than a classic mastiff breed. Their mobility was severely hampered by excessive bone; they were quite unlike the huge but more active spike-collared flock guardians I once saw in northern Spain, actually working for their keep. The Sarplaninac, the big Yugoslavian herder, looked a fine breed, but I find it very difficult to distinguish this breed from the Kraski Ovcar or Karst Shepherd Dog from Slovenia. Both were entered and I really needed an expert on each breed to enlighten me on their differences. Both resembled a wolf-grey Estrela Mountain Dog. The Tibetan Mastiff entry was impressive, with many looking far bigger than the ones I see here, and with a wider range of coat colours. The Russian Owtcharkas were imposing dogs and not to be trifled with.

David Hancock, writing on the Dortmund World Dog Show in *Dogs Monthly* (2003)

The Shepherd's Mastiff

The shepherd's masty, that is for the folde, must neither be so gaunt nor so swifte as the greyhound, nor so fatte nor so heavy as the masty of the house; but verie strong, and able to fighte and follow the chase, that he may beat away the wolfe or other beasts, and to follow the theefe, and so recover the prey. And therefore his body should be rather long than short and thick; in all other points he must agree with the ban-dog. His head must be great and smooth and full of veins; his ears great and hanging; his joints long; his fore legs shorter than his hinder; but verie straight and great.

Conrad Heresbatch, *Four Bookes of Husbandrie* (1586), translated by Barnaby Grooge

As discussed in the previous section, powerful dogs bred to protect livestock have been utilized from the upland areas of Iberia in the west, right across to Iran and on to the highlands of Eastern Europe, from mountainous Balkan regions in the south and

Shepherd and his dogs in High Zerayshan, Tajikistan.

Shepherd and his dogs in the Caucasus.

Shepherd's mastiff, left foreground in Cuyp's The Negro Page, *1660.*

BELOW: Shepherd's mastiff, right foreground in Pillemont School, Mountain Landscape.

Shepherd's mastiff, centre foreground in Froment's 1476 depiction.

Shepherd's mastiff, centre in Heures de Rohan, *1415.*

Shepherd's mastiff, right foreground in de Crescens' Book of Husbandry.

OPPOSITE PAGE
TOP LEFT: *Fierce-looking shepherd's 'terrier': a print by J. Ward, c.1790.*

BOTTOM: *Shepherd's mastiff in Italy in Roos's landscape of 1657.*

BELOW: *Powerful English flock guardian in Landseer's* A Sleeping Dog, *1850.*

northwards to former Soviet states. Sometimes they are called shepherd dogs, sometimes mountain dogs, and a few dubbed 'mastiffs', despite the more precise use of that word in modern times. Their coat colours can vary from solid white to dark-grey and from a rich russet to solid black, often with tan. Many that developed as breeds are no longer used as herd-protectors and their numbers in northwest Europe seriously declined when draught dogs became a victim of the mechanized age. A number of shared features connect these far-flung types: a dense weatherproof jacket, a substantial build, an impressive magnanimity and a strong instinct to guard livestock placed under their supervision. As a group, they would be most accurately described as the flock guardians; in Britain in the distant past they were referred to as 'shepherd's mastiffs', but they were valued all over Europe, as the quote at the head of this section, and its source, indicates.

If you look at pastoral scenes in paintings from past centuries you can soon identify the widespread use of such protective dogs: Cuyp's 1660 portrayal of *The Negro Page* (left foreground); *The Extensive Mountainous Landscape with a Herdsman Driving his Flock* from the circle of Jean-Baptiste Pillemont

(1727–1808; right, foreground); *The Virgin in the Burning Bush* (detail) by Nicolas Froment (1476; centre foreground); *The Annunciation to the Shepherds* from Master of the Heures de Rohan (*c.*1410–20; centre); Pierre de Crescens' *Leading Animals to Pasture* from his fifteenth-century *Book of Husbandry* (right foreground); and Philipp Pieter Roos's 1680 painting of an Italianate landscape showing a shepherd and his dog resting by a pool. You can soon see

a common type of dog: a powerful, fierce-looking, usually spike-collared animal. Landseer picked up this kind of tough-minded, strongly made sheepdog in his *A Sleeping Dog* of *c*.1850, as did the painting by J. Ward, etched by H.R. Cook in 1790, of *The Shepherd's 'Terrier'*. To this day, in Northern Spain, the Balkans and in Eastern Europe, you can still find spike-collared flock guardians continuing this work. The mastiff type was perfectly exemplified in an early seventeenth century Flemish School depiction of a wedding procession entering a village.

Ancient Value

The ancients knew the value of big resolute dogs to guard their livestock. Aristotle, writing around 2300BC in *The History of Animals*, stated that: 'Of the Molossian breed of dogs, such as are employed

Shepherd's mastiff, centre foreground in The Wedding Party, *Flemish School, c.1620.*

in the chase are pretty much the same as those else-where; but sheepdogs of this breed are superior to the others in size, and in the courage with which they face the attacks of wild animals.' Varro wrote around 2000BC: 'Dogs…are of the greatest import-ance to us who feed the woolly flock, for the dog is the guardian of such cattle as lack the means to defend themselves, chiefly sheep and goats. For the wolf is wont to lie in wait for them and we oppose our dogs to him as defenders.' He went on to de-scribe these 'guardians' as having a stubby jaw with projecting fangs, a large head, thick shoulders and neck and of 'a leonine appearance'; those words describe a primitive mastiff.

Wolf Threat
Our contemporary affection for the wolf would not have been shared by those living in remote villages in India or a number of European countries in the middle ages. Wolves, operating in packs, have long threatened livestock and sought human prey when desperate for food. Powerful dogs of the flock-guarding type were needed to protect livestock, and strong-headed, very fast hounds were needed

to course them. Hunting wolves for sport may not appeal to twenty-first-century sympathies, but that should not lessen our admiration for wolfhounds, their bravery and athleticism in the hunt, when wolf numbers required checking. But the shepherd's mas-tiff didn't have the protection of the pack; theirs was a lonelier task, tied to their flock and their pasture, often unnumbered. Their dedicated flock protection in remote areas deserves our admiration. In his *The Illustrated Book of the Dog* (1879), Vero Shaw noted:

> In countries where the wolf is common and the lion not unknown, their penchant for mutton had to be guarded against, and for such use, it is probable that a more powerful and fiercer dog was employed than our modern collie. Indeed this is the case at the present day; and in Thibet the large black-and-tan Mastiffs of the country are used to guard the flocks and herds.

Robert Ekvall, writing in 1963, found twenty-one dogs of Tibetan Mastiff type, or three-and-a-half dogs per tent, when living for several weeks in an en-campment of just six tents.

The Tibetan Dogs

Time and time again you will find writers on these breeds linking them with an origin from the Tibetan 'Mastiff'. But I believe all such big mountain dogs or shepherd dogs share a common origin and came south with migrating people, ending up in the Pyrenees, the Alps, the Balkans and the foothills of the Himalayas. I can find no evidence of the Tibetan Mastiff existing before the Kuvasz, for example. It disappoints me, therefore, to see the St Bernard being bred more like a mastiff than a mountain dog. Historically, the hospice dogs were much more like the other mountain breeds and did not feature the massive head, loose lips and excessive dewlaps of the modern pedigree St Bernard. I can never see the rationale in extolling the proud history of a breed and then perpetuating that breed in a different mould. Huge dogs have a magnanimity, a munificence and a majesty all of their own and simply don't need exaggeration to promote themselves or win our admiration.

The Tibetan Mastiff has recovered from the absurd claims of Victorian and early twentieth-century zoologists, natural historians and even some archaeologists that the breed represented the original mastiff, whence came all mastiff types in the West. They are bred now to resemble what they have always been – big, strong, livestock-protection dogs, thick-coated, strong-muzzled and physically extremely robust. In their *The Tibetan Mastiff – Legendary Guardian of the Himalayas* (1989), Ann Rohrer and Cathy Flamholtz wrote:

> The Tibetan Mastiff holds a very special place in the hearts of the nomadic sheepherders. Perhaps they, above all, can truly appreciate the breed. The nomads, with their black yak-hair tents and large flocks of sheep, goats and yaks, come to resemble whole towns, temporarily halted in their eternal wandering. They live life on the move, roving from one highland pasture to another.

In this informative book, the authors describe the caravan dogs, used to protect a convoy of goods for trading, including livestock. They point out that:

> Appearance was of no particular importance to the caravan man. In order to effectively perform his job, however, the caravan dog had to have certain attributes. Imposing size, heavy bone, power and agility were musts. However, size could never be so exaggerated that it interfered with function. A giant cumbersome dog just couldn't keep up with the rigors of caravan travel.

There is a strong message there for all breeders of large pastoral dogs. It is worth a look at this classic

Tibetan Mastiff today.

Tibetan Mastiff in its homeland.

example of such a dog to assess its contemporary quality.

The Breed in Britain
It was good to read, in a critique on the Tibetan Mastiff Club Show of 2003, these admiring words:

> It is some years since I have judged the breed in this country and was amazed to see what progress has been made in uniformity of type and conformity to the Standard. Gone are the square, long-legged, plush-coated, Chow-headed dogs of yesteryear… Most were well ribbed-up with length of ribcage and compact loin, giving the desired body:height ratio. There has been a big improvement in strength of hindquarters and set of hocks.

All the points made are of importance to such a breed. The Finnish judge of the breed at Crufts in 2007 made these observations: 'The entry at Crufts posed me with many problems as the variation in type was extensive. The dogs ranged from tall and leggy to small and low to the ground. Several were long cast whereas some were too short in body and too high on the leg.' Such comments are worrying; this judge pointed out that similar problems had been encountered but overcome in Finland. When I saw the breed at the Helsinki World Dog Show, I was impressed with the quality there. In 2009, judges of the breed here reported some alarming faults: poor hind movement, clicking hock joints, straight stifles and too long a hock (in other words exaggerated angulation), faulty front movement, weak hocks and too close a movement in the hind legs. A year later, a judge expressed disappointment in the quality of movement, lack of layback in shoulder, weak and close rear movement with the exhibits showing good breed type having less quality than those without. But in 2012, it was reassuring to read a critique stating: 'I enjoyed seeing the progress that has been made since I last judged the breed in 2009. Fronts have improved greatly and rear angulation is better. Rear movement is improving, though still some way to lose cow hocks completely.' This is a magnificent ancient breed, developed in the hardest of schools and meriting the very best custodianship, especially here, as it is officially deemed to be a British breed, having been first registered here.

Medieval Laws
Any breed developed to drive off fierce and savage predators needs the strength, stamina and intense dedication to do so. Such powerful dogs have long been valued. In medieval times, there were laws under which some court fines were assessed in terms of wolves' tongues. At one time, the yearly tax in Wales was established at 300 wolves' heads. France was one country particularly populated by wolves; as early as 1467, Louis XI created a special wolf-hunting office, whose top member was appointed from the highest families in the land. In the French province of Gevaudan in the 1760s one wolf is alleged to have killed more than fifty people, the majority women and children. At the end of the French revolution in 1797, forty people were killed by wolves along with tens of thousands of sheep, goats and horses, and, in some remote districts not a single watchdog was left alive. The dense forests led to the French mainly hunting them with packs of scenthounds rather than coursing them with faster hounds. But in the remote pastures, the shepherd relied on his 'mastiff'.

Use in the Hunt
In Britain, once the wolf had been exterminated, the need for flock guardians or shepherd's mastiffs disappeared, but all over Europe, strapping herding dogs continued to be favoured, if only to protect

flocks and herds being driven to distant pastures and markets from human threats and village curs. The drovers of Britain used the Smithfield Sheepdog (a leggy, shaggy-haired shepherd dog, named after the London market of that name), which became the Old English Sheepdog and in Wales the Welsh Hillman. Some of the fiercer ones became involved in the European stag, wolf and boar hunts, not as hounds, but as 'matins', expendable 'catch-dogs', sacrificed at the kill to save the more valuable, better-bred hounds. Artists such as Hondius, Oudry, Snyders and de Vos all captured both the ferocity and the canine sacrifice in such dangerous employment.

Local Trial

Perhaps inspired by living in the Windrush Valley in Oxfordshire, classic grazing fields for drovers en route to markets to the southeast, I once tried my two young Bullmastiffs as flock guardians, with the consent of a local farmer. Handicapped by not having been weaned alongside sheep, but naturally protective and responsive to new training, the two powerful dogs soon understood that they were to guard the fields and me, the temporary shepherd. They responded immediately to any dogs passing by (a public footpath crossed the pasture) and soon learned to ignore the sheep (and the prospect of mutton!) But the most informative reaction was from the sheep; they very quickly relaxed with two big dogs lying down in their field and, more importantly, followed the dogs when I led them around the perimeter of their pasture. If it's not wishful thinking, the sheep seemed to know they were expected to follow the dogs – and did so. The relaxed, laid-back attitude of the hefty dogs no doubt removed any hint of threat to the sheep from them. But I could see at once the immense value to a shepherd of a powerful dog, left alone to guard his flock.

The ease of modern living has led to our devaluing the contribution made throughout human history by the flock protectors, but our ancestors prized them and developed them as highly impressive, extraordinarily robust, canine specimens. We must be careful with the surviving breeds not to substitute

Author's Bullmastiff settling down as shepherd's mastiff.

Sheep instinctively following the author's Bullmastiff.

show-ring criteria for functional need. Huge cow-hocked, straight-stifled, over-coated, under-muscled shepherd's mastiffs would not have lasted long in the demanding pastures of past centuries. Our respect both for our rural heritage and those breeds surviving man's changing requirements needs to be demonstrated by a seeking of soundness before 'stance' and fitness ahead of flashiness. These quite remarkable faithful, selfless, admirable dogs, often killed by marauding packs of predatory wolves, deserve no less. In fairly recent times, in North America, between 1985 and 2005, eighty-three livestock protection dogs were killed by wolves in the Rocky Mountain states alone, according to C. and J. Urbigkit's review of 2010 published in the *Sheep and Goat Research Journal* (Vol. 25). In 2013, a report from the Zoological Society of London reported that the grey wolf population in the world had quadrupled in forty years to more

than 11,500. In Greece alone, farmers are paid more than £1 million in compensation for the 32,000 sheep and goats, 2,000 cattle and 2,000 horses and donkeys killed by wolves each year. With around 330 sheep currently being killed annually by bears, reintroduced from the Czech Republic into the Pyrenees, perhaps the reintroduction too of the shepherd's mastiff, more determined than the mountain dogs, would be timely.

> Many hundreds of years ago, when our island was principally primeval forest, with few clearings, it must necessarily have been infested with wolves, bears, and the lesser British carnivorae, and to protect the flocks and herds it must have been requisite to have a large and powerful dog, able to cope with such formidable and destructive foes, able to undergo any amount of fatigue, and with a jacket to withstand all vicissitudes of weather, for his avocation was an everyday one; day and night, and in all weathers, was he watching and battling with heat and storm and marauding foes. What other dog but the old English sheepdog possesses attributes necessary for the multifarious duties urged upon such a business?

Rawdon Lee, quoting the leading expert on the breed at that time, Dr Edwardes-Ker of Woodbridge, Suffolk, in *Modern Dogs of Great Britain and Ireland (Non-Sporting Division,* 1894*)*.

Steppe Guardians

> The wolf-like Turkoman or Natolian watch-dog… is rugged and fierce, with erect ears and rather furry tail. Its jaws are very powerful. This race is used by the Turkoman hordes as the guardian of their cattle and tents, and extends from central high Asia to the Bosphorus. It is also employed in Persia by the wandering tribes for the same purpose… It is a shaggy animal, nearly so large as a Newfoundland, and very fierce and powerful.
>
> W.C.L. Martin, *The History of the Dog* (1845)

From Pasture to Poseur
The imposing dogs of the flock-guarding or mountain dog breeds from around the world have long found favour in Britain. Impressive breeds from Portugal in the west to Hungary in the east and from Turkey in the

Central Asian Owtcharka.

BELOW: Show Champion Central Asian Owtcharka.

south to Germany in the north have found their way here. But the huge and often quite fierce pastoral dogs of Russia have yet to attract favour. Russian breeds like the Borzoi and the Samoyed have long been admired here and are now very much part of our dog show world. But the flock guardians or owtcharkas from Central Asia, the Caucasus and Southern Russia, now the Ukraine, despite appearing at world dog shows, do not feature here. There were plenty at the World Dog Show held in Helsinki in 1998; some were very resentful of other dogs, many being muzzled, even in the ring. Several were 32 inches at the withers.

Owtcharka Types

These distinct breeds are powerful, assertive and very protective dogs of some stature but not exactly pets in our sense of the word. The Caucasian sheepdog is

Caucasian Shepherd Dog.

BELOW: The lost Shepherd's Mastiff of the Swiss Alps – the Alpine Mastiff.

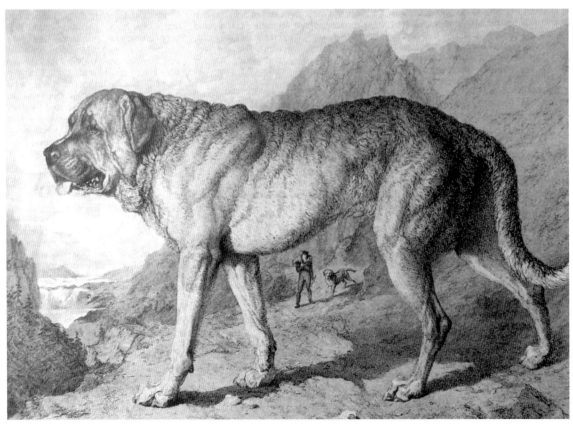

ABOVE: Karst Sheepdog of Yugoslavia.

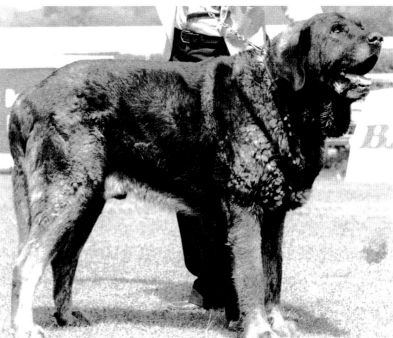

Spanish Mastiff of 1983.

very much like the Karst or Istrian sheepdog, the Sar Planinac or Macedonian/Illyrian sheepdog and similar to the brindle form of the Spanish Mastiff. There are, not surprisingly given the distances involved, different varieties of the Caucasian dog: the massive thickset type from Checheno-Ingush, northeast of the Caucasus; the taller lighter type from Azerbaijan in the southeast towards Azarbayjan-e-Sharqi in Iran; the smaller, squarer type of Dagestan, east of the Caucasus; and the big rangier Kangalian from the border area between Georgia and Turkey. Some experts claim that the best and most uniform specimens actually come from Georgia. Their restriction to these remote areas has led to these dogs being largely unknown in the West. They are becoming better known in eastern European countries and in the

TOP LEFT: Estrela Mountain Dog.

TOP RIGHT: Anatolian Shepherd Dog.

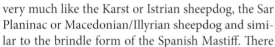

Tibetan Mastiff.

USA, where they became recognized, as the breed of Caucasian Mountain Dog, by the United Kennel Club in 1995.

If you lined up a Caucasian Owtcharka, a Carpathian Shepherd, a Karst, a Sar Planinac, a Spanish Mastiff, an Estrela Mountain Dog, an Anatolian Shepherd Dog and a Tibetan Mastiff, in a brindle or wolf-grey coat, and kept in mind the lost shepherd's mastiff of the Swiss Alps or Alpine Mastiff of old, you could soon see how function decided form in such breeds, as well as how very similar is their type. This, despite the immense distance from the Atlantic in the west to the Caspian Sea in the east. If you lined up parti-coloured specimens of the Rafeiro do Alentejo from Portugal, the Pyrenean Mastiff, the Pyrenean Mountain Dog, the Anatolian Shepherd Dog, the Mioritic Shepherd and the Bucovina Shepherd of Romania, again the similarities would be startling. To do their work as flock guardians, mountain dogs or steppe dogs have to have thick, weatherproof coats, size and substance, great stamina and robustness and a strongly developed protective instinct. Making use of this natural guarding instinct, the owtcharka type has been crossed with a St Bernard to produce the Moscow Guard Dog, a huge, imposing protection dog, now becoming favoured in Russia.

The Central Asian Owtcharka needs less coat but all the other attributes listed above to do its work. The breed is found from the east of the Urals to areas of Siberia and south into Mongolia. The best examples today tend to be in Turkmenistan, where it has been

Caucasian Owtcharka.

recognized as 'a national treasure'; they can also be encountered in Uzbekistan, Kazakhstan and Tajikistan. Their coats are shorter, but their skin is thicker than the other owtcharka breeds, and their ears and tails are normally cropped. They remind me of a smooth St Bernard. They resemble too the bigger forms of shepherd's dog once depicted here, when used in times past as a shepherd's mastiff or flock guardian. The Central Asian is a powerful breed, having been used as a hunting dog on boar and bear because of its bravery and dash. Those with tan markings over their eyebrows have been dubbed the 'four-eyed Mongolian Dogs'.

The third owtcharka breed is the South Russian, white, off-white or grey, long-haired, over 30 inches at the shoulder and weighing around 165lb. They

Parti-coloured Rafeiro do Alentejo.

South Russian Owtcharka.

Reinagle's Old English Sheepdog.

remind me a little of the early depictions of our Old English Sheepdog, as portrayed by Reinagle, for example. They are similar to the Hungarian Komondor, without that coat texture, being used, like the latter, on the steppes, only in their case in the Ukraine. This south Russian breed is not one to be trifled with; it is known as 'the white giant' in some areas of its homeland and is often harshly treated. There is an old Russian saying that states that a 'pampered South Russian is a killer'! The military have found uses for them but their export is not encouraged. Despite their reputation for 'hair-trigger aggression', you have to admire a breed that can survive such a hard climate, such fearsome predators and stern handlers, over many centuries. Their aggression may have been the key to their survival.

Innate protectiveness in dogs does bring with it intense loyalty, as owners of dogs from the flock-

guarding breeds will know. I was not surprised to learn of the Caucasian Owtcharka, left behind when deposed leader Aslan Abashidze was exiled from Adzharia in western Georgia in 2004, being reunited with his owner in Moscow after his excessive pining moved all who witnessed it. Abashidze, for all his faults, has been credited with saving this breed from extinction. He was said to have had around eighty of these dogs, subsequently auctioned off by the Georgian dog breeders' federation. The breed is reported to have guarded the Soviet side of the Berlin Wall. Their sheer size and immediate suspicion of strangers has led to their employment as guard dogs within Russia. I believe it is incorrect to describe such a breed as aggressive; rather the flock-guarding breeds are overtly protective, of their owners and his property, a most valuable instinct for shepherds and drovers to utilize.

Pastoral Guards Valued

German travel writer Johann Kohl, in his *Journeys in South Russia* (1841), described the shepherds there and their dogs:

> The shepherds make their evening meal round a blazing fire, with their twenty watchful dogs encircling them… Between every two shepherds three or four dogs are placed, also at equal distances from each other. In order to make the dogs stay on their respective posts, a piece of an old cloak or sheepskin is laid on the spot…as each knows his own, he is sure to lie down wherever he finds it.

Kohl visited Scotland around 1844 and described a drover's dog seen there as a 'wild, shaggy wolf-dog'. Such a dog was often described as a shepherd's mastiff.

In his *Researches into the History of the British Dog* (1866), George Jesse quotes a Mrs Atkinson as saying of the flock guardian of Tartary she saw near Omsk in West Siberia: 'As I looked at her I thought I never saw anything more beautiful; she was a steppe dog; her coat was jet black, ears long and pendant, her tail long and bushy; indeed, it was a princely animal.' All

over Tartary too, these huge flock-guarding breeds were valued. One old saying there goes, 'To ask an Usbek to sell his wife would be no affront, but to ask him to sell his dog, an unpardonable insult'. Not a very modern view!

The Turkish Kangal

The travels of steppe nomads into Europe and the establishment of the Ottoman Empire ensured that such dogs became known further afield, from southeast Europe, including the Balkans, to southeast Russia and northwest to Austria and a part of Hungary. Ash records a misadventure with an Albanian flock guarding dog in 1859, the writer dubbing it the 'Albanian king of dogs, who is undoubtedly first cousin to the Turkish one.' This account was sparked by a visit to the Islington Dog Show and a sight of Frank Buckland's Turkish Guard Dog being exhibited there. Hamilton Smith writes in 1840 of the dogs used in Persia to guard flocks of sheep, the dog of Natolia, stating they were a deep yellowish-red, with a few of them black and white – 'believed to be cross-breeds'. Smith records that a similar dog was found in Central Asia to the Bosphorus.

Anatolian Shepherd Dog.

Turkish Kangal Dog.

Fanciers of Anatolian Shepherd Dogs might find that of interest, although the title of their breed still causes controversy. Firstly they are not shepherd dogs in the strict sense; secondly, in their native country, the black-faced ones are called Karabash dogs and the white ones Akbash dogs, (now a separate breed in the USA); and thirdly, the Kangal Dog is the title favoured by many (and now recognized separately by the KC). In a country the size of Turkey it is likely that local differences would be found in the national flock-guarding dog. People in Muslim countries are sometimes alleged to despise dogs but Ash quotes a 1662 account that states that 'There is no people in the world that looks after its dogs and horses as well as the Turk.' Perhaps there is a worldwide difference of attitude between those who use dogs and those who don't.

The recognition, outside Turkey of their national dog, the Kangal Dog, tells you much about lobbying in the show world and not much about the pursuit of accuracy in breed titles by the various kennel clubs of the world. Enthusiasts are vital in any breed, but when they follow their own path, despite neither researching thoroughly nor respecting the country of origin's position on their national breed, they can be a menace. The flock guardian/livestock-protection dog of Turkey is the Kangal Dog. The recognition by the KC here of the breed, in 1983, under the title of Anatolian Sheepdogs, then Anatolian (Karabash) Dogs, has long been disputed. Thirty years ago, I was invited to speak

at the annual seminar of the English breed club by the leading enthusiast here, the late Natalka Czartoryska, about the background and likely history of the breed. On presenting my doubts about the validity of both the KC-accepted title and different *breeds* for this Turkish dog, based on evidence given to me by Susan Goldhor, Director of Agricultural Research at the School of Oriental and African Studies and supported by Dr Sebastian Payne, a British zoo-archaeologist, specializing in the origins of domestic animals in Turkey, in 1982 (also provided to the Chairman of the KC of the time), it was made abundantly clear to me that my views were unacceptable. Now, the KC has recognized the Turkish Kangal Dog but only alongside the continuing recognition of the Anatolian Shepherd Dog. This important step is a result of the work of Margaret Mellor, whose influential book, with Lesley Tahtakilic, *The Kangal Dog of Turkey* (2009), is the best breed book and *the* convincingly argued case for the correct title.

I suspect that this impressive breed has influenced this type of dog across a wide spectrum; their phenotype, temperament and identical use is found in any number of countries, especially those adjacent to Turkey or once part of the Ottoman Empire. An acquaintance of mine, who, unusually, travelled widely in Albania in the 1990s, found identical dogs there performing their time-honoured role. The influence of the Kangal Dog can be seen in the Balkan flock-guarding breeds. Such links are important; if and when a breed is found to have inherited defects, other related breeds need to be examined too, in their own long-term interests. The Kangal Dog of Central Turkey is expected to have a coat with solid colours varying from sand to pale grey, with the black mask considered 'characteristic'. The white dog, or Akbash Dog, of Western Turkey has made good progress in North America. The KC has decreed that, from 2005, in their breed of Anatolian Shepherd Dog, all coat colours are acceptable, with or without the black mask. The KC recognized the Turkish Kangal Dog in 2005. It could be that in the course of time, every solid-coloured, sand to pale-grey dog with a black mask, is transferred to the Turkish Kangal Dog register, with the other type lapsing, out of a paucity of registrations.

United States Programme

Earlier, I referred to the Livestock Protection Dog programme in the United States, in which the

Sar Planinac.

BELOW: The Komondor.

The Kuvasz.

employment of powerful flock-guarding breeds like the steppe dogs has been studied and then applied by Ray and Lorna Coppinger, both biologists. Their subsequent breeding programme has led to around a thousand dogs being placed with farmers and ranchers across 35 states. These dogs, selectively bred to produce ideal flock guarding specimens, come from Italian Maremma, Yugoslavian Sar Planinac, Anatolian Shepherd Dog, Hungarian Komondor and Pyrenean Mountain Dog stock, often inter-bred. Brought up from their first days of mobility as pups with sheep, these dogs are now being successfully used to deter predators, much to the gain of sheep farmers. Unlike herding dogs which respond to human commands, these guard dogs have to function without human intervention. These dogs learn not to guard livestock in set locations but to move with the sheep and patrol the area the sheep are grazing in at any one time.

This is the system used by shepherds from the steppes of Hungary and Russia to the highlands of Tibet in the east and of the Iberian peninsula in the west, even taken to Uruguay by the Spanish colonists,

leading to the emergence of the Uruguayan sheepdog, so like a Pyrenean Mastiff. James Murray, in his *A Summer in the Pyrenees* (1837), observed that 'The Pyrenean shepherd, his dog, and his flock, seem to understand each other's duties. Mutual security and affection are the bonds which unite them.' Those few words are an apt summary of the shepherd-sheepdog partnership, which goes way beyond mere dog-ownership. The use of Anatolians to protect goats from cheetahs, baboons, jackals and caracals in Namibia is another present-day example of the value of the timeless employment of big, strapping dogs to protect livestock.

The Hungarian Dogs

The Hungarian pastoral breeds, with the exception of the unique Puli, mirror the form of other nations' dogs: the Kuvasz resembles the Tatra and Pyrenean Mountain Dogs, the Komondor has a distinct Bergamasco look to it, the Mudi resembles the spitz herders and the Pumi looks like a Labrit, as function influences form. In their book *Dogs of Hungary* (1977), Sarkany and Ocsag wrote:

The nomadic shepherds were always aware of the value of a good working companion: they kept two types of dog, the big white guard dogs who took over the flock at night, and the small active sheep dog, the Puli, who actually worked the flock by day. The shepherds protected the characteristics of their dogs by taking care that the two types did not cross-breed, and by ruthlessly culling out weak specimens.

They went on to point out that sheepdogs had to endure great extremes of temperature, variations of over 40° C between summer and winter, with wind chill adding to the challenge. The two quite different big white flock-guarding breeds were favoured in the same country, grazing areas being rather different where each was patronized. The Kuvasz was kept in the mountainous areas, sometimes in what were termed white villages, where only white livestock-protection dogs were tolerated. The Polish Kuvasz-equivalent is in the Tatra Mountain pastures (with their Lowland Sheepdog equating with the Puli), while the Slovakian Kuvasz is at home in the higher Carpathians and Romania has the Carpathian Sheepdog. The Komondor was very much the steppe flock guardian of Hungary. The movement of sheep from pasture to pasture has rarely observed national borders.

Worldwide Role

The Smithfield sheepdog may have been our nearest equivalent to the fearsome flock guardians of the steppes. There are many depictions of powerful, very protective larger editions of our surviving collie breeds in paintings of past centuries. But the Tasmanian Smithfields of Graham Rigby in Australia (*see* Chapter 2) may well represent the last examples of our lost flock guardians. Once predators such as lynx and wolf have been removed, the need for these dogs lapses. But wherever we raise livestock in areas featuring such predators, the protective instincts of these dogs become valued once again.

Unwise Imports

Perhaps we should admire them from afar, for all these powerful livestock-protection breeds would find urban living in western countries intolerable. When I see such highly protective dogs at foreign shows, usually securely muzzled and justifiably so,

I ponder the provisions of our foolish Dangerous Dogs Act. We are not free to import breeds like the Fila Brasileiro, the Japanese Tosa and the Dogo Argentino, recognized as the national breed of each of their native countries. When I see them at overseas shows they behave immaculately, both with people and other dogs. Their owners shake their heads in disbelief when I tell them of our law-makers. Our global reputation for common sense, moderation and an enlightened attitude to animals has been undermined. Foreign breeds renowned for their overt protectiveness, like the owtcharkas, can paradoxically but rightly enter our country freely. I am strongly against breed-specific legislation; the law as it stands protects nobody. Dogs of every breed can be successfully socialized; any individual dog of any breed can transgress if not adequately socialized. But it is asking a great deal to expect a big, free-ranging, highly independent dog from a remote part of the world to become, overnight, an urban pet. We have to respect its heritage ahead of our selfish desires.

Big, naturally protective sheepdogs like the owtcharkas of Russia, the Kuvasz breeds of Hungary, Slovakia and Poland and the spaghetti-coated Komondor have long served the shepherds of the steppes and been greatly valued by them. Now, in the New World, their value is being recognized anew. It is a rich heritage and one to be treasured. Brave, determined protective dogs in any country deserve our admiration. The Tibetan Mastiff has been bred down to be an acceptable companion dog in the developed countries; most mountain dogs are best left where they belong.

There is one breed that brings the best of this type of dog to our more crowded world – the Leonberger of today, created in the flock guardian mould. It may never have carried out this timeless role, but for me this impressive breed epitomizes both the character and the stature of such admirable, selfless dogs – gentle giants of imposing grandeur, forever ready to serve.

In all pastoral countries and in all times the dog has been man's chosen and most useful help-meet as guardian of the sheepfold. Originally and in mountainous lands a massive dog was used to protect the flocks and herds against predatory wolves – one who was capable unaided of tackling a wolf... The shepherd's

Leonberger atop a Mountain *by Conradyn Cunaeus, c. 1880.*

dog of the Pyrenees and of the Himalayan mountains remains a mastiff, and at one time our English Mastiff was used as a guardian of cattle and sheep. Gradually, as the wolf disappeared, a gentler dog was needed to round-up our flocks on the pastures and to drive cattle to market, and so evolved our shepherds' dogs of the downs and wolds and the various breeds and strains of Collie that follow their active lives among the fells and dales of the Border and on the wind-swept hillsides of Scotland.

Robert Leighton, *The Complete Book of the Dog* (1922)

CHAPTER 2

THE HERDING BREEDS

The British Contribution

Let us now turn to the shepherd's dog of our own is-land and the adjacent parts of the continent, which offers several varieties, more or less differing from each other. One breed from the north is covered with a deep woolly coat, capable of felting; the colour is generally grey; another breed, that generally depicted, is covered with long flowing hair, and the tail is full and bushy; the colour is in general black, with tanned limbs and muzzle, varied occasionally by white on the breast. In both the muzzle is acute, and the ears erect, or nearly so. There is a third and larger breed, called the drover's dog…

W.C.L. Martin, *The History of the Dog* (1845)

In medieval times, as discussed in the previous sec-tion, livestock was protected by huge dogs known as shepherd's mastiffs; the word 'mastiff' being used here to describe a large mongrel not as used today to describe a pedigree breed. As large wild preda-tors disappeared from Britain, the need for such dogs disappeared too, but our Old English Sheepdog type may well have descended from such dogs. As the forested areas were reduced, the dogs of the for-est shepherd had to find a new role; it is likely that the working sheepdog or collie of today comes from such dogs. In 1840 there were over 10 million sheep in Britain, needing pasture *and* herding dogs. In some areas it was customary to use multi-purpose dogs on farms, rather as in Ireland the versatile Kerry Blue and soft-coated Wheaten terriers were stock dogs, farm terriers and guard dogs – just as the varieties of the Schnauzer were employed in Ger-many. Drovers needed to feed themselves on their long journeys and used a sheepdog cross greyhound,

The Working Sheepdog of Britain in a coloured print, 1905.

*Old English Sheepdogs in
a coloured print from 1917
entitled* On Guard.

BOTTOM LEFT: *The Smithfield
Lurcher, blend of Greyhound
and Smithfield Collie.*

BOTTOM RIGHT: *The
Australian Kelpie, developed
from Scottish dogs in the late
nineteenth century.*

known as a lurcher, to fill their pots with meat. The Smooth Collie is considered by some experts to have developed from such a cross.

In the far north of the British Isles were the Kelpies of the Orkneys (now reborn in Australia), leggy dogs used to get grazing stock out to small islands at low tide, the bigger Scottish collies (with their rough, smooth and bearded variants) of the Highlands and what we now call Border Collies in the Lowlands and northernmost English counties. Shetland had its own type, smaller and more of a house dog. Cumberland too had its own sheepdog, some looking more like a German Shepherd Dog than its own collie relatives, others bearing almost the beardie coat. The original Border Collie type may have been forest sheepdogs (referred to as 'ramhunts' in some accounts) used to keep stock in clearings, constantly circling them to keep the flock together and deter predators.

In time, selective breeding developed these instinctive skills, leading to such dogs becoming the

Westmoreland scene, showing leggy, short-haired sheepdog, c.1900.

BELOW: *Lake District valley, with sheepdog midway between Beardie and Collie.*

national herding breed. In Wales there were distinct types like the Welsh Hillman, a handsome red-coated dog, the Black and Tan Sheepdog and the Welsh Collie, often predominately white. In Ireland the tri-colour Galway Sheepdog, a strapping black, tan and white dog, and the Glenwherry Collie of Antrim, a

wall-eyed merle dog, were favoured. In his book *The Dog* (1933), James Dickie refers to a letter from Galway, a century old, that stated:

> The sheepdog in this country is rather a handsome animal. It is a very well-made dog with a long, thick coat which makes it appear much larger than it is, and a long, well-furnished tail…The upper part of their body is nearly black, as is also that of the head and tail; the rest of their body, legs and the fringe of the tail is light brown and the lower part of the face lighter still. All sheep-dogs in this part of the country are marked as I have described and are unlike any I have ever seen in England.

Those words should be enough to spark interest in a restoration of such a distinctive dog. In Leinster, particularly in County Wicklow, a red merle bobtailed collie was utilized. Merino sheep were imported into the Kilkenny area, together with a Spanish shepherd who used blasts on a horn to call his sheep. A pure strain of solid black or black and tan, sometimes chocolate or bronze-coloured collie was once favoured in Sutherland and Ross, with some experts linking them with Scandinavian herding dogs.

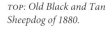

TOP: *Old Black and Tan Sheepdog of 1880.*

Welsh shepherd with two Old Welsh Grey Sheepdogs and Terrier, c.1898.

The Collies of Scotland

'The English form of Sheepdog is, as far as I can find, described in earlier times than is the Scotch Collie; and I think it not improbable that the latter may be in part derived from the former and the Scotch Greyhound.' Those words from such a verbose chronicler of the dogs of the British Isles as Hugh Dalziel in his *British Dogs* (1888) reveals the widespread ignorance of the forms of pastoral dog in Britain in the nineteenth century. Although, to be fair, some of today's Smooth Collies can be distinctly 'greyhoundy', certainly more than their sister breed. In his *The Dogs of the British Islands* (1878), 'Stonehenge' wrote, rather unhelpfully:

In Scotland and the north of England, as well as in Wales, a great variety of breeds is used for tending sheep, depending greatly on the locality in which they are employed, and on the kind of sheep adopted in it… In Wales there is certainly, as far as I know, no special breed of sheepdog, and the same may be said of the north of England, where, however, the colley (often improperly called Scotch), more or les pure, is employed by nearly half the shepherds of that district, the remainder resembling the type known by that name in many respects, but not all.

Should the word 'collie' be restricted to Scottish sheepdogs, with the English ones not called Border Collies but 'Borders Sheepdogs' after their use on the borders of the flock, rather than in the border country between England and Scotland? Writers in the eighteenth and nineteenth centuries used the word collie or colley very loosely. In *The Illustrated Book of the Dog* (1879), Vero Shaw wrote:

There has been an attempt made by one or two writers in *The Live Stock Journal* – which devotes no inconsiderable portion of its pages to canine matters – to designate this dog the Highland Collie, but there was an utter absence of any reasoning in justification of claiming for the Highlands of Scotland the honour of being the peculiar home of the Collie. We are rather disposed to think that the pastoral dales of the Lowlands of Scotland and the North of England have had more to do with breeding the dog to his present high state of perfection as a shepherd than the North Highlands…

He went on to stress that shepherds cared little of pedigree but bred entirely for performance.

In his *Non-Sporting Dogs* (1905), Frank Townend Barton wrote:

Smooth-coated sheep-dogs are found in every county of Great Britain, and farmers and shepherds are very fond of them, many being splendid animals at their work. In breeding smooth-coated collies the chief difficulty presenting itself is in connection with the coat; so many specimens being mixtures. With careful

Rough Collie, early twentieth century, shorter coated.

Rough Collie of today, far too heavily coated.

BOTTOM LEFT: Smooth Collie of the 1930s.

selection and perseverance much more might have been done for the smooth coats. Certainly they have not the handsome appearance of their rough-coated brethren.

In his *Our Dogs* (1907), Gordon Stables wrote: 'The smooth-coated dog...although found in the Highlands, is a Lowland dog, with a Lowland coat and Lowland ways, and more at home among cattle than sheep.' Today we have two separate breeds of Scottish Collie and not just distinguished by length of coat.

No Pure Origin

Those breed historians seeking a long and pure origin for the collies of Scotland would be wise to study the words of William Stephens on such dogs in *The Kennel Encyclopaedia* of 1907:

> In the first Volume of the Stud Book, 78 'Sheep Dogs and Scotch Collies' were registered up to the year 1874... Only 18 had pedigrees, and only three of these extended beyond sire and dam. There is no doubt that, some years ago, the Gordon Setter cross was introduced, the consequence of which was the production of black dogs with bright mahogany-tan markings, thin in coat, and possessing a Setter's 'Flag', instead of pale tan markings, dense coat and thick brush.

Stephens went on to point out: 'The great fault now met with is unduly exaggerated (Borzoi type

The Collie Nero by Lucy Waller, 1890: broad-headed and thick-coated.

of) head which is always accompanied by a stupid and vacant expression – quite unlike the intelligent expression of the true collie.' He would not have admired some of the Collie heads appearing in today's show rings.

In *The Popular Collie* (1960), Margaret Osborne wrote:

> Unfortunately, far more recently than this date [the end of the eighteenth century], infusions of different blood were introduced into the Collie, usually to satisfy a whim for a special point: the cross with the Gordon Setter was made to enrich the tan; with the Irish Setter in a misplaced attempt to enrich the sable; with the Borzoi to increase the length of head. As a result of the Irish Setter cross the words 'setter red most objectionable' came to be included in the earlier standards of the breed, and even today we all too often see the horrible results of the Borzoi cross in the receding-skulled, roman-nosed horrors which masquerade under the name of Collie.

It seems that Collie breeders would clandestinely out-cross to achieve a change in a previous century, but forbid an out-cross to remedy its after-effects

in a succeeding century; an out-cross to a different shorter-muzzled, broader-headed breed could so easily breed away from such an unwanted feature.

Critics of the Collie's head and show ring alterations have long been at work. In his *The Dog* of 1933, James Dickie gave the view:

> About sixty years ago the collie became a fashionable pet, and thereafter two new strains developed, the rough and the smooth show collies. It was then laid down that the head should be long, narrow and sharp, but not domed; since then dogs have been

Scottish Collie at work, Gourlay Steell, 1869.

BOTTOM: Sheep in a Scottish Landscape *by J.W. Morris, 1867, depicting local collie.*

bred entirely without a stop and with extraordinarily narrow heads. The brain-pan, in fact, has been bred out of them, with the natural result that, compared with his working ancestor, the show collie is little better than a congenital idiot. The popularity of show collies is on the wane. The smooth variety was never common, and the rough variety, having been 'perfected' and become a fool in the process, is rapidly being superseded by dogs of less size and more brains.

His prediction about popularity was, thirty years later, somewhat wide of the mark, but the severity of his words, with a forthrightness unlikely to be matched in dog books of today, do illustrate the depth of

Rough Collie Moss View Superior by Ward Binks, 1930, not over-coated.

feeling over the changes in this breed brought about by show-ring fanciers.

Damage by Promotion

In 1908, there were over 1,200 Rough Collies and 170 Smooth Collies registered with the KC; 100 years later, in 2008, the figures were: 1,171 Roughs and 43 Smooths, the latter's very survival being threatened. Twenty years earlier, however, over 8,000 Roughs were registered, indicating the fickleness of the pedigree dog world and indeed the public response to the promotion on film of a breed. The 'Lassie' films gave enormous exposure to the Rough Collie; the Dulux paint commercial gave very damaging temporary exposure of the Old English Sheepdog, with rescue centres being overwhelmed by the breed in due course.

The pedigree dog world itself has not always been kind to the pastoral breeds, with the Rough Collie being a prime example. William Arkwright, the great working gundog expert, writing in *The Kennel Gazette* in July 1888, had this to say:

> 'fancies', locust like, appear to have settled on the Collie, and, unless we can exterminate them, they will most assuredly exterminate the Collie. 'Fanciers' have recently determined that a Collie shall have an enormous head, an enormous coat, and enormous limbs, and that by these three 'points' shall he stand or fall in the judging ring; so they have commenced

Head Study of a Collie by H. Watts, 1893; no sign of alien blood, just a worker.

> to graft on to the breed the jaw of an alligator, the coat of an Angora goat, and the clumsy bone of a St Bernard. A 'cobby' dog with short neck, straight thick shoulders, hollow back, and small straight tail, but graced with a very long snout and a very heavy jacket, is already common at our shows, and increases and multiplies... First of all, the Collie is intended for use, for definite work, and, as soon as we find ourselves breeding dogs that cannot gallop, jump, 'rough it', aye, and *think* too, we may be certain that, whatever he may have got hold of, it is not a sheepdog...

In an editorial in the June 1890 issue of *The Kennel Gazette* the writer asked:

> turn to sheepdogs: how many collies of the present day, who have won prizes, could clear a high hurdle or scamper over the backs of a flock of sheep to turn it?...the sheepdog is now a companion and not trained for work, many, we are afraid, would hardly be good for a long gallop, or could do more than run a mile or so behind a slow carriage.

Old-style Working Sheepdog; utility ahead of handsomeness.

The Scotch collie (working type) 1930.

Mr James Scott's Kep, one of the most prefect working collies in Scotland at the time,1912.

Thirty years later, successful show Collies changed hands for extraordinary sums: Ch Squire of Tytton went to the USA for £1,250 and Ch Ormskirk Emerald was sold here for £1,300, huge sums at that time. The pedigree pastoral dog now had value a long way from the pastures and pens; in the show world such a dog could do no work yet be highly priced entirely on its appearance – and after its show career, its breeding potential. Inevitably, following very different criteria, showman and shepherd sought quite different attributes in their dogs. The shepherd didn't have a need for a dog admired for its looks alone, he needed a worker, a gifted worker, almost another pair of hands and eyes.

Acquiring Sagacity

A passage from W.H. Pyne's *The Costumes of Great Britain* (1808) provides some insight into the life of a Highland shepherd:

> The dog, by being constantly the companion of the Highland shepherd, acquires sagacity, far superior to what is common to the brute creation; appearing to comprehend all his master's commands… The shepherd, who is acquainted with the best spots for pasture, and who watches for prognostics of the weather, manages the flock accordingly, by the aid of the dog, who drives the sheep sometimes to the summit of a mountain, and at other times, to a particular spot upon its side, or into a deep glen, acting by the signals of his master; who stands on a conspicuous height, shouting his directions, and waving his crook, which the intelligent animal comprehends at a surprising distance.

The Highland Shepherd from W.H. Pyne's
The Costumes of Great Britain, *1808.*

Pyne went on to describe the ability of the dog to single out individual sheep:

> The shepherd at the time of collecting the flock in the evening for the purpose of counting it, fixes his crook in the ground, and stands a few paces therefrom: the dog drives the sheep between the crook and his master, who numbers them as they pass; but if a straggler goes on the outside, and mixes with those who have passed muster, the dog immediately pursues, singles him out, and brings him back.

Against that background, it is not pleasing to give the opinion that the Rough and Smooth Collies and the Shetland Sheepdog did not survive the show interest in them of the late nineteenth and early twentieth centuries, with their working lives now ended. I have seen sheepdogs in the Lake District looking exactly like the depictions of Smooth Collies in the late nineteenth century. I have also seen miniature collies with smooth coats that have cropped up in working litters; if the Shetland Sheepdog had been named as the Miniature Collie, in two coats, it may

The Smithfield Drover from W.H. Pyne's The Costumes of Great Britain, *1808.*

Early Shetland Sheepdog – lacking the heavy coat of today.

have survived as a working sheepdog in the pastures. Breeds like the Poodle, the Pinscher and the Schnauzer have thrived in different sizes – it can be done!

The Sheepdog of the Shetland Isles

> In Orkney, on the pasture lands round the Scapa Flow, and especially on the island of Hoy, such miniature Collies were frequently to be seen a generation ago; but in later years they have been more closely associated with the Shetlands, where they were locally known as the Toonie Dog – name derived from their work of guarding the croft, or farm… North Sea fishermen and other visitors brought specimens of the breed to the mainland to keep as pets, and I have seen more than one in the seaports of East Anglia. It was from a Lowestoft fisherman that Mrs Feilden got a brood bitch whose puppies were afterwards shown at Crufts.
>
> Robert Leighton, *The Complete Book of the Dog* (1922)

If you look at portrayals of the Sheltie in the show ring of a century ago, you could be forgiven for thinking it was then a quite different breed. While this could be said of a number of breeds, in this one I very much prefer the 1913 specimens. If you look at photographs of Thynne's Kilravock dogs – such as Laddie, a fine tricolour; the mainly white Cleopatra; Gipsy Love, a black and tan with a truly weatherproof coat; Eureka, a beautifully balanced bitch; and Flora Modal, an excellent tricolour – you can see the sound foundation of any future breed. They all had strong, wide-skulled heads, thick but not long coats and, unlike some of the chicken-boned contemporary dogs, ample bone and broad chests. From such stock could have come a really impressive breed. In due course, the Eltham Park kennel continued this type, but already, in their dogs, you could detect the heavier coat

The Sheltie of today, far more heavily coated than its predecessors.

Ch. Hurly Burly (top) and Farne of Greyhill (bottom) owned by Miss Mary Grey.

and lighter bone. They were much more collie-like than today's dogs and why not? The Houghton Hill kennel became influential but this led to over-use of this line, bringing a more refined head – continued in the Exford line. If the type exemplified in the 1920s, with Mary Grey's Hurly Burly and Farne of Greyhill both fine examples, had been perpetuated then perhaps the drift towards being a Toy breed could have been averted. If this breed is to deserve its title of Sheepdog it has to justify that proud tag.

In his *Dogs and I* (1928), sportsman and judge Harding Cox wrote:

> The Shetland is a very small sheep dog, but it may well be *too small*! Already some of the prize winners are below the proper standard of inches and weight. They are *not* 'Toy' dogs, therefore any attempt to degrade them to such a level should be severely frowned upon and condemned. Judges take notice!

Shelties of today.

A dog looking more like a longer-backed Pomeranian, or 'all fluff and no puff', as one disillusioned Sheltie fancier put it to me, has no right to be named or considered as a sheepdog. In *Hutchinson's Dog Encyclopaedia* of 1934, the breed has these words on it:

> ...there are two distinct types of Shetland Sheepdog, but both are registered under the same name, a fact that has led to considerable difficulty and argument. The one variety is very like the Collie dog of the eighteenth and early nineteenth centuries, before the days of registration, and the other is a miniature of the show Collie type... This rather unfortunate state of affairs has divided the breeders into two camps, and it is to be regretted that it did not at the same time divide the dogs...

Is this a discussion to be resumed if this breed is to establish lasting type?

Such criticism from 'outside the breed' will be resented but what are the breed experts – those appointed to judge future breeding stock– saying, not so much on type but on quality? Here are some of their post-show critique comments: 'I found just seven dogs in the entry with anything like the correct conformation... There is more to a Sheltie than a big coat and a pretty face...' (2011); '...breeders and exhibitors seem to be concentrating more on head, expression and fullness of coat to the detriment of construction...' (2011); 'my main concern is that correct front angulation, as stated in the Standard, is now almost nonexistent. Judges have been bemoaning this in critiques for well over 30 years...' (2012); 'I was disappointed to find so many steep upper arms and straight shoulders, in spite of so many critiques pointing this out from time to time, people don't seem to be able to understand that it applies, in many cases, to their own dogs and they continue to breed from bitches with the problem to dogs who also have the problem.' (2013). Against that background, it is quite astounding to read a critique, from the 2013 Richmond Championship Show, by the Shetland Sheepdog judge, that reads: 'The Shelties were the highest entry of the day. A couple of major faults creeping into the breed that must be watched carefully, there was quite a few who lacked forechest and showed steep upper arms, this restricts movement. Also quite a few narrow muzzles spoilt...' Major

Precious trinity: William Pease, born 1880, with his farm collie Fly and horse.

Farm Collie preserved at the Natural History Museum, Tring.

faults *creeping in*! After over thirty years of these very faults being regularly reported in this breed, along comes a judge who thinks they are new! No wonder breeds regress!

Of course there are some top-class Shelties; I have long liked the Stormhead dogs, having first seen them in the mid-1950s. In recent times, I have seen sound dogs from the Myter kennel of Mrs Mylee and Miss Shannon Thomas in Buckinghamshire, their Myter Guilty Pleasure JW in particular. It is good too to see fewer timid Shelties in the ring, with exhibits once looking as though they'd rather be anywhere else. Over a thousand Shelties are bred each year; this is a situation where an overview, with remedy in mind, from outside the breed is surely justified. This could so easily be the perfect companion breed.

The British Working Sheepdog

The late arrival of the Border Collie onto the show scene has led to some 'beautification', but their use is ever more widespread, from the pastures to the hearth, to the agility, obedience, fly-ball and disabled-assistance support dog roles – all with great success, making this perhaps the most versatile breed in history. These are difficult days for farmers and farm dogs. The glamorous Rough Collie may grace film-sets and the likeable Bobtail may star in paint advertisements but neither breed works any more. The world famous and unsurpassable Border Collie now features in the show ring, but only after considerable opposition from the International Sheep Dog Society (ISDS), which rightly feared a loss of functional ability and working physique. These dogs may

have moved from the pastures to city streets but really they are only spiritually happy when working, and quite a few are too hyperactive to make good house pets. (I had one that when alert carried his tail high and was the toughest dog I ever had, active till seventeen years old. When I wrote of this in *Dogs Monthly*, reader Christine Foord wrote in to say her collies had this feature too and were clever and assertive. Such a feature, if demonstrated on an exhibit in the show ring, however good the dog, would lead to the dog being unplaced. It is claimed also, without evidence, that such a tail carriage is associated with restricted rear extension – not true with my dog. John Holmes, an expert on sheepdogs, once told me that this raised tail often depicts increased determination in the dog concerned, no bad thing in a working animal.)

The challenge for their fanciers is to breed them for their new role without losing their essential characteristics, for that is how all breeds survive. The fairly recent arrival of the breed on to the benches needs to be balanced against the long-established trial scene. As pointed out in the June 1983 Newsletter of the ISDS, when considering early pedigree registrations:

> The Kennel Club Gazette in its May 1983 edition, gives some interesting statistics: it shows the registrations for Border Collies since 1978. They read as follows:- Border Collies registered in 1978 – 368; in 1979 – 843; in 1980 – 735; in 1981 – 718; in 1982 – 756. Compare these figures to the Society's registrations which have run consistently at 6,500 approximately for each of the years in question.

Such background gives some balance to the contemporary show scene, where town-dwelling owners are all too often unaware of the roots of their breed. Owners of show Border Collies are usually aware of the blood behind their dogs; Paul Turnbull's Blue, registered with the ISDS on merit in 1984, was used on KC-registered bitches with some success.

Challenging Review Task
It is far from easy to review the shepherd dogs of Britain covered by the titles of Border Collie (when registered with the KC) or working sheepdog (usually registered with the ISDS, although KC-registered dogs described as working sheepdogs do compete in agility, obedience and fly-ball contests).

In the pastures you see highly efficient if not always very handsome dogs, diligently performing their centuries-old tasks. In the show ring, from the ringside, it is reassuring to view top-quality dogs such as Australian and English Ch Waveney Kozmonant, Fayken I am A Legend, and his litter-sister Fayken Indecent Proposal, judged to be Border Collie of the year and runner-up respectively in 2013. But, in the same year, it's alarming to read one judge's report that states:

> I haven't been around the show world for about four years. The Border Collies presented to me came in four different types. Slab-sided and narrow headed (athletic). Square incorrect height to length ratio,

incorrect forehand, i.e. forward placed shoulder, steep upper arm and square croup, short-coupled (majority). Dwarf small usually profuse coat (glamorous). A finer version of an Australian Shepherd especially in the head and stifle area. This made my judging to The Standard very difficult... This dip in quality happens in dog breeding where the generation of 'greats' is weakened in the next generation. This is not a slur on breeders, etc. It is what is available in the gene pool, how it is used, and if there are no lines with 'nicks' in them, then mediocre rules until such matings are found.

Clearly now is the time for inspired selection of breeding stock, strict observance of the Breed Standard and the pursuit of soundness so often demonstrated in the trials dogs.

The Trials Dogs

Competitions between dogs and their owners have long been a feature of rural life. They have been accused of developing dogs principally for the trials themselves: spaniels too 'hot' for your average shooter to handle and retrievers too light-boned for sustained work in the sporting field and 'flashier' sheepdogs to satisfy *their* appeal for the judges. But a desire to compete was behind the first sheepdog trial, run between ten dogs at Bala in North Wales, in 1873. As

TOP: The Border Collie: Britain's, and arguably the world's best herding dog.

Dogs of the pastures – bred for work, not to be pets.

'Strong-eyed' sheepdog at work.

BELOW RIGHT: *Old Hemp, father of the modern working collie.*

Eric Halsall has pointed out in *Sheepdogs – My Faithful Friends* (1980):

> A trial is simply planned to assess ability and is obviously of great practical value in determining the qualities of the dogs taking part. Good dogs can, and do, delight in their prowess; the human braggards – whose dogs perform wonderful feats on the hill! – have their teeth drawn; and the watchers choose their potential breeding stock. Wherever sheep are farmed, trials are held and in today's competition when entries reach towards a hundred, even at the remotest trials, it is a very good collie that wins.

It is good to know that there are now field trials for show collies, whether Border or Beardie. Herding sheep makes unique demands on a dog; their role depends on control. Some should only be used on cattle; some excel with large flocks; all trial dogs have to practise with half a dozen sheep and every sheepdog is an individual.

The 'Strong-Eyed' Sheepdog

In this role, a certain type of dog is needed. The dog's instinctive defence of territory is harnessed to guard a pasture. The dogs then, without human direction, place themselves between an approaching predator and the stock in their remote pasture. This

is in stark contrast with the herding breeds, those hyperactive dogs that stalk, chase, bully, bark at and even bite sheep to impose their will on them. These are the 'header-stalkers', using classic canine predatory behaviour, inherited from wild ancestors. They usually feature the prick ears and long muzzles of those wild ancestors, although drop-eared dogs like the Pointers and Setters of the shooting field also make use of this instinctive 'restrained' focus. These dogs have to be controlled by human voice or whistle. Just as the Beardie combined the skills

of driving and herding, the shorter-coated working sheepdog, usually described as a 'collie', using the 'header-stalker' technique rather than that of the flock guardian, not only matched them but suited the changing ways of farming. As the railways did away with the need for drovers and the acreage of common grazing land decreased, there was a need for dogs able to move stock from one fenced pasture to another, to pen them for shearing and health checks and get them on to vehicles for market. It is likely that these shorter-coated farm collies were not widely used in Wales and southern England until the livestock industry adapted to new transport opportunities. The Border Collie, or working sheepdog of sheepdog trial fame, is the best known 'strong-eyed' breed in the world, so-called because it exerts control over sheep by assertive eye contact and aggressive body positioning.

In his *The Farmer's Dog* (1975), John Holmes wrote:

To revert to the question of 'eye', this is a subject which is often misunderstood. First of all 'strong eye' is not essential in the working dog and I have known many excellent 'loose-eyed' dogs. It can be, and often is, a liability rather than an asset… It is, in fact, a comparatively recent innovation, having been developed to its present-day strength only since sheepdog trials started, and then solely in the type of sheepdog which proved most successful at the trials.

But in *Sheepdogs at Work* (1979), Tony Iley wrote:

In approximately 1790 the presence of 'eye' was recorded by James Hogg, the Ettrick shepherd-poet. He refers to it in a matter of fact way without surprise, leading us to believe that it was not a new innovation… James Scott of Overhall, Hawick (International Champion 1908 and 1909), said that he had not seen 'eye' in dogs until 1875, when he saw it in a bitch owned by John Crozier, a herd at Teviot Water, who got her from Northumberland. Because of this it can be concluded that 'eye' developed in various isolated families of dogs in the period between 1740 and 1870. At this time it would not be widespread, and its value would not be fully realized until the early trials began, starting with the first trial at Bala in Merioneth, Wales, in 1873.

In 1894, the supremely capable Old Hemp, reputed to have 'eyes that blazed', became the father of today's working collie. He died in 1901 but not before siring over 200 top-class offspring.

The ability of a dog to identify individual animals is illustrated by an anecdote in the Rev. Charles Williams's *Dogs and Their Ways* (1863):

Lord Truro told Lord Brougham of a drover's dog, whose sagacious conduct he observed when he happened on one occasion to meet a drove. The man had brought seventeen out of twenty oxen from a field, leaving the remaining three there mixed with another herd. He then said to the dog, 'Go, fetch them,' and he went and singled out those very three.

Different terrain and difficult sheep-rearing country led to different instincts being instilled in the sheepdogs. In their stunningly illustrated *Hill Shepherd – A Photographic Essay* of 1989, John and Eliza Forder wrote:

'Cur' or 'barking' dogs have been used in the Lake District for generations and are bred especially for the job of shifting sheep in difficult terrain. They are trained to bring sheep away from crags, cliffs and undergrowth, while a sheepdog from lower, 'cleaner' country may resort to sinking its teeth into them through sheer frustration. Herdwick sheep, local to Lakeland, will outwit shepherds and dogs if they can.

Waist-high bracken, unfenced pastures and cruelly concealed crags challenge both dog and shepherd;

Westmoreland shepherd with his rough-haired dogs.

they simply *have to* work as a team in this timeless rural scene.

The Revival of the Welsh Sheepdog

For over a decade the Welsh Sheepdog Society, formed in 1998, has been working to revive a distinct variety of collie based on their traditional form in Wales. They run a register of purebred stock dogs and hold demonstrations. Bigger than Border Collies

and often blue merle (in the Plynlimon and Devil's Bridge area), tricoloured (black and tan in Tywyn), red-tan (down the Cardigan coast) and white, or a lighter sable and white, Welsh Sheepdogs are 'loose-eyed' herders but valued for their stamina and robustness. With powerful shoulder muscles, folded ears, broad-muzzled faces and big strong feet, they excel in driving the bigger flocks and have a characteristic high tail carriage when working. The initial trawl for suitable breeding stock produced around 200 likely dogs, with 80 selected as foundation stock; over 1,000 are now registered with the society. They were famed as drovers' dogs, able to get large herds to market; in North Wales a big grey variety was favoured. Bobtailed dogs are found in southeast Wales, but they cannot be registered with the society. In pursuit of a bigger gene pool, enquiries have been made in Patagonia, where Welsh settlers developed the Barboucho from the dogs they took with them. The enterprise of these enthusiasts is heart-warming; the world of the pastoral dog needs such enlightened energy to ensure that old working dog breeds are respected once again.

A wholly new breed is being developed in Wales, called the Welsh Mountain Dog, resembling the old Galway Sheepdog and from a combination of breeds to suit a purpose. This handsome breed, created by Welsh breeder Lyn Kinsey, is a blend of the Bernese Mountain Dog, the Border Collie and the Loughlander, the

TOP: *Suffolk shepherds and their dogs, dogs bred for the pastures not for show.*

Red smooth Welsh Sheepdog bitch Penry Saphire, owned by Adeline Jones, bred by Gary Gullimore-Pike.
ADELINE JONES

BOTTOM: KyiApso of Tibet. TARA DARLING, COURTESY OF DOGS IN CANADA

latter created in Durham by Sue Curle-Lane by blending the blood of the Bernese Mountain Dog with that of the Newfoundland. The new Welsh breed is not as prone to the ailments that afflict many large breeds, has a sunny disposition and sound temperament, very much resembling a big, strongly built Border Collie, an admirable companion in rural areas. The pastoral breeds of Britain may come and go but they form an important part of the worldwide scene both in variety and, especially, in quality.

The Harsh-Haired Herding Dogs

Distinguished by Coat

Livestock-farming – the rearing, herding and eventually getting stock to market – has long been a hard living not a gentle pastime. Before the days of rail and wheeled transporters, the sheep and cattle, and therefore the shepherds and their dogs, 'hoofed' it. The dogs were either robust or they didn't survive. The drovers needed strong, substantial dogs, able to travel huge distances and protect the stock, as the Bouviers or drover-dogs of the Low Countries demonstrate. The Lake District farmers needed a leggier dog than those in Kent; the moors shepherds needed robust, agile dogs with immense stamina. Function, as always with dogs, decided form. In time, transhumance led to the development of the

mountain dogs/flock guardians, herding needs gave us the shepherd dogs and within them, specialists committed to the 'living fence' role, like the German Shepherd Dog, or the flock herders, like the Bearded Collie of Scotland and some parts of England. In the shepherd's vocabulary, words now lost to us have

Cao da Serra de Aires – Portuguese Sheepdog.

meaning: a shag was a shaggy, rough-coated dog, a hirsel was the dog used for sorting livestock into groups and a haggard was a dog used on the flanks of the flock. The Border Collie may have got its name, not from the border of Scotland and England, but from its skill on the *borders of the flock*. But the Beardie's name came from its coat and its physical impression. A more accurate title might have been the Harsh-haired Collie, for it's the coat texture rather than the chin-hair that distinguishes the type.

The harsh-haired or goat-haired group is represented in most areas of Europe: the Cao da Serra de Aires and the less well-known Barbado da Terceira (a Bobtail look-alike) from the Azores but seen too in Portugal, the Briard and the Picardy from France, the Pyrenean Sheepdog, the Gos d'Atura of Catalonia, the Fonni Sheepdog of Sardinia, the German Sheep Poodle, the Lowland Sheepdog of Poland, the South Russian Owtcharka, the Tibetan Kyi

Apso (Kyi meaning dog, Apso meaning bearded) or Humli Dog, the Schapendoes of Holland and, from the British Isles, the Bearded Collie, the Old English Sheepdog and the now-extinct Old Welsh Grey, Blue Shag and Smithfield Sheepdogs. This group of dogs is also represented in the Egyptian Sheepdog, the Armant, and the Patagonian Sheepdog, which may be an offshoot of the Old Welsh Grey, introduced by migrating Welsh settlers. The Tibetan 'Terrier' too may belong here. As mentioned in Chapter 1, a glance at Reinagle's portrayal of *A Shepherd's Dog* of two centuries ago could have given you the impression that he was depicting a Briard or a South Russian Owtcharka rather than an Old English Sheepdog, such are the similarities in appearance of this type of pastoral dog.

Corded or Felted Coat

In some areas where prolonged wind-chill exposure was met, corded (felted when uncared for) coats like those of the Komondor, the Bergamasco and the Puli were needed. But the coat texture and length produced was originally always in pursuit of a purpose and never appearance. The herding breeds were developed by essentially practical men, in eternal combat against the elements and wild predators,

The Komondor of Hungary.

men who quickly discarded weedy or faulty dogs. I know of no old print or early photograph or painting that depicts the longer-haired herding breeds with the excessive length of coat displayed by many of their successor breeds at modern shows. Too heavy or too long a coat is a needless imposition on a working dog. Most of the Beardies I see in the show ring nowadays display such a length of silky coat as to obscure the natural lines of the dog's body, which is contrary to the Breed Standard. The Standard of the Old English Sheepdog places no restriction on the length of coat at all. The penalties of excessive coat length are discussed in Chapter 4. (The early breed founders in both the Old English Sheepdog and the Bearded Collie warned very clearly against letting the breed's coat become increasingly lengthened by

The Bergamasco of Italy.

The Schapendoes – the Dutch Beardie.

Picardy Sheepdogs.

BOTTOM RIGHT: *Cotswold shepherd with local Beardie, c.1890.*

show-ring fanciers disrespectful of the breeds' working origins.)

European Cousins

The goat-haired sheepdogs have long existed as a distinct type all over Europe, but all lack coverage in canine literature. If you compare their distribution with that of the big flock guardians of the high pastures like the Maremma, the Estrela Mountain Dog, the Caucasian Owtcharkas, the Kuvasz, the Tibetan 'Mastiff' and the Bergamasco, and then with the various types of Dutch and Belgian Shepherd Dogs, the Border Collie, the Beauceron, the Algerian Sheepdog, the Berger de Picardie, the rough and smooth Collies and the now extinct Welsh Hillman, you can soon see how climate, function and terrain determined type. Against that background, therefore, I don't believe there is really any need to seek an origin for, say, the Bearded Collie in dogs off a Polish ship in the sixteenth century or any other foreign ancestry, as frequently claimed. If you want a long-haired sheepdog, breed one selectively from the longer-coated specimens of sheepdog stock! The international distribution of dogs that herd sheep, long-haired, rough-coated or smooth, demonstrates that the differing coat lengths occur naturally and have been perpetuated and enhanced by line-breeding down the centuries to stabilize one particular coat. In time a desired coat length can be fixed and the various breeds, or varieties within a breed, evolved. Not surprisingly, coat lengths can be linked with specific

needs in particular areas and developed with other breed characteristics. With pedigree dog breeding being only just over a century old it is easy to overlook the fact that breed types evolved in many cases over at least five centuries.

Jim Dunsford – still working his Beardie at seventy-one, on Salisbury Plain in 1937.

Credible Origins

I can find neither evidence nor any credibility in the stories that the longer-haired herding dogs all originated in one country and spread out from there. I believe it is likely that the herding dogs brought south by the migrating Indo-Europeans roughly four thousand years ago were the prototypal dogs and since then they have gradually evolved into the types and with the physical features demanded by location, function and local preferences. In Britain, Bearded Collies have been inter-bred with the Old English type and the working sheepdogs of the Border Collie type for centuries. This is not to say of course that in some areas a definite type was not preferred and kept distinct. I believe it is likely that the shaggier sheepdogs were called Beards (or Hirsels) in Scotland, Haggards in Ireland, Greys in Wales and Shags in England, where the bigger ones were used as drovers' dogs and dubbed Bobtails, and, if in a blue-grey coat, Blue Shags.

The Bearded Collie

In *The Illustrated Book of the Dog* (1881), Vero Shaw quotes *The Live Stock Journal* of 1878, in which

Gordon Phillips of Glenlivet writes on the 'rough-coated' Collie. It is forgivable to assume that his words refer to the pedigree Rough Collie, but he was describing a *shaggy* sheepdog, *not* the longer-haired variety of the Scottish Collie. A précis of his words is of considerable value to Bearded Collie fanciers. Phillips wrote that: it is seldom if ever seen purebred in the north of Scotland; it is shaggy-coated, thick-skinned, with short powerful limbs; shepherds prefer it for its endurance of cold and fatigue and its ability as a driver, considering it the best dog for sheep; the size of an ordinary collie but a good deal deeper-chested and flatter in the forehead; a dark grey in colour, short-tailed, at home among the drift and snow, finely adapted for hill climbing.

He wrote that this type of shaggy-coated collie instinctively made a wide sweep, with shepherds stating that they can safely trust 200 or 300 sheep 'to the sagacity of this valuable dog, which does not hurry or push, but drives them as coolly and as cautiously as if its master were present'. Vero Shaw produced an illustration of the collie described by

Pioneer breeder Panmure Gordon and his Bearded Collie. MARY EVANS PICTURE LIBRARY

Bearded Collie depicted by Edmund Bristow in 1826.

Phillips, adding that, 'It is impossible to give any standard for judging this variety. General appearance, tail, strength, and shagginess without too much length of coat, should be taken into consideration.' Shepherds were known to refer to such collies as goat-haired collies due to the texture of their coats. Early depictions of the breed show them with shaggy but not long coats.

Place of Origin

Comparable thinking has led some to claim that Peebleshire is the true home of the Beardie, Dorset the real home of the Bobtail, the Lake District the original base for the Border Collie and Snowdonia the home of the Old Welsh Grey. But Beardies have long been favoured in northwest England and, being utilized by drovers, could be found wherever there was a vibrant sheep trade; the Smithfield Sheepdog, the bigger Beardie-type, being associated with the sheep-market towns and areas of eastern England. There were differences between the longer-haired sheepdogs found in the Highlands and those working in the border regions. In Rawdon Lee's *Modern Dogs of Great Britain and Ireland (Non-Sporting Division)* of 1894, he stated:

I certainly agree with the author of *The Dogs of Scotland,* [Thomson Gray], when he says that the two

varieties as found in Scotland and England are identical... As a fact, the old English sheepdog is pretty common in almost every county in England, but is most often found as the dog of the farm in the midland and southern counties, and as assistant to the drover in the metropolitan and other cattle markets of our large centres.

It would be surprising if shepherds in each region didn't favour *their* type of harsh-haired sheep and cattle dog; that's how breeds are founded. Pioneer breeder Panmure Gordon, writing in 1898 to

Unexaggerated Beardie of 1902.

Thomson Gray, gave the view that the breed was actually raised as a tracker in stalking and often had staghound blood.

Beardies' Style

Beardies work in a different style from that of their shorter-haired fellow working sheepdogs; although they can display the same ground-hugging creeping gait, they are not silent or 'strong-eyed' but excel at collecting and then retaining sheep in big groups. This capability made them most useful to drovers and butchers. The goat-haired collies were favoured by renowned drovers such as McDonald of Skye around 1930, then shepherds like Tom Muirhead of Dunsyre a few decades later. Brian Plummer, the country sports writer, bought Muirhead's kennel of Beardies, describing the white-headed ones as willing to 'face the devil himself', because of their hardness. More

recently, Graham Nicholson's Working Bearded Collie Foundation aimed to continue their work. Lynne Sharpe, with her Brambledale dogs in Carmarthenshire, has continued to breed for a working dog, both in anatomy and instinct; if I were going to buy a Beardie, I'd purchase one from her kennel.

I understand that in the early days of trying to breed pure Beardies it was not unusual to find a couple of pups in a litter looking more like Border Collies. The early registrations of sheepdogs with the International Sheepdog Society listed rough, smooth and bearded types but farmers often interbred dogs with different coats and ear carriage. The Bobtail was also used as a drovers' dog, like the Bouviers on mainland Europe; I can remember an old grazier on Salisbury Plain fifty years ago telling me how the instinctive skills of the Bobtails varied: some preferring to lead the sheep, others to drive them as a flock and yet others to guard a flank. This instinctive behaviour occurred in young, untrained dogs.

Limited Base

I understand that every pedigree Bearded Collie registered in the world can be traced back to just twelve dogs, a small genetic base. With just one dog registered in 1948, we had nearly 2,000 registered forty years later, now reduced to well under 1,000 being registered annually. This fine breed will need wise breeders if it is to retain its characteristics, robustness and virility. Already, in Canada, I've seen the breed described as having set a record for 'the breed ruined in the shortest possible time'. It is surely vital to breed every ancient breed true to its heritage rather than for those who see only cosmetic appeal. The Beardie should be a medium-sized dog not a rival to the Old English Sheepdog. The Beardie should be long-backed (but not as long-backed as some show-ring specimens today) and its eyes should be visible, not concealed. I like the phrase used in the outline description of the breed in *Our Dogs* in December 1898: 'The face should have a sharp, inquiring expression'. Facial expressions can tell you a lot about dogs as well as people! Beardies are clever dogs and this, together with their determination and tractability, has led lurcher breeders to utilize their blood, as have Deerhound breeders of old, although no shepherd would want Deerhound blood in his stock. This

Bearded Collie of today.

Old English Sheepdog of today.

particular group of herding dogs readily arouse our affection; it is even more important that they are afforded our respect, respect for their true type and soundness. It is disrespectful just to breed to meet show ring criteria.

The Old English Dog

THE OLD ENGLISH BOB-TAILED SHEEP-DOG: This is a shaggy-coated, hard-haired, hard-headed, rough-and-right sort of a dog without much of a tail, very often seen accompanying the drovers of the southern counties. I have seen some of them, not pretty only, but particularly beautiful, and seemingly possessed of a high degree of intelligence. I dare say if they were as much admired as the Highland Collie they would become refined in their manners, but refinement isn't a strong point with the Bob-tailed Sheep-dog, any more than it is with his master.

Gordon Stables, *Our Friend the Dog* (1907)

It is likely that dogs such as the Bobtail or Old English Sheepdog in southern England and the Beardie or Bearded Collie in northern England and Scotland were the flock guardians and then the drovers' dogs. When a sizeable flock was being patrolled by dogs at night, each dog could be located by the shepherd through its distinctive bark. The Bearded Collie gives tongue when working, unlike its relative the Border Collie or working sheepdog, as the unregistered ones

Old English Sheepdog originally depicted in 1811.

Old English Sheepdog of 1905.

tend to be called. The Old English sheepdog has the steady, ambling, energy-saving gait of the long-distance walker; the Bearded Collie, which was expected to herd too, has a quicker effortless, gliding walk. The Bobtail excelled as a stockyard guard; both these heavier-coated breeds were shorn with the sheep and 'salved' with a mixture of tar and oil as an insect-repellent and weather-proofer. Both were very much outdoor breeds!

It is hard not to be an admirer of this distinctive old working breed. The general public is fond of it but understandably nervous of having to care for a coat that has just about got out of hand. I know of no old photograph of this breed that depicts it as heavy-coated as the dogs are today. This is a betrayal of type and a punishment for the breed; in time, this issue could lead to it becoming a vulnerable breed, with a low level of breeding stock. Only 429 were registered in 2012; compared to 763 in 2001, 1,269 in 1997, 2,138 in 1992 and 5,731 in 1979. Any breed that loses 5,000 annual registrations in three decades is in worrying decline. When experienced, knowledgeable experts on this breed like Jean Gould, Gwen Mogford and Ann Arch (who, wisely, got her first Bobtail from the Shepton kennel of the Tilleys) express concern about how the breed is being presented, judged and bred, there is *genuine* cause for concern. In summary, their concerns, set out in the dog press in the late 1990s were: excessive preparation before show-ring appearances, comic presentation – installing pom-poms on the exhibits' heads, moving the dogs too fast in the ring, platitudinous critiques, incorrect skulls with no stop, soft, woolly coat texture, narrow, almost tubular

bodies, incorrect hock joints, weakness in action on the move, no rise in the loin and overdone silhouettes. In time, such flaws can become permanent, but I cannot see huge changes being made and I fear for the breed. There *are* times when the KC should step forward and act as the ultimate guardian of a breed in serious decline.

A remarkably frank critique on this breed after a 2003 breed club show makes some telling points: 'I last judged the breed at Windsor some three years ago, I thought then, the breed had deteriorated to such an extent that this was as bad as it was likely to get… I was naive to believe such a thing…' This judge went on to point out that breed clubs have a role as custodians of the breed, with the task of protecting it and encouraging betterment. If breed clubs cannot achieve 'betterment' in their breed, who can? Very few Bobtails undergo hip and eye tests; should not an overseeing body like the KC insist on mandatory health checks in a breed where the dogs' best interests are being neglected? If a breed with a shaggy coat gets taken over by the grooming zealots, who realigns them towards putting soundness of anatomy before coat care? Intervention from above quite rightly causes resentment and suspicion, but on rare occasions it can be for good. If not, how can this delightful breed be saved ?

Continental Types
Other harsh-haired dogs, often born with naturally short tails, somewhat smaller than ours, are the Pyrenean Sheepdog or Berger des Pyrenees – known in their locality as Labrits, the Gos D'Atura of Catalonia (recently recognized by our KC as the Catalan Sheepdog) and the Polski Owczarek Nizinny or Polish Lowland Sheepdog. Some specimens in these breeds that are born with tails can be seen undocked. The Portuguese Sheepdog or Cao da Serra de Aires, known as the 'monkey dog' for its heavy eyebrows, beard and moustache, and the Catalan Sheepdog both feature the full tail, the latter breed carrying it gaily when working. The Portuguese dog, the Schapendoes of Holland, the Berger de Picardie, the Catalan Sheepdog and our own Bearded Collie are astonishingly similar in appearance, a significant fact if, one day, gene pools need enlarging. The smaller versions of the Italian Bergamasco, especially when they are young and

The Labrit of the Pyrenees.

their coats less developed, also look very much like these dogs, indicating a strong natural type. Their coats reflect the climate and temperatures found in their pastures.

The French Breeds

In France the Berger de Brie or Briard and the Picardy sheepdog represent their bouvier or drovers' dog and their Berger de Beauce or Beauceron equates to the German Shepherd Dog. The Briard is reputed to have accompanied Napoleon's armies, (perhaps creating the Armant found in Egypt), driving sheep for his quartermasters. In the more densely farmed areas of central France, the shepherds had to keep close control of their flocks. So they used a team of dogs – one called the 'foot' dog, to collect strays, another called the 'hand' dog, to work close to the shepherd, and a third, known as the 'borders' dog, to patrol the perimeter of the grazing area. This latter task demanded the most training, with this dog covering nearly 60 miles each working day.

The Pyrenean Sheepdog (rough-faced).

BOTTOM LEFT: *The Pyrenean Sheepdog (smooth-faced).*

BOTTOM RIGHT: *The Pyrenean Sheepdog, the descendant of the old Mastin, from Johnson's* Pyrenees Costumes, *1832.*

The Berger de Brie, sometimes called the Bouvier de Brie, has the same shoulder height as the Bouvier des Flandres but not the forequarter bulk. I get depressed when I read again the old fallacy of this breed originating in a Barbet-Beauceron cross, based on appearance presumably but denied entirely by history. The Briard has existed in its own right for as long as the Beauceron and belongs to a type that breeds true all over Europe. Of far greater interest is the observation that this breed type appears wherever the Celts settled. Celtic dogs have long featured griffon-like coats and the Briard has been prized for the sheer harshness of its coat texture. Some display the

Afghan Hound ring-tail and others the setter-type tail, rather than the 'hook-tail' desired; I do hope one of these doesn't become a breed point fad – a low-slung tail of any type is surely less important than essential soundness in the breed.

The most numerous of the French sheepdog breeds, the Briard, has, like many of the multi-talented herding breeds, been used widely, as a police dog, Red

The Portuguese Beardie: Cao da Serra de Aires.

Cross dog, sentry dog and ammunition carrier. The Marquis de Lafayette brought dogs of this type to North America to work with sheep. The Club Français du Chien Berger de Brie was not formed, however, until 1897, despite one of the breed being placed first in the class for sheepdogs at the first French dog show held in Paris over thirty years earlier. In the modern breed I have concern still about their temperament, especially excessive shyness, having learned long ago the deceptive and unpredictable nature of this feature. But there seems to be a responsible breed club in Britain working to improve every aspect of the breed here.

The Common Dog of Europe
The Pyrenean Sheepdog or Labrit comes in two varieties: smooth-faced and rough-faced. But as with so many herding breeds, this one could vary from one valley to the next. The Azun dog was more like a Schipperke of Belgium, the St-Béat dog like a miniature Old English Sheepdog and the Ariège dog much more muscular than either. Eventually the Arbazzie and Bagnères dogs were considered to be the type to be standardized. The rough-faced Pyrenean Sheepdog is of the Beardie type, a breed type also found, as mentioned earlier, in Catalonia as the Gos d'Atura, in Portugal as the Cao da Serra de Aires, in Egypt as the Armant, in Holland as the Schapendoes and in Poland as the Polski Owczarek Nizinny or Polish Lowland Sheepdog. This type could be described as

'the common dog of Europe', so widespread is its form – a tribute to its earned value. The Labrit is a 32lb dog, 18in high, dark fawn with black hairs or light grey with white markings, with a harlequin factor too; the long-haired variety has the thick, wavy, harsh-haired coat of the beardie type; the smooth-muzzled variety has the flatter coat – longer on the tail. The Picardy Sheepdog is heavier, taller, with a more wiry coat in fawn or shades of grey, with its prick ears assisting breed recognition, for all these continental beardie types come from a common mould.

The Spanish and Portuguese Breeds
The Catalan Sheepdog or Gos d'Atura Catala is a 40lb, 20in-high, fawn, reddish-brown, grey or black and white sheep herding dog, with the classic long, flat, rough or harsh-haired coat of the beardie family of pastoral dogs. The Portuguese Sheepdog or Cao da Serra de Aires is a 38lb, 20in-high, fawn, grey or grey with black or tan sheep herding dog with the usual long, slightly wavy, harsh-haired coat of the beardie family, sometimes called the 'monkey dog' because of its facial hair. The Catalan dog is proving popular in England. I have been impressed by the specimens I have seen at shows, but it is not easy to differentiate between the Spanish and Portuguese dogs when the coat colour is similar; I have seen working Beardies too looking much like these overseas breeds, the type being so constant. In striving to give each of these breeds a distinct breed identity I hope that small idiosyncrasies are not stressed to the detriment of an overall sound dog.

The German Beardie – Rauh-haarige Schäferhund.

The Dutch and German Breeds

The Dutch Beardie, the Schapendoes, comes from the northern province of Drenthe. It was used to move large flocks of sheep and has the predictable type for such a breed: 18in tall, 35lb in weight, with a long, wavy harsh-haired coat, usually in blue-grey to black but with all colours acceptable, although the distinctive blue-with-black seems to have become its breed type. The breed was almost lost in the Second World War but fancier P.M.C. Toepoel collected the remaining specimens together to restore the breed. The FCI recognized the restored breed in 1989. In Germany, there was once a shaggy-coated smaller sheepdog, but, like the Hutespitz, the Schafpudel, or sheep-poodle, seems to have been lost. This type displayed the corded coat, hence the poodle tag, and has been linked to the Hungarian Puli, although varieties of coat texture in pastoral dogs has been known to crop up within the same litter, with out-crossing not being involved.

The Polish and Hungarian Breeds

Poland and Hungary also have their heavier-coated type of herding dog, in addition to their big flock-guarding breeds, mentioned in Chapter 1. The Polish

ABOVE: *The Hungarian Puli.*

The Polish Beardie – Polski Owcarek Nizinny.

Unusual Hungarian Puli in a falko or apricot coat.

Lowland Sheepdog, sometimes called the Valee Sheep-dog, is also just under 20in high, 40lb in weight and with a coarse, dense, thick, harsh-haired coat, available in all colours but mainly seen in piebald. With sixty-five registered in 2012, their future in Britain looks firmly based but not entirely secure; a breed's popularity with the show fraternity can change without regard to the merit of a breed, especially an imported one, as the Maremma Sheepdog illustrates. The corded-coated Hungarian Puli may have been the foundation stock of Hungarian herders, with the big ones eventually becoming recognized as the Komondor and developed as a separate breed of flock guardian.

Staying with the Flock
The sheep-herding dogs quite often went with flocks of sheep when these changed hands, and sometimes

Beardie with Leicester sheep, c.1862. FARMER'S WEEKLY MAGAZINE

countries too. It is, in my view, quite absurd to claim that the different herding breeds, especially when they occur in the same country, are completely unrelated. It is entirely fair, however, to state that line-breeding for distinct 'type' has been practised for several hundred years in a number of areas. This has in the past not been done to perpetuate breed points but to meet local demands of climate and temperature, as well as role – whether for herding or just protection. Nowadays, more sophisticated Western dog breeders, especially those in North America, have elected to place breed differences high on their list of breeding priorities; for shepherds in remote, testing conditions such an approach would be more than a luxury. Their dogs were bred for performance not prettiness. To take just one example: length of coat would support the dog's function *not* inhibit it. Similarly, the texture of coat was for weatherproofing not glamour. Breeding away from functional need always penalizes the dog. This is discussed in Chapter 3.

The Heelers

These are the cattle-drivers; the hoof-dodgers, the nip 'n' duck dogs.

> In bygone days the Welsh shepherds were accustomed to use a dog called a 'heeler', whose duty it was to drive the sheep away from the lowland pastures and force them back into the hills, the lower feed being reserved for the winter, when the hills were out of reach because of snow. These were mostly curs who bit the sheep and drove them off by force, but now the Welsh usually use their old dogs – the Bob-tails – who drive the sheep in any direction the shepherd wishes, and who can attain to a very high degree of perfection through their training.
>
> W.L. Puxley, *Collies and Sheep-Dogs* (1948)

I first became aware of the heeler's skill in an unusual way: playing football with a fellow twelve-year-old who had a Pembrokeshire Welsh Corgi. The dog 'played' football with us, and every time it was threatened by a swinging foot, it flattened instinctively and the foot cleared its head. This was done with remarkable timing. I was impressed; later on, when this dog was mated to a local terrier, I obtained a pup, such

Driving horses in the Campagna, Rome, 1880.

was my admiration. This 'drop-flat' technique is a vital survival technique when back-kicking hooves respond to a small dog's quick nip. Clever, experienced heelers will nip the rear foot that the cow is standing on, rather than the one free to kick. The approach is nearly always from behind: a quick nip and away. Watching a farmer drive cattle up a ramp at the Bath and West Show, many years ago, using a small terrier-like dog, I asked him what kind of dog he had; he replied that 'she's a nip 'n' duck dog'. It's an instinctive inherited skill related to the dog's size and agility. My Border Collies could drive cattle, heeler-fashion, but found moving horses too perilous. An Italian colleague, however, has told me of collie-like dogs there quite able to move or round up horses without mishap, but they were specialists. I have seen spitz-type 'sheepdogs' rounding up ponies in Iceland using this technique.

This heeling skill was valuable when cattle needed to be moved: in markets or when loading lorries or railway trucks. Short-legged, terrier-like heelers were not an unusual sight in Britain in the last

two centuries. If they had been gundogs or hounds whole libraries would be filled with tales of their deeds, but they were used by shepherds and stockmen not squires so little has been recorded of them. But when, as a student over sixty years ago, I had summer jobs on farms, it was not unusual to come across small, nondescript foxy-headed dogs working cattle. I was reminded of them a few years later when, on an expedition to Norwegian Lapland, I came across Buhund-type dogs on the farms there and Lapphund-type dogs accompanying the Lapps on reindeer drives. The Germans have lost their heeler: the red-brown cattle dog known as the Siegerlander Altdeutsche Hirtenhund or Kuhhund (cowdog).

Dogs of the Vikings

There has been speculation that the Welsh Corgis were taken to Wales by Viking invaders, with the Vallhund of Sweden identified as the source. I am not aware of the 'nip and duck' instincts of Scandinavian breeds, like the Vallhund, the Buhund or the

Swedish Vallhund at Crufts in 1992.

BOTTOM RIGHT: *English Farm Collie with ACD appearance.*

BOTTOM LEFT: *Australian Cattle Dog.*

Lapphund, but the Vallhund, while having its own distinct breed type, is remarkably similar to the Pembroke Welsh Corgi. The Senjahund of Finmark is noticeably similar to our surviving English heeler, the Lancashire breed.

Pastoral breeds accompanied migrants perhaps more than other types, rivalled only by hounds in value. It is easy to spot British influences in pastoral dogs used in former colonies. I have seen working sheepdogs here that could easily be taken

Norwegian Buhund at Bath Dog Show, 2013.

Bobtailed Heeler of the Black Mountain.

for Australian Cattle Dogs or Australian Shepherds. These Australian dogs are covered later. When sheep were traded, the sheepdogs were often traded with them. In 1982 the *Smithsonian Magazine* in the United States produced a theoretical model of neoteny in dogs that indicated the development of the dog in various stages throughout domestication. This study showed heelers, huskies and corgis in the first move away from the wild dog, followed by the header-stalkers, the hunters and herders, then the other types, with the flock-protection dogs, with their blunter heads and drop ears, a much later development. Head shape and ear carriage can have an influence on capability.

Black Mountain Dogs

Here is a mental exercise for all owners of Corgis, Lancashire Heelers and Australian Cattle Dogs. Imagine going into a field of hefty lively bullocks, then getting down on your hands and knees and picturing the menace faced by your dogs when the cattle surround and threaten you. I write this from my memory of a story told to me on the Black Mountain on the Herefordshire/Welsh border, when I was researching the bobtailed heelers found there. A cat-

tle farmer told me of when he once had a diabetic attack when in a field containing twelve well-grown bullocks. He 'came to' surrounded by determined bullocks but protected by two of his heelers. Lying vulnerably on the ground, he saw the menace his dogs experienced every day, and, for the very first time, from their perspective. This experience gave him a new respect for his agile, steadfast and highly focussed dogs. Every year in Britain dog-walkers are harmed by defensive cows, usually with calves, when walking in pastureland.

On the Black Mountain, these dogs were not to be trifled with; I was warned not to get out of my car when visiting farms guarded by them until the farmer emerged to control them. The lady photographer sent by the magazine that commissioned my article ignored or forgot this advice and sacrificed a nearly new pair of wellies! These dogs lived on farms that gave the word remote its full meaning. Without mental toughness and great agility they would never survive their calling. Any 30lb dog facing a 1-ton beast has my admiration; facing a dozen, with horns as well as hoofs, takes a very special kind of dog. Dogs serving man by herding horses, driving cattle or corralling wild bulls survive through their great agility, but they are chosen for their courage. Without courage, they wouldn't be exercising their agility. They are remarkable dogs.

Emms's depiction of a bobtailed collie of 1904.

BOTTOM RIGHT: *Bessie – a Corgi by Edward Aistrop, c. 1900.*

Cur Dog Heritage

We tend to use the word 'cur' in a derogatory manner these days, but the word was originally used to describe a nondescript working dog rather than a definite type. In *The Sportsman's Cabinet* (1803), such a dog was described as:

> In colour the Cur is of a black brindled or of a dingy grizzled brown, having generally a white neck and some white about the belly, face, and legs; sharp nose; ears half pricked, and the points pendulous; coat mostly long, rough, and matted, particularly about the haunches, giving him a ragged appearance, to which his posterior nakedness greatly contributes, the most of the breed being whelped with a stumpy tail.

That sums up rather well many of the dogs I saw on the Black Mountain; researchers should never dismiss the word 'cur' as just derogatory.

The Welsh Heelers

In 2012, there were only 371 Pembrokeshire Welsh Corgis newly registered with the Kennel Club, and just 108 of the Cardiganshire variety. Originally classified as one breed, with only ten being first registered in 1925, on their recognition, in 1950 there were well over 4,000 Pembrokes registered but only just under 170 of the Cardigan variety. Statistically it could be argued that the latter is maintaining its position better than the former, but it is the Cardigan that is listed as vulnerable. Patronage from the royal family led to the astonishing rise in popularity of the Pembroke dog and it has retained a steadfast bunch of fanciers. This Welsh heeler has kept its perky nature and natural assertiveness, but has lost some of the ruggedness of the earlier types. It takes courage and technique to drive cattle, a dog lacking agility being at a distinct disadvantage. Nipping a 1-ton bull then avoiding its resultant kick demands special qualities but they

have to be backed by the anatomy supporting the mental approach.

The origins of such heeler-cattle dogs are often the subject of fierce debate and remarkable ignorance from strangely revered dog writers. E.C. Ash, in his *Practical Dog Book* (1930), wrote: '…they are a cross of Shetland Sheepdog with the Sealyham Terrier, and possibly Border Terrier…' But nine years

later he was writing: 'I am of the opinion…that the Welsh Corgi (Pembroke) is an Alsatian cross.' About that time, Theo Marples wrote: 'Probably the Welsh Sheepdog and the Bull Terrier had a hand in his making.' Clifford Hubbard, however, who made a comprehensive study of the Welsh breeds, linked the Pembroke variety with Flemish weavers who settled in the Haverfordwest area in the eleventh century. He considered that these migrants brought their Schipperke-like dogs with them to provide an essential ingredient in the emerging breed. Hubbard knew a great deal about both Welsh dogs and pastoral dogs across the globe.

TOP LEFT: *Howitt-Lodge's depiction in 1928 of the founder of the Cardigan Corgi as a show dog – Bob Llywd.*

TOP RIGHT: *Merle Cardiganshire Welsh Corgi of today.*

Tailed Pembrokeshire Welsh Corgi of today.

Comparable Types

We tend to think of the Schipperke as a solid-black, tail-less dog, associated with Belgian barges and a breed title derived from 'little skipper'. But there are solid fawn and solid blue varieties, some with tails, and another school of thought links them with dwarf Groenendaels, with a breed title derived from 'little shepherd'. This has some appeal for me; I see distinct resemblances between the Schipperke, the Norwegian Buhund, the Iceland Farm Dog, the Norwegian Lundehund, the Norrbottenspets and the Vallhund of Sweden, the West Siberian Laika and the Corgis of Wales. There is a corgi-like breed in Croatia, called the Medi, already saved from extinction and being shown. It is always worth keeping in mind that useful dogs travelled with tribes or migrants across many centuries and across many borders.

The English Heeler

But what about the only surviving English heeler breed, the Lancashire Heeler? With just over 100 being registered annually, this breed now appears to have been saved and have a sound future. This is very good news, firstly because we have lost too many of our native pastoral breeds, and, secondly because this is a breed well worth saving. A foot high, smooth-coated, black and tan or liver and tan, lively and perky by nature, it represents an ideal companion dog for many households. I do hope the show-ring fanciers keep faith with the historic design of this breed and not produce, in time, Dachshund-like specimens with snipy jaws, bent legs and too low-to-ground a build.

ABOVE LEFT: Portrait of a Lancashire Heeler by Juliet McLeod of 1951 (before recognition).

Liver and tan Lancashire Heeler.

FULL COAT, LONG LEGS, SHORT BODY.

SMALL CAT-LIKE EARS

NARROW HEAD, EARS TOO CLOSE TO-GETHER

LARGE ROUNDED EARS.

GOOD EARS.

CROOKED FRONT.

BOWED FRONT.

GOOD FRONT.

Faults in the Pembrokeshire Corgi (1934).

DIPPY BACK, CURLED TAIL, SMALL EARS

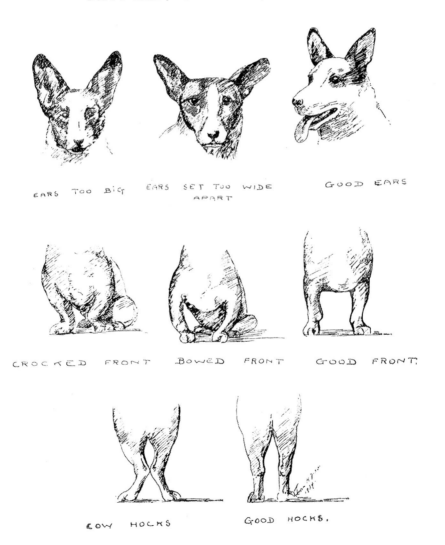

EARS TOO BIG   EARS SET TOO WIDE   GOOD EARS
                     APART

CROCKED FRONT   BOWED FRONT   GOOD FRONT

COW HOCKS   GOOD HOCKS.

Faults in the Cardiganshire Corgi.

This is essentially a natural, unexaggerated working breed, deserving to be conserved as just that. A specialist show judge for Lancashire Heelers at Crufts in 2013 concluded that:

> There is still a bewildering variation in type in the lower classes, but there were enough compact exhibits with level toplines and high set tails for me to end up with a really exciting line-up in both sexes. I was delighted too that for the first time when judging the breed, all the exhibits appeared sound and not one of them hopped.

There is cause for enthusiasm over this breed's future there. There is encouragement too from the news that a Lancashire Heeler, Bellsmond Spirits Shadow over Triphazard, went Best in Show at an all-breeds show in 2013 in Finland, from the 400 dogs entered, in a country where some of the best judges reside. From the ringside, I like the look of Ch Doddsline Kristen and his progeny. However, the last two decades have not been good for British heeler breeds.

Heelers on Show

The comments by judges on the three British heeler breeds in recent years provides an immediate and expert view of these breeds and the state of them today. The Crufts judge of Pembroke Welsh Corgis in 1997 recorded:

> Presentation was very good, sometimes too good, however the breed in general has a lot of problems, the main ones being movement, toplines and feet. Too many people are running after the latest winning dog without any thought as to how it will fit in with their own breeding plan. This results in the vast type variances we are seeing and the poor movement…

The Crufts judge of Cardigan Welsh Corgis in 1995 wrote: 'The main problem however is rear construction and rear action, too many lack the drive and follow through that are a must in a working dog. They would not last on the hill pastures which they used to work and the old farmers would give them short shrift…' The Crufts judge of Lancashire Heelers in 2002 wrote: '…movement is still poor, we must never lose sight of what this dog was bred for…' In 2003, a Championship Show judge recorded on Cardigan

Corgis: 'I was somewhat disturbed to see so many straight fronts and bad shoulder placements and hope we can focus on returning the type and soundness we had a few years ago.' The Crufts qualifiers of the foregoing decade would have been bred from, whatever their quality, and produced the dogs reported on here.

Built-In Flaws
A Lancashire Heeler judge, at a 2003 show recorded: '…there is cause for concern as I think fronts are getting worse…for an active working breed conformation and soundness must come first.' But does it? That same year, a Pembroke Corgi judge gave the view that: 'Movement was bad on some (both ends), poor shoulders too… Where are those good old breeders?' Four years earlier, a Cardigan Corgi judge (at LKA) had concluded:

> One thing which seems apparent in the breed today is lack of length of stride, the Cardigan is a herding dog and should be able to outpace the normal walking pace of its owner. Unfortunately this is not always the case and stilted hind action is far too prevalent; poor conformation and movement lacking drive was seen in many exhibits…

At a different show:

> I find it very difficult to understand why someone would want to show a dog that does not conform to the Breed Standard in breed type and just as importantly movement. If poor specimens are continually used in breeding programmes, i.e. poor movers and bad toplines – which now seems to be the norm when you look around – I think we can say goodbye to the breed as we have known it.

That makes disturbing reading, coming as it does from an accepted expert on the breed. It is not as though such faults had not been pointed out in the past, as the two images here, from 1934, illustrate.

Perpetuating Faults
In 1956 the experienced sheepdog breeder John Holmes, writing in the dog press on Corgis, stated:

> It is interesting to note that it is only in show dogs that bone is considered of great importance. Among

those who keep collies, terriers, etc., purely for work, it is never mentioned… I cannot see any reason why we should let it become a fad and try to breed Corgis with about twice as much bone as they really require…

Overlooking the hound fraternity's fascination with bone, I agree with the point he makes. Why bestow on a pastoral breed a physical feature it never needed in the pastures? Far better to concentrate on avoiding the perpetuation of acquired faults, the sure sign of a breed 'going downhill'. In 2005, a Lancashire Heeler judge concluded:

What on earth has happened to this lovely breed?… I find it hard to believe that the breeders have lost the plot so completely. I was startled at the lack of quality which was here today. Dogs of all shapes and sizes, too light boned, too big, badly constructed, indifferent heads, eyes and expressions, appalling fronts… Fronts are the worst I have seen in the breed… I think the breeders need a wake up call…

In 2009 the Crufts judge of Pembroke Corgis wrote:

Last year after Crufts, Albert Wight (the 2008 Crufts judge) had some harsh words to say about the breed and I must admit I can see his point. I know it's easy to romanticize the past but remembering the 70s and

early 80s, the 'Yorkshire' era with all those wonderful tricolours…it's hard to deny that we're not going through a vintage period in the 00s.

If you consult such reports on the British heeler breeds, it is clear that there is a discernible lack of wisdom within the breeds and this is alarming. With registrations falling and judges voicing considerable disquiet, there is much to be done to safeguard the future of these fine breeds; a clear statement setting out what a working dog needs to function, back to basics if you like, is desperately required.

Cattle-Dog Heritage

The larger cattle dogs overseas are well worth studying. It is interesting that dogs used with cattle range from those substantial enough to impose their will – like the Rottweiler, the Fila breeds, for example the Fila de Sao Miguel, the Presa breeds, such as the Perro de Presa Mallorquin/Ca de Bou or cow-dog of Mallorca (Fila and Presa identifying the 'gripping' breeds), the Bardino Majero of the Canary Isles and the Perro Cimarron of Uruguay – down to the little heelers. All these dogs need considerable courage but the little breeds especially so. They combine skill with guts. As long as man needs beef and milk, he will need clever, brave dogs to support him. Butchers may no longer need strong-headed dogs to pin cattle at abattoirs or markets and the droves have long lost

Perro de Presa Mallorquin or Ca de Bou (cowdog of Mallorca) at World Dog Show.

Fila de Sao Miguel.

their role. But stockmen in many countries still need cattle dogs, dogs agile enough to dodge lashing hooves and sometimes thrusting horns too, yet brave enough to undertake the task in the first place. These are not just another breed or collection of breeds. They are very remarkable dogs. As the lifestyle of modern man heads towards total urbanization, sporting and pastoral breeds face an uncertain future. We dispense with their skills at our peril; it would be foolish indeed to assume that the uncertainties of the future will not in any foreseeable circumstances present a need of such unique talents.

It may be that an international organization of pastoral breeds is called for; most countries have developed their own breeds in this field and common challenges have to be faced if a sound future for such admirable creatures is to be planned. I would hate to see brave and talented dogs like these wholly unemployed and just left to fade away. Cattle dogs have never enjoyed noble patronage, featured in fine art or carved a niche for themselves away from the pastures. That may not strengthen their image but should not weaken their case for conservation. The Filas or holding dogs, in particular, face serious threats in the developed world as ignorant law-makers punish them for the misdeeds of their owners. Yet from the stock-pen to the boar hunt such dogs merely did man's bidding; they are well equipped to continue this in many different ways for a long time to come.

Heeler of the Black Mountain working a longhorn.

Drovers' dogs are singularly prompt in their actions, and all who have watched them in the crowded, noisy, tumultuous assemblage of man and beast, that used weekly to occur in Smithfield, must have observed their intelligence and courage. Nor in the busy streets of London, through which drove after drove of cattle were taken, could the same qualities fail to be noticed by any sagacious looker-on. These dogs were accustomed to bite severely, and always attacked the heels of the cattle, so that even a fierce bull was easily driven by one of them.

Charles Williams, *Dogs and Their Ways* (1863)

Herders Abroad

Pastoral Dog Need
Up to 1000BC, something like four-fifths of Europe north of the Alps and the Pyrenees was covered by dense forest. Over the next 200 years, extensive clearance by farmers provided the basis for new growth through local trade, notably from the fairs dating from the time of Charlemagne. This growth brought an unprecedented demand for herding dogs, both to control herds and get them to market. Bruges became the chief European wool manufacturing town and medieval Flanders and its neighbours produced a wide range of driving dogs, as the Bouvier breeds demonstrate. As increasing urbanization occurs in

Europe, the pastoral breeds are vulnerable; yet, much further east, old breeds are being lost too. The Tooroochan Sheepdog of Siberia may now be lost as a distinct breed, their past value forgotten. The need for guarding and moving sheep has lessened or been mechanized.

ABOVE: The Shepherd and the Sea, *etching by Lecouteux, c.1885, showing prototypal Briards.*

Beauceron herding sheep: Going to Pasture *by Sangston Truesdell.*

In the sixteenth century Spain had 3 million sheep and exported them both to her neighbours and to her new territories. The main trade was overland to France over the Pyrenees, with dogs playing a major role in their safe passage. In 1840, France had over 5 million sheep in her pastures. Two hundred and fifty years ago, the Danes were sending 80,000 head of cattle a year to Germany by driving them overland using dogs. The routes taken by the various drovers with their herding dogs crossed every European boundary and it would be unwise to claim purity of descent for the different national breeds of today. These European drovers used dogs like the Bouvier type and sharper, quicker-moving dogs like the herding breeds of Western Europe today.

Pastoral Breeds of the Low Countries

> The Groenendael and its kindred spirits, the Malinois and Tervueren, I could not find in work on any Belgian farms, and the trials I found were those for police type work. The intelligent traits of the Groenendael have been utilized by the police for their requirements, and in many countries the breed has been evolved for the show bench. This is the fate of many West European working dogs. Only once in the Black Forest of Germany have I seen an Alsatian, the German Shepherd Dog, in action with a flock of sheep.

Those words by Eric Halsall in his *Sheepdogs – My Faithful Friends* (1980) tell a sad story of an ever-decreasing use of the dogs of the pastures. But this

Belgian Shepherd Dog – Malinois.

Belgian Shepherd Dog – Groenendael.

Belgian Shepherd Dog – Laekenois.

neglect is not new, rooted not in human whim, but created by an increasingly urban landscape and as the livestock market changes its nature. The herding breeds may have suffered less than the flock guardians, but having lived in Central Europe on three different occasions, been based in Gibraltar for a year, as well as attending half a dozen World Dog Shows all over Europe, I am very aware of the decline in use of the pastoral breeds and their drift to the show bench – or oblivion.

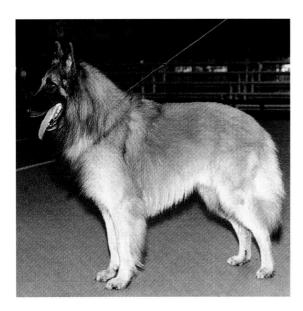

Belgian Shepherd Dog - Tervueren.

The Belgian Breeds

The herding breeds have been just as neglected abroad as in Britain. In Belgium, for example, their four varieties of shepherd dog, named after the region of their development – Tervueren, Groenendael, Malinois and Laekenois – were unrecognized and not bred to type until the invaluable work of Professor Reul of the Cureghem Veterinary School bore fruit at the end of the nineteenth century. I find the Malinois most impressive, with Liz Richardson's Sabrefield kennel distinguishing itself both in the ring and at trials, fly-ball and agility. It is claimed I know by the FCI and some national kennel clubs that the Bouvier des Flandres (or drover's dog of Flanders) is Belgian, but the breed developed when Flanders, a medieval principality spanning what is now Holland, France and Belgium, was French, although there was once Spanish influence there too. There can be a distinct resemblance between the Bouvier des Flandres, the rough-haired variety of the Dutch Shepherd Dog and the Laekenois, especially when all three were working types. Similarly, location has led to the Bouvier des Ardennes, a breed reminiscent of the Pumi of Hungary, another Belgian drover's dog, showing signs of French pastoral breeds, although, again, we must remember that the old Ardennes region occupied what is now parts of Belgium, Luxemburg and northern France. Working dogs do not relate to modern national boundaries, much more to routes to markets and grazing rights. As I point out throughout this book, breeds are a modern phenomenon.

The Background to the Bouviers

Few breeds of dog developed in isolation from their function. Against this background, the Bouvier des Flandres became associated with the agricultural plain of Flanders and enjoyed a wide variety of names: *vuilbaard* (dirty beard), *koe hund* (cow dog) and *toucheur de boeufs* (cattle-mover or drover). When cattle and sheep were transported to market and ports by rail and truck, concern was expressed for the dogs of the local drovers, rugged handsome

The Bouvier des Ardennes.

The Bouvier des Flandres.

dogs conforming to an identifiable type. In 1910 the Bouvier was first exhibited as four varieties, the Bouvier de Roulers, for example, being bigger and black, but in 1912 the growing band of enthusiasts combined forces to standardize these into one. Then the Great War played havoc with the breeding stock and it was left to a Belgian Army veterinary surgeon, Captain Darby, who by saving some good specimens founded the modern breed through his sire Ch Nic de Sottegem. By 1922, the breed club had agreed the desired type and drafted a breed standard.

Since then the Bouvier has become more a personal guard dog, police or army dog than a pastoral breed but has remained essentially a working dog. The first American standard was approved in 1959, and revised in 1975 following the sensible Franco-Belgian agreement. With the breed type now agreed internationally, the Bouvier is gaining in strength in many widely separated countries on sheer merit. I am more than a little puzzled though why the colour chocolate-brown should be so disliked and severely punished in the breed; if an otherwise good pup emerges in this colour, why consign it to the bucket? In Holland, however, they do favour a rough-haired shepherd dog, with a short or smoother-haired and a long-haired variety too. My memory of Bouviers in the early 1960s, when living on the Continent, is the Belgians and the French preferring the taller, rangier types and the Dutch favouring the cobbier, shorter-legged type.

The Dutch Breeds

Not surprisingly, there is some similarity between the pastoral breeds of Holland and those of Belgium: a

ABOVE: *Dutch Shepherd Dog – rough-haired.*

Dutch Shepherd Dog – short-haired.

shepherd dog with a number of varieties, originating in location but manifested in coat texture, but with the addition of their Beardie, the Schapendoes, no surviving Bouvier but a general farm dog, the Smoushond, that may have had the same role as Ireland's Kerry Blue and Wheaten Terriers – all-round farm dogs, especially around the yard itself. The Dutch Shepherd Dog is little known in Britain but has three attractive variations: short-, long- and rough-coated, with the last-named having a distinct look of the Belgian Laekenois in some specimens and a hint of Bouvier in the larger ones. The Schapendoes has been covered in an earlier section, under the harsh-haired herding type found, each only slightly different, in half a dozen European countries.

The German Breeds

In Germany now there is but one surviving breed of shepherd dog. Yet there were once distinct variations of it too: smooth-coated dogs; the white sheepdogs of Pomerania (the Pommerscher Hutehund, once tried by a Dorset farmer and shown at Crufts in 1919), the heavier-coated dogs of Bavaria and the south and the lighter-coloured dogs of Prussia. In the early days of the twentieth century, merle and wire-coated German Shepherd Dogs existed in the breed, with one well-known bitch of the 1920s, Lori Maier, featuring this coat texture, now no longer favoured. The Hutespitz, a big, thick-coated, white and fawn herding dog was once widely used in northern Germany. In the January 1884 edition of *The Kennel Gazette* there was a piece on German Sheepdogs that made some interesting observations:

> Mr Beckmann in *Der Hund* thus describes the three types of dog found. 'The rough-coated race has a hard coat with hardly any gloss, dry to the touch…the lower side of the tail becomes a stiff brush, the belly and hinder part of the legs are feathered. The colour is mostly a deep black or iron-grey… The colours alluded to above are occur in the rough-coated dogs also… In our country (Leipzig Saxony), on the Lower Rhine and about Westphalia these dogs are given the preference and we see them often in company with the numerous droves which are being weekly exported into France and Belgium…these rough-coated dogs come originally from the Hanoverian country.'

The writer went on to describe the other two types: the long-haired race, with a shaggy coat, parted along the spine, blue-grey in colour but also yellowish-white and the short or smooth-haired race, often

The first Pomeranian Sheepdogs imported into Britain, the property of Mr A.D. Ingrams who exhibited them at Cruft's in 1939.

German long- and short-haired sheepdogs of 1900.

MIDDLE LEFT: *German Shepherd Dog and two 'Sheep-poodles' at early English show, 1893.*

BOTTOM LEFT: *The Hovawart.*

BOTTOM RIGHT: *A 1904 depiction of a German Sheepdog.*

docked and black and tan in colour – 'come across here and there all over the country'. The accompanying sketch showed two of the types.

Working on three separate occasions in Westphalia and visiting the more remote farming areas, I never once found a German Shepherd Dog working with sheep (I therefore deal with this breed in Chapter 6) but noticed golden-coated Hovawarts guarding the farmyards and, as ratting dogs, small pinschers being used, similar to the modern breeds of Miniature Pinscher and Schnauzer. The German breed of Schnauzer is a classic example of a versatile farm breed: the Riesenschnauzer, or Giant Schnauzer, was the drover and farm guard, the standard Schnauzer was the yard dog and the miniature version the ratter. On Irish farms I found the Wheaten and Kerry Blue Terriers being used as all-round farm dogs in exactly the same way, with the unclipped Wheatens closely resembling Bouviers and Schnauzers. The quaintly named sheep-poodle of Germany that displayed a corded coat is probably now extinct, as is the old blue merle smooth-coated German Shepherd Dog, very much like our Smooth Collie.

French Farm Dogs

Only comparatively recently have we in Britain come to appreciate and then value the herding or herd-protecting breeds of France. But nowadays, with twelve Pyrenean Sheepdogs (rough-faced), nineteen Beaucerons and 126 Briards registered with the Kennel Club in 2012 to reinforce the 105 Pyrenean Mountain Dogs, our acknowledgement of their many agreeable qualities is manifesting itself; all the French herding breeds resemble other European breeds too. The Berger de Brie or Briard is like

A Briard of today.

the Schafpudel of Germany, the Berger de Beauce is similar to our own smooth collie, the Berger de Picardie resembles our long-lost Smithfield Sheepdog, the Berger des Pyrenees looks like the Schapendoes of Holland, the Catalan Sheepdog and our Bearded Collie, by type, as function and climate decided form. Lesser known varieties like the Berger des Pyrenees a face rasee, or smooth-faced Pyrenean Sheepdog, the Berger du Langedoc or Farou, the Berger de Bresse, the Berger de Savoie and the Labrit from Les Landes in the southwest show how different areas can produce their own types, rather as the Galway Sheepdog, the Glenwherry Collie, the Welsh Hillman, the Black and Tan Collie and the Old Welsh Grey existed in the British Isles.

The French herding breed which impresses me the most in that country, however, is the Beauceron, a strapping, handsome dog with the majesty of the Akita and the alertness of the Dobermann. (I strongly suspect that Herr Dobermann resorted to Beauceron blood in the creation of his breed.) Black and tan or harlequin and sometimes dubbed '*bas rouge*' or red stockings because of its red-tan legs, the Beauceron is little known outside France but is now recognized by our KC (and has an Interim Standard), with impressive stock here reinforced by two young

French shepherd in the Pyrenees with his Labrit.

dogs recently imported from Slovakia. A big, robust, powerful, muscular but not heavy breed, 26in at the withers, very strong-minded and rather fierce in appearance, it is one of the few breeds whose strength of will you can sense, and while it lacks the 'strong eye' of our working sheepdogs, its work with cattle is in the brusque no-nonsense style.

The French conduct the Nationale d'Elevage for the breed, attracting over 600 Beaucerons for a variety of tests, spanning conformation, temperament, obedience and herding, leading to very comprehensive assessment awards. The breed has been used by both the French army and the police and my French friends tell me they were originally hunting dogs used on boar and stag, representing an ancient French type. The harlequin factor is found in hounds, as the Dunker hound, the Great Dane and the Dachshund illustrate; the 'merling' of the Beauceron is more like the hound colouration than that found in collies. French shepherds believed that double dew-claws on the hind legs denoted herding skill in a dog, and the Beauceron features this unusual addition today. The Farou or Berger du Languedoc, also called the Berger de Camargue and Chien de Larzac, is probably a southern version of the Beauceron.

The Lost Breeds

The Labrit, probably getting its name from the town of that name in the south of France (although some

suggest it comes from de la Brie, since it is Briard-like and there was a tendency in the nineteenth century to call all French smooth-haired shepherd dogs *chiens de Beauce* and all coarse-haired dogs *chiens de Brie*) has now been embraced by the Pyrenean Sheepdog. The Berger de Bresse is almost certainly now lost to us and the Berger de Savoie, Beauceron-like but drop-eared, may too not have survived. Little is heard of the Picardie Sheepdog. We have probably lost more types of herding dog all over Europe than of any other group; the pastoral scene changed dramatically in the twentieth century and the advent of the pedigree dog has seen human whim play its part too. But this group of dogs has given man supremely loyal and devoted service over many centuries and whether French in origin or British deserve our gratitude.

TOP: *Blue merle Beauceron.*

Berger du Languedoc.

The Spanish Breeds

Further west, in Iberia, neglected or overlooked native breeds are becoming recognized as the canine heritage of each nation is at last being valued by the show fraternity; in Spain, for example, at the 2013 Madrid show, the Garafiano Sheepdog, from the Canaries, was paraded, followed by three other native breeds. The Carea Leones, from around Leon, sometimes called the Leonese Sheepdog or the Perro de Pastor Vasco, the Carea Castellano Manchego and the Euskal Artzain Txakurra, or Basque Shepherd Dog, were introduced to the curious onlookers in the main ring programme. The latter, surviving in northern Spain in the Bilbao region, now has its own preservation society/breed club and determinedly loyal fanciers. It is not unusual either to find the Australian Shepherd linked with Basque shepherds emigrating to Australia in the nineteenth century. The Catalan Sheepdog, or Gos D'Atura, is now becoming known in Britain, with thirty-two registered with the KC in 2012. The pastoral dogs of the Pyrenees, ranging from the huge mountain dog (on the French side) or Patou, the still-substantial Mastiff (on the Spanish side, also called the Mastin d'Aragon or the Navarro Mastiff) and the Beardie-like sheepdog or Gos D'Atura, have already been described. There is also the Majorca Sheepdog or Mallorquin Shepherd, a general farm dog, in two coats, short and long, and usually black.

ABOVE: The Labrit or Pyrenean Sheepdog. PATRICIA LORE, COURTESY OF BRYAN CUMMINS

Gos d'Atura or Catalan Sheepdogs.

The Garafiano Sheepdog. POZO

It has been difficult for some time to research the Spanish pastoral breeds. I first read of them in Clifford Hubbard's two books of the late 1940s: *The Observer's Book of Dogs* (1947) and *Working Dogs of the World* (1947). He seemed unaware, however, of the breeds referred to at the start of my previous paragraph. When living in Gibraltar for a year in the mid-1960s and camping in more remote parts of the Spanish hinterland, I found it difficult to identify their pastoral *breeds* as such. I saw Basque Shepherd Dogs near San Sebastian, in red-tan or merle or harlequin coats, but also in two types, one for the higher pastures, the other for the lowland ones. I saw black merle Leonese Sheepdogs and black and buckskin Manchegos, with the huge Spanish Mastiffs much smaller in the high pastures than at shows or when used as guard dogs. Along the Portuguese/Spanish border, I found it hard to distinguish the Estrela Mountain Dogs from the Spanish Mastiffs used by shepherds in that region. But at the World Dog Show, held in Oporto, the breed differences were quite apparent. The shepherds seemed to care little about 'unique type' considered

so precious by show fanciers and often prized ahead of physical soundness; for them performance was all.

The Portuguese Breeds

The Portuguese pastoral breeds are as varied as, yet almost matching in type, those of neighbouring Spain, ranging from the Castro Laboreiro, the cattle dog of the north, the Estrela Mountain Dog from the central highlands – a classic flock guardian – the Rafeiro do Alentejo from the south and the Beardie-type, the Cao da Serra de Aires, a

Head study of a Rafeiro do Alentejo.

The Castro Laboreiro of Portugal.

shaggy-coated sheep-herder. I have in Portugal come across the last-named and thought at first it was a Catalan Sheepdog, so alike, to me, were the two breeds. And, on the same peninsula of Iberia, is this surprising? The Estrela is now well-established outside Portugal, though their registrations here are sadly going down, year on year. The Rafeiro dog I have never seen outside Portugal, but been very impressed with them in their pasturelands. They may lack the eye-appeal of their more glamorous cousin from further north, but looked impressive, very serious about their work and probably a better watchdog. They have a wider range of coat colours and look much more like a working dog. The Castro Laboreiro can be remarkably Labrador-like, often displaying an otter tail; could they be linked, remembering the Portuguese presence off Eastern Canada in past centuries?

Eastern European Breeds

In Hungary, the distinctive Puli, Pumi and Mudi breeds still perform as movers of livestock, with the much larger Komondor and Kuvasz breeds acting as flock guardians. Only the Puli is seen in Britain's

The Pumi of Hungary.

show rings in any numbers, but the Komondor and Kuvasz are recognized. In *Dogs of Hungary* (1977), Pal Sarkany and Imre Ocsag wrote:

> It seems likely that the majority of the nine native recognized and registered breeds arrived in the Carpathian Basin during the Great Migration preceding the Magyars, the Huns and Avars, then with the Magyars and later on with the immigrating Pechenegs and Cumanians as their sheepdogs and hunting dogs… The Puli is the ancient sheep dog of Hungary. He has worked sheep on the plains of the Puszta since the 9th century, and has survived quite simply because he was, and still is, physically and temperamentally superlative for the work… Mudis are bred largely by shepherds and herdsmen… For a century the word 'Pumi' was confused with the word 'Puli'. 'Pumi' may have been derived from 'Puli'…the breed emerged about the 17th or 18th century…

More likely, when compared to the development of sheepdogs elsewhere, is that the Puli arose from longer-haired or corded 'sports' from the Pumi or Mudi, two breeds much more like each other, with the Pumi closely resembling the type displayed by the Labrit of the French Pyrenees.

The Mudi of Hungary – spitz-like.

Breeds such as Romania's Mioritic Shepherd, the Bucovina Shepherd, the Carpathian Shepherd (once just called the Romanian Shepherd and very similar to the Mioritic dog but heavier-headed) and the solid black, shiny-coated, well-named Raven Dog have been presented at their country's shows for the first time. In Bulgaria, they have their Karakachan Dog, named after the Karakachan people, semi-nomadic livestock keepers and breeders. In Poland, the livestock-protection dog is the Tatra Mountain Dog, resembling the Maremma in Italy, the Pyrenean Mountain Dog of France, the Kuvasz of Hungary and, especially, the Slovakian Shepherd Dog or Liptok. The Polish herder is their Lowland Sheepdog, now well known in Britain and covered in the section on the bearded types.

The Scandinavian Breeds

The Scandinavians still have their herding dogs, of the classic spitz type of the arctic north, and surprisingly similar in each country. When on an exploration trip to one of Iceland's ice caps, Hofsjokull, in the middle of the last century, I was intrigued to see what looked like a prick-eared, bushy-tailed collie on several farms there. Known locally as the Islandske Spidshunde and used to round up ponies

ABOVE: *Norwegian Buhund at Crufts, 1998.*

An Iceland Farm Dog today.

The Finnish Lapphund.

as well as sheep, they have earned mentions both by Dr Caius and Shakespeare. The Icelandic Sheepdog is long established and very collie-like, as is the Buhund or cattle dog of Norway, now becoming known in our show rings. The northern Scandinavian herding dogs range from the corgi-like to the collie-like, with the Norwegian Senjahund and the Swedish Vastgotaspets or Vallhund exemplifying the former and the maastehund of the Lofoten Islands, and the Finnish, Swedish and Lapponian Herders resembling the latter. The corgi-type heelers, like the Vallhund, have to be agile, quick and alert, if only to survive. As cattle dogs, as discussed in an earlier section, they have to learn to bite the hind foot that is bearing weight, giving them that extra split second to duck or flatten to avoid the reacting hefty kick. They learn too to attack alternate feet, rather than repeating the first attempt, just to gain a little more surprise.

The Finnish Lapphund seems to be making progress here, although it was only recognized by the Finnish KC in the 1950s and separated from the smooth variety in 1967. This breed was introduced into Britain by Roger and Sue Dunger (Sulyka) and their enthusiasm has done much to promote this attractive breed here. Hardy, double-coated, working dogs, they have been bred by the Sami people of Lapland in northern Scandinavia for centuries to herd their reindeer. I have watched in fascination similar dogs carrying out this task in northern Norway, near Jaeggesvarre Glacier, when on an expedition there over half a century ago – a timeless scene.

Dogs in the Faeroe Islands
The Danish Faeroe Islands have links with both Iceland and the Shetland Isles so their sheepdogs are of interest for the pastoral breeds of those two locations. In *The Sporting Magazine* of 1809, there was a piece on these dogs that read:

> Dogs in the Ferroe Islands: A proper sheepdog in Ferroe must never bark when employed in the fields, lest the sheep should be rendered wilder than they are. There are in these islands several kinds of dogs; the oldest breed have rather a long pointed muzzle, and short erect ears; but most of them have their ears half or entirely hanging down, stand pretty high on their legs, and are smooth-haired. A smaller kind of dog is kept for driving the sheep down from the inclosures when they jump over the fences in summer. The principal property of these dogs is to bark.

When you look at the Iceland Sheepdog and then early representations of the Shetland Sheepdog, and recall their role, the sheepdog diaspora brings considerable uniformity in the working dogs developed and employed in it.

Colonial Needs
A different type of stock dog was required by settlers in the wide-open spaces of America and Australia. Despite taking their herding dogs from Britain with them, the early colonists found a need to adapt them to local conditions. In Australia this produced the Barb or black Kelpie, the Kelpie and the Australian Cattle Dog. The striking resemblance

The Barb depicted in 1908.

to old forms of our native breeds in these emergent breeds is undeniable. I have seen working collies in Britain that could pass at first glance as one of the Australian breed. The Australian Shepherd owes more to the United States for its development, but is very similar to the bobtailed sheepdogs of the Black Mountain, on the Hereford border with Wales. In New Zealand, the Huntaway was produced, a barker rather than a silent worker like our collie but still reminiscent of our old black and tan sheepdog. These Antipodean breeds are covered in more detail below.

Antipodean Herders

Anyone who has read Robert Hughes's *The Fatal Shore* (1988) will retain a lifelong admiration for those who went to Australia in its earliest years of development by Europeans. This admiration must be extended too to the dogs that accompanied the earliest settlers. Certainly, on the long, arduous journey out there, dogs would have suffered as much as any human, if not more. It is worth remembering that when considering the surviving breeds of Australian, and indeed New Zealand, dogs. It is hardly surprising that breeds like the Australian Cattle Dog, the Kelpie and the Huntaway of New Zealand are among the toughest breeds of dog in the world. Writing in the *South African Merino Breeders Journal* in 1941, Mr W. Ross's article 'Training a Sheepdog' stated:

> As far as we are concerned, there are only the Border Collie and the Kelpie to choose from…the Kelpie is an Australian breed. It varies a lot in colour and size and probably springs from the same source as the Border Collie, with possibly some admixture of blood far back. That does not, however, detract from its present value. You will probably find the Border Collie is more obedient and stylish while the Kelpie is hardier.

TOP LEFT: *A Kelpie working sheep in Australia.*

Australian Cattle Dog – UK import.

Australian Cattle Dog.

New Zealand farmer with his Huntaway.

This hardiness is an immense benefit in an unforgiving sheep rearing country such as Australia; sheep farmers are not looking for pets – in any country.

Australian Shepherd – it has the same colour range as our Border Collie.

It is hardly likely that ornamental dogs would have accompanied the early transport ships to Australia and New Zealand; it is certain that dogs valuable enough to have merited passage in this way would be workers: herding dogs, hounds or terriers. Dogs in these categories would have gone on this long hazardous voyage because they would bring benefits at the far end to their owners. It is not good sense, however, to link them with contemporary breeds because breeds were not valued in the eighteenth and early nineteenth centuries; function ruled. On the other hand, it is of value to link them with the common dogs of England at that time.

Sheep and cattle being taken to the Antipodes would have been accompanied by herding dogs. Terriers and hounds would have been valued as vermin-controllers and pot-fillers. Big, strapping mastiff-type dogs would have been valued as guard dogs and seizing dogs. Later on, sportsmen would take gundogs and packhounds. This, I believe, is the background for considering the development of breeds down under. The Australian Cattle Dog is often stated to have come from a mixture of smooth merle collies, dingo, Dalmatian and black and tan Kelpie. The dingo blood is stated in one Australian publication to have introduced silent working, the red coat colour and the heeling instinct. The last point is explained in these words: 'A dingo trait is to silently creep up behind an animal and bite, and these cross pups followed this style of heeling.'

Red merle Border Collie.

BOTTOM: *Bull Terrier of a type that may have contributed to the ACD's make-up.*

A reasonable response to this, to me, incredible statement would be: British working sheepdogs work silently; red merle is in the collie gene pool – it doesn't need an infusion of dingo blood; and the heeling instinct was present in British herding dogs before any Europeans reached Australia, ask any Welsh Corgi or Lancashire Heeler breed historian. As for the infusion of Dalmatian blood, can you truly imagine any hard-bitten weather-beaten cattle farmer introducing the blood of a spotted coach dog to, as the Australian publication puts it, 'give the progeny a love of horses and a sense of responsibility for guarding their master's possessions'? My working sheepdogs loved horses and were naturally protective of me, my family and our 'possessions'. Why did no English farmer find it necessary to infuse his working pastoral dogs with Dalmatian blood?

Noreen Clark, in her 2003 book, *A Dog Called Blue, The Australian Cattle Dog and the Stumpy Tail Cattle Dog 1840–2000*, an excellent piece of research on these breeds, provides authoritative background to this subject. Her researches show that the Dalmatian theory was invented by an Australian dog

'expert' called Kaleski, with no evidence whatsoever, perhaps going on an uninformed hunch to account for the blue ticking in the breed's coat. Genetic research alone has shown that a quite different gene is responsible for this and one that is not present in Dalmatians. Despite this incontrovertible contradiction of Kaleski's theory, we have the KC, in their official Illustrated Breed Standards, published at regular intervals by Ebury Press, stating: 'Behind the Australian

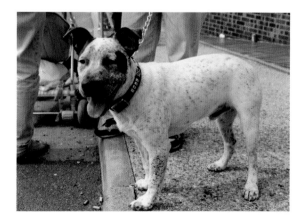

Stumpy tail cattle dog.

Cattle Dog are breeds such as the Dingo, the Kelpie, the Dalmatian and the Bull Terrier, but the breed has been purebred since the mid-1890s.' Apart from the fact that the dingo is not a breed, it is not impressive for a publication that really should be authoritative to be so totally wrong.

The Australian Cattle Dog is respected in many countries for its mental toughness, physical robustness and serious approach to work. In his *Hunting Big Game with Dogs in Africa*, the American Er M. Shelley gave an admiring pen picture of one of these dogs. He described her as:

> …a wonderful hunting dog. She could trail nearly as well as a hound, and, when it came to fighting in dense places, I have never seen a dog that could compare with her. She possessed the power and had the courage to force a lion from place to place in dense cover, while large packs of dogs could not move him

at all. In after years she was used by Mr Rainey to bring both lions and leopards out of dense reed beds, where his entire pack of forty or fifty hounds and Airedales could not move them.

That is some tribute from a man with immense experience in hunting big game. I have pointed out that the theory that the Australian Cattle Dog came from root stock of two Scottish blue merle working collies crossed with dingo, with Dalmatian and Kelpie blood introduced later, is unsubstantiated. I see Bull Terrier features in the anatomies of many ACDs but am told that the out-cross to the Bull Terrier was not considered a success and not favoured. The dingo blood is alleged to have produced the inclination to creep up behind cattle and bite them. But there has never been a shortage of British working collies with the instinct to get behind stock and nip it into compliance. I once owned two working sheepdogs that would nip the

Mr Bridges' Kelpie, a Queensland sheepdog winner that was crossed with Dingo blood.

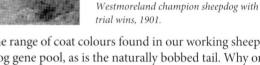

<small>BELOW LEFT:</small> *A black merle Westmoreland champion sheepdog with trial wins, 1901.*

hocks of cattle as a herding tactic without any training to do so.

Sources of Blood

I suspect that the blue-mottled or speckled coat of this quite admirable Australian breed has given rise to such weird conclusions, and was certainly behind Kaleski's invention. As mentioned in an earlier section, it is not unusual too to find the Australian Shepherd linked with Basque shepherds emigrating to Australia in the nineteenth century. But this attractive breed displays the range of coat colours found in our working sheepdog gene pool, as is the naturally bobbed tail. Why on earth would colonist-farmers, living in a tough climate in a new land, rush to use Spanish dogs when their own were so proficient – it makes no sense at all. An Australian fancier of the Stumpy Tail Cattle Dog told me a comparable calumny, that this breed developed from the Smithfield Sheepdog, brought out from England, hence the bobtail.

Firstly, the Smithfield Sheepdog was like a leggy Old English Sheepdog, usually sporting a full tail; secondly the naturally bobbed tail occurs in working sheepdogs, as those on farms on the Black Mountain on the Welsh/Herefordshire border indicate to this day. To claim a false provenance for any modern breed degrades that breed; to restate a false origin demeans the fanciers of that breed; to record for posterity a false compilation for a breed in defiance of historical facts is simply deceitful. I could believe, however, that the so-called Tasmanian Smithfield could be descended from our Smithfield dog; it is sizable, shaggy and a very competent all-round sheepdog. Perhaps the Tasmanian dog could be used to improve some of the sad examples of the Old English Sheepdog being proudly shown in Britain.

One Australian breed to do well here is the Cattle Dog, already supported by a devoted collection of fanciers, with as many being registered annually as our own Smooth Collie. When I told my Australian colleagues some twenty years ago that a British

Ally, a Tasmanian Smithfield (naturally tailless), of Graham Rigby, Tasmania, 2003.

BELOW: *Over-coated Old English Sheepdog.*

breeder had imported a pregnant ACD bitch, the response was 'Oh no! These dogs are not pets!' And I could understand such a reaction. But this bitch was imported by John and Mary Holmes, who had a greater knowledge of dogs, especially working dogs, than most. Sadly deafness appeared in the litter born to this bitch, a red speckle from the Landmaster Kennels in Adelaide. This problem was tackled by breeders here and in its native country; honesty and openness always helps to reduce inheritable defects in any breed.

Essentially Working Breeds
I have been able to benefit from studying a CD Rom, kindly sent to me by ACD-expert Noreen Clark, referred to earlier, that portrays specimens of the breed, whelped before 1950 and going right back to Hall's Heelers of around 1890. Each of the dogs depicted could have been described as a working sheepdog from the UK. There was no detectable sign, in dogs spanning sixty years of the breed's development, of dingo, Bull Terrier or Dalmatian influence. Most of these dogs were leggier than the contemporary breed. I do hope the requirement for the breed to be slightly longer from the point of shoulder to

Aussie Shepherd at UK working test.

BELOW LEFT: Australian Shepherd in Border Collie pelage.

the buttocks than the dog's height at the withers isn't being overdone. This is a working breed par excellence and one deservedly admired by all who come into contact with it.

The Australian Shepherd, perhaps better named the American Shepherd – for that is where it was promoted and developed – is very much an active, alert, eager to work breed. It has an attractive and remarkably wide range of coat colours, but no more so than our own native equivalent. It has a naturally bobbed tail, just as some of our native working sheepdogs do. It is becoming popular here, with eighty-seven registered in 2001 against not one ten years ago. In 2012, 124 were registered here and I saw some excellent specimens at the Bath Dog Show in 2013. Two recent

critiques have however issued warnings. Australian Shepherds, Ch Show, 2011:

> …after almost 20 years exhibiting and judging Aus Shepherds, it was disconcerting to see so many fine-boned exhibits often with accompanying narrow heads. The breed's purpose is to work cattle and sheep. Too many exhibits on the day were lacking in the required muscle, while several exhibits were over-angulated at the rear; yes, they may look good when standing but they lack drive on the move.

Australian Shepherds, Ch Show, 2012: 'Front angulations were poor in many, giving the impression of stuffy necks and stilted front movement… Please remember this is a working stock dog and should be able to work all day under all conditions, so should be well made and sound.'

Importance of Heritage
When I was in northern Spain a few decades ago, returning home from a year in Gibraltar, I recalled the alleged link between this breed and Basque dogs. I was mainly researching a breed called the Euskal Artzain Txakurra, or Basque Sheepdog, but I enquired about merle sheepdogs being used by Basque shepherds. No livestock breeder, archivist or dog historian there could provide substance to the claim that such dogs had gone to Australia with sheep in a previous

century. In my car, I had my own working sheepdog. A Spanish farmer looked at him and said: 'Remember, our dogs have never worked as your dogs do!' If that is so, why would hard-pressed Australian

sheep farmers, working in a harsh climate for sheep and dogs, wish to weaken the blood of their highly competent, 'strong-eyed' sheepdogs, even if such Basque dogs were available at all? But the Kennel

TOP: Liver and tan Kelpie.

Powerful, fit Australian Cattle Dog – a superb working dog.

Club's official history of this breed presents this claim as proven. Their evidence would be of more than passing interest! Accurate breed histories are so undervalued; when throwbacks occur or inheritable conditions rear their ugly heads, ancestry really does matter. So often when mismarked pups crop up a misalliance is blamed when it is merely the extended dormant gene pool manifesting itself.

The Australian Kelpie is alleged to have a diverse gene pool, perhaps because it has a far wider range of coat colours, based on black and its derivatives, with strange claims of 'Russian Collie' origin and an Eve-like ancestry from one bitch called 'Kelpie'. I prefer to link them with the old fox-collies of Scotland. As Iris Combe points out in her *Herding Dogs* of 1987, the crofters on the Western Isles in the nineteenth century used Kelpies (called just that) to work cattle and which were determined enough to make the cattle swim at low tide from one island to another. These dogs were described as bear-like, with similarities to Scandinavian herding dogs and a hint of Viking introduction.

The Kelpie is finding increasing favour in North America – as is the Australian Shepherd, with outstanding dogs in Canada such as Chs Bayshore Stonehaven Heart Breaker, Clearfires Hang Onto Yer Hat and Clearfires Dreaming In Colour. A miniature form of the breed is being developed too, with Shadylanes Gamblin Girl at Stoverly a fine example.

Australian Initiative

In late 2013, in Sydney, the Working Dog Alliance, a newly formed, not-for-profit, charitable organization, set up with a federal government grant – as part of the Australian Animal Welfare Strategy – held its inaugural meeting. The lectures covered topics such as 'Measuring and investigating factors that affect the performance of working dogs, their handlers and dog-handling teams'. One of the Alliance's five directors is Mia Cobb, who worked for nearly ten years as the Manager of the Guide Dogs of Victoria training kennel. She supports the view of working sheepdog expert, Matthew Johnson (who trained Tom, a Kelpie, termed a 'wonder-dog' and sold for Aus$12,000) that the livestock industry was very much underrepresented in this new alliance. It would be good to see a comparable set-up here, with perhaps the ISDS leading the way. In many countries 'top dogs such as Tom are treated royally but lower-rated working sheepdogs so often fare less well.

The New Zealand Special

These dogs of Australia are matched in toughness by the Huntaway of New Zealand, a 'bark-collie', for

A Huntaway – with responsibilities!

Paddy, a fine Huntaway. DAVID
AND NICKY DAVIES

BELOW: *Ruby, a powerful
Huntaway from the Killibrae
kennel of Rachel Scrimgeour.*

Ruby: A Killibrae Huntaway in superb physical condition.
RACHEL SCRIMGEOUR

want of a better description. Strongly made black or black and tan dogs, they have been accredited with Labrador blood, but if you were a sheep farmer would you introduce retriever blood? The habit of Victorian dog writers, who on seeing a breed for the first time, immediately linked it with a local look-alike, has been echoed by some contemporary writers but is seriously flawed. There are any number of black and tan smooth-haired pastoral dog breeds, ranging from the Beauceron of France to the Entlebucher and Appenzeller of Switzerland. If you were seeking the creation of a pastoral dog, why use non-pastoral dog blood when you can capitalize on inherent talent waiting to be drawn out? What herding qualities does non-pastoral dog blood bring?

In November, in New Zealand, actually at Huntersville, the Huntaway Festival is held. It begins with a dog-barking competition! For the Huntaway Championship, each dog is required to work three sheep up a slope for about a quarter of a mile passing through three sets of flags. Each set is 22yds apart and arranged in a zigzag course, the dog having to bark before going through the second set of flags, or be disqualified. Twelve minutes is the time allotted for this course. For the dog, accurate movement and utter concentration is essential. The trial Huntaway has to demonstrate that it can handle three sheep; the dog

is expected to be forthright in method without panicking the sheep. When sheep are jammed by sheer numbers, the Huntaway will 'mount' the flock, or run over the backs of the sheep, just as the old English sheepdogs of Sussex once did. Brian Davies, a sheep farmer in Sennybridge, now uses this breed, having seen them working in New Zealand. He finds they make the sheep less nervous; the Huntaway's barking seems less of a menace than the silent stalking threat of a collie. Bark-power can be more useful than eye-power in some herding situations. These Antipodean herding dogs were developed in testing conditions; their ancestors survived the voyage and the demands of opening up a new country. Prize them!

African Herders

In *Dogs and their Ways* (1863), Charles Williams wrote on the cattle dogs of the Hottentots of South Africa, stating:

When the Hottentot takes his turn to go with the herds to pasture, he is accompanied by his dog or dogs. None have more skill in watching and driving the cattle than these have. While the herds are on their way, they are incessant in their attentions to the flank and rear, barking sagaciously to keep them in the proper line. On arriving at the place where the

By protecting livestock, the Kangal Dog helps the cheetah to survive, because farmers have no reason to kill the big cat.
ANDREW HARRINGTON

cattle are to graze for that day, the dogs employ themselves, without bidding, partly to fetch in stragglers and keep the cattle together, and partly in scouring the fields in the neighbourhood of the herds, which they do from time to time when required, in a body, to keep off the wild beasts.

Atlas Sheepdog, an all-white specimen.

Those words could have been applied to many different tribes and countries over many centuries; such is the international need and value of the pastoral dog to man. Farmers in Namibia have benefited from the 300-plus Turkish Kangal Dogs sent there by the Cheetah Conservation Fund and now extended to Kenya, to protect both cattle and cheetahs by deterring the latter from grazing herds without their lives being threatened.

The Atlas Sheepdog of Morocco, also known as the Aidi or Kabyle Dog, is claimed to be a rarity, a pastoral breed of non-European origin. The Kabyles were the aborigines of Barbary and kept sheep, cattle, goats, camels and donkeys. Employed as a drover but with a nasty reputation as a guard dog, these dogs are prized for their versatility and selectively bred for their alertness and aggression. The Algerian Sheepdog may simply be a French dog imported by settlers; it certainly has a definite Berger de Beauce look about it. Another ancient breed, the Canaan dog of Israel, was restored literally from the wild by Dr Menzel in the late 1930s. She found, amongst the feral dogs of what was then Palestine, a distinct

ABOVE: *The Algerian Sheepdog.*

The Canaan Dog – the desert herder.

'collie' strain, believed to be abandoned herding dogs of the Bedouin. Once restored by a careful breeding programme, they excelled as guide dogs for the blind, sentry and messenger dogs and in sheepdog trials; 400 of them were trained for mine detection work in World War II. Strangely, the Canaan Dog has a definite 'spitz' look to it, featuring the bushy curled tail and prick ears of the northern dogs.

It would a worthy action if some enthusiast were to attempt the re-creation of the Old Welsh Grey sheepdog using the blood of the Patagonian Sheepdog or Barboucho. This dog is believed to have descended from the old Welsh breed after Welsh settlers took their dogs with them to the Chubut valley at the turn of the twentieth century. Known for centuries in Sardinia is the Fonni Sheepdog, a strongly made goat-haired sheepdog, looking a little like both a Picardy Sheepdog and a Labrit, and perhaps related to it. The beardie type is famous for its cleverness and quick response to training, the French army making good use of both Briard and the Labrit as messengers in the Great War.

In India, the Dhangari Sheepdogs of Maharashtra have a distinct Border Collie look about them. They are used for herding in the Western Ghats, where huge flocks of goats and sheep are grazed. They move with the caravan, acting as sentries at night, but also hunting

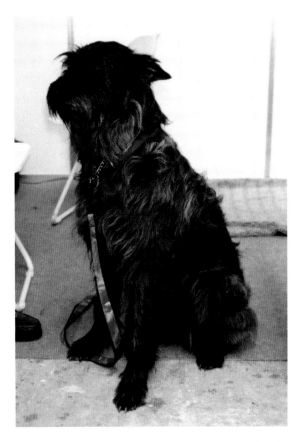

ABOVE: *The Fonni Sheepdog of Sardinia.*

Dhangari Sheepdog from Maharashtra.

Mr W.K. Taunton's Afghan Dog Khelat, which was brought to this country after an Afghan war, and was probably the only one of its kind seen in the UK. It somewhat resembled an Old English Sheepdog.

for small local game. Twenty inches high and around 25 pounds in weight, they are usually black with white on the brisket, underbelly and legs. With a reputation for being the best dogs in rough or mountainous terrain, extremely hardy and breeding true to type, they may now be lost to us as, when on the move with their nomadic owners, they breed with local dogs and lose identity. The Vikhan is a big flock protector in the Chitral region of northwest Pakistan, often wearing the classic spiked iron collar to protect the throat, their wool being spun to produce fabric for winter clothing. The Bhutia and the Bisben in the Himalayas may also have been lost; related to the Tibetan dogs, they are big, substantial herder-flock guardians with long, shaggy hair in winter that is shed in summer. Renowned for their fierceness towards strangers, they are remarkably robust, famed for their hardiness in extreme weather conditions. The famous Mastiff breeder W.K. Taunton

exhibited an 'Afghan Sheepdog' called Khelat in 1920 that may have belonged either to this breed or an allied one, such as the Bangara Mastiff.

American Herders

In the United States a survey in the 1940s revealed that their most numerous breed was the humble farm collie, still looking much like its British ancestor. One American Kennel Club recognizes these dogs as a formal breed, known as the English Shepherd. They also have a breed they call the McNab dog, a smooth collie descended from sheepdogs taken to California in 1885. But inevitably the Americans had to meet their own cattle dog needs and a breed now known as the Catahoula Leopard Dog was created. Catahoulas are essentially gathering dogs, having a natural tendency to circle to the other side of stock, opposite the handler. They specialize in gathering rough wild cattle and

ABOVE: *Red and grey Leopard Dogs working cattle.* LOUDENSLAGER

English Shepherd Dog. DOGS IN CANADA MAGAZINE

even hogs. They track the stock, bring it to bay rather like a hound, bark loudly to attract the stockmen and often work in teams. They remind me of the Portuguese Cattle Dog, Cao de Castro Laboreiro, which has a comparable function as a herd protector and drover. Catahoulas are unlikely, in their unique marbled-harlequin or black merle coats, to be confused with another breed.

American dog breeders are not slow to develop their own variant of another nation's breed, as the American Cocker Spaniel, the American Bulldog, the American Staffordshire Terrier and the American Water Spaniel demonstrate. They sometimes refashion a breed name – as with their so-called English Shepherd and the Amstaff – but don't shy away from renaming a refashioned variety – as their King and Shiloh Shepherds indicate. They also recognize the merits of an all-white GSD. In producing their own shepherd dog, the Shiloh Shepherd, they claim it is more like the old-style GSD, heavier-boned, more heavily coated and more muscular than the modern German dog.

ABOVE LEFT: *Shiloh Shepherd.*
DOGS IN CANADA *MAGAZINE*

The Catahoula Leopard Dog.

The Florida Cow Dog.

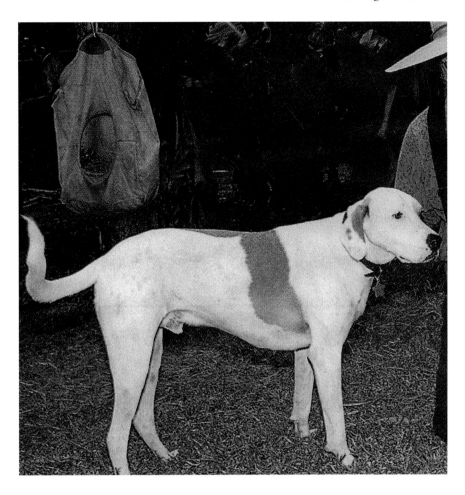

It could be that in such a way old farm breeds are restored to their original type. The American and Australian pastoral breeds are often more robust than some of ours. The English Shepherd is very similar to the so-called Australian Shepherd, also developed in the USA, and often naturally 'bobbed' and 'loose-eyed' too. (American dog breeders have produced a miniature version of both, but as companion dogs.) Registered as a breed with the United Kennel Club (UKC) but not the American KC, their equivalent of ours, they are mainly farm dogs, usually tricoloured or black and tan, and have a sound reputation as workers. In a highly individual coat comes their Blue Lacy, mostly slate-blue, sometimes with tan, and with a formidable reputation as a cattle dog of great resolve. They all but died out until enthusiast H.C. Wilkes in 1975 ensured their survival with a revitalized breeding programme. Brought 'out west' by the Lacy brothers around 1848, and about 45lb in weight, when solid gun-metal grey there is a distinct 'reduced Weimaraner' look to them. Like the Catahoula Leopard Dog, they are unlikely ever to be confused with another breed, truly all-American. In Florida they have developed their own drover's dog, the Florida Cow Dog, a strongly built, often lemon and white, smooth-haired dog, worked in teams and alleged to be able to keep a herd together throughout an overnight stop.

The American Cattle-Pinning Dog
In modern America, a breed called the American Bulldog, but more like a Bullmastiff than a Bulldog, and now well-known here, is still used to drive wayward cattle and to catch hogs, a very dangerous

activity and one in which the dog can be killed. These powerful, resolute dogs hurl themselves at the hog, which weighs three times more than they do, and seize it by the ear, hanging on despite every effort of the enraged hog to shake them off or harm them. The sheer, almost reckless bravery of such dogs is quite remarkable. Not classic pastoral dogs but livestock-penning dogs, they match the role of the Cane Corso in Italy, the Rottweiler in Germany and the Bardino and Perro de Presa Mallorquin in the Mediterranean. When judging American Bulldogs, I have striven to emphasize the importance of agility, speed and balance in a breed destined for such a role. But their fanciers have been obsessed with size in their dogs – both in weight and height at the withers, almost prizing sheer bulk at the expense of functional capability. When judging Victorian Bulldogs – dogs reshaped like their distant ancestors rather than designed to win in the show ring, where the short muzzle and enormous head is strangely desired – I try hard to choose the more athletic exhibits. Real Bulldogs were either athletic or dead!

ABOVE LEFT: The Bardino of the Canaries, a fierce herder.

The Fila de Sao Miguel – a gripping breed, used on wayward cattle.

Cattle or Butchers' Dogs

In the Mediterranean islands the Cao de Bou (cow dog) and the Fila de Sao Miguel are used as cattle-drivers. The Sicilians developed a cattle dog, called the Branchiero, that worked in a unique way, leaping at the head of the herd leader to turn it in the required direction. It resembled the Rottweiler, another one-time cattle dog and also alternatively called 'Butcher's Dog'. Stockmen and butchers have long had a need for powerful dogs that could hold, pin or grip wayward cattle, difficult rams or highly determined boars, especially in places where the herd ran semi-wild. Predictably they opted to employ 'catch' or 'capture' dogs from the hunting field. These dogs developed from the hunting mastiffs used by primitive hunters to pull down aurochs, buffalo and wild bulls before the invention of firearms. These holding dogs were used quite extensively as the emergent types subsequently demonstrated: the Bullenbeisser in Germany, the Niederlandischer Bollbeisser of the Netherlands, the Cao de Bou in Mallorca (their breed titles alone revealing their function), the Fila (literally 'seizing' or 'pinning' dog) Brasileiro of Brazil, the Perro de Presa (literally 'gripping dog') Canario from the Canaries. Such dogs needed power with speed, agility with skilful timing and great resolve backed by instinctive judgement; they did not need massive bulk and great size – impressive in the show ring, disastrous in the stockyard!

In *Dogs and their Ways* (1863), Charles Williams recorded:

> On the arrival of vessels with livestock in our West Indian colonies, the drover or cattle-dog of Cuba and Terra Firma is often of great service. The oxen are hoisted out by a sling passed round the base of the horns…and allowed to fall into the water…one or two dogs catch the bewildered animal by the ears, one on each side, force it to swim in the direction of the landing-place, and instantly let go their hold when they feel it touches the ground; for then the ox naturally walks up to the shore.

In this act by determined dogs there is a combination of astonishing resolve, immense natural skill and instinctive tactics when faced with a giant ox that is terrified and panicking, which deserves great admiration.

The Multi-Purpose Farm Dogs

In *Farmers in Prehistoric Britain* (2011), Francis Pryor writes:

> Sheep are well-known for being worked with dogs in the open, but it is less generally known that dogs are very useful in the farmyard too. Daily during winter I use my dog to remove animals from an area where I want to replace food; when the fly season starts I use her to move stock towards the dip bath… On my own, I would be hard-pressed to persuade unwilling ewes to take their annual bath, but my border collie, Jess, has powers of persuasion in her raptor-like eyes that I simply do not possess.

In her charming and beautifully illustrated *Rural Portraits – Scottish Native Farm Animals, Characters and Landscapes* (2003), Polly Pullar writes:

> It can be very hard to find a good all round dog that does everything required of it. Some farmers end up with many collies, each suited to a particular type of sheep work. The best dogs on a mixed farm are those that will not only single out a ewe and never lose sight of her even when she is fleeing across the heather with a huge group of others, but also help to bring in the cows.

Farm dogs have to be versatile.

In Ireland, I've seen the Kerry Blue and Wheaten Terriers used as multi-purpose farm dogs, able to undertake just about every canine role on the farm. Farmers overseas needed small dogs too; to control pests such as rats, to act as turnspit dogs in the farmhouse kitchen and to go to ground when foxes were hunted. The smallest could do all three tasks but had to be very small to fit into the cage round the spit and work the treadmill without too much discomfort. In Britain, the work was considered too arduous to be done on successive days and so a team of dogs was used, leading to the expression 'every dog has his day'. In Germany the Schnauzer varieties provided the range of canine skills around the farm. In Russia, the Laika breeds

Cattle dog in Ireland working a Kerry bull, 1861.

offered a similar versatility, the large ones acting as herders and the small ones as yard dogs and ratters. All over the world, dogs, whether employed to drive cattle, sheep, goats or reindeer, to guard farmsteads or flocks, to kill foxes or rats or 'hold' an individual animal, were bred with just one object in mind: their function. This criterion, ruthlessly pursued, demanded physical and mental soundness, robustness of health and responsiveness to training. We no longer do so in the developed world and our crowded veterinary surgeries demonstrate the foolishness of this daily.

Beauceron working cattle in France; working type is precious.

CHAPTER 3

THE WORKING FORMAT

Shaping the Functional Dog

Unfortunately, far more recently than this date [the end of the eighteenth century], infusions of different blood were introduced into the Collie, usually to satisfy a whim for a special point: the cross with the Gordon Setter was made to enrich the tan; with the Irish Setter in a misplaced attempt to enrich the sable; with the Borzoi to increase the length of head. As a result of the Irish Setter cross the words 'setter red most objectionable' came to be included in the earlier standards of the breed, and even today we all too often see the horrible results of the Borzoi cross in the receding-skulled, roman-nosed horrors which masquerade under the name of Collie.

Margaret Osborne, *The Popular Collie* (1960)

Cosmetic Changes

The above quote, already used to make a point in Chapter 2, reveals one consistent element – all the out-crosses were made for cosmetic not functional reasons. Now that breed health, breed purity and instructions to show-ring judges are all receiving much merited attention, there is one extremely important aspect of pedigree dog breeding and showing that deserves attention. It would be sad if

we lost breeds to the perpetual pursuit of prettiness backed by prolonged inbreeding, more than regrettable if we lost breeds to rogue genes and monstrous if judges rewarded exhibits displaying harmful exaggerations. Sad, regrettable and monstrous too if our precious breeds are bred to the wrong template; the show ring has changed a number of breeds, not for the better; fashion, fad and pressure from influential kennels can impose a changed type on a breed. Gradual changes, viewed initially as slight exaggerations, develop into bigger ones, reactions to docking in breeds not previously docked and 'the fashion of the day' can all contribute to the classic fundamental type in a distinctive breed being reshaped. This reshaping can be whimsical in origin, untraditional in effect, even harmful in its manifestation, but as time passes, can become acceptable. Damage by design causes as much discomfort and distress to dogs as many health problems.

The shape of a breed, its physical form or morphology, should result from its functional design, be protected by its Breed Standard, guarded by its breed clubs and treasured across the generations of its breed devotees as its unique identity. But all too often breed points become breed exaggerations as close breeding overplays its hand. In this way, long

Old English Sheepdogs, from left to right: Stylish Boy; Village Lass and Hidden Mystery, two puppies; and Bouncing Lass. All were owned by Charles Frohman and were multiple show winners.

ears become ground-draggers, short legs become castors, long spines become centipedal, long coats become overcoats, slack eyelids become dustpans and short muzzles become dental and respiratory handicaps. It is easy to argue that the Kennel Club should be overseeing breed continuation or protecting the morphological integrity of a breed, if only on health grounds. But the first stop is surely the breed clubs. The KC should look over their shoulders and may have failed to do so, but that shouldn't let breed clubs off the hook. Who allowed the Collie-Borzoi cross? Who watched as the Shetland Sheepdog became more coat than dog? Who allowed the Welsh Corgi's legs to all but disappear?

How did the two varieties of Shetland Sheepdog (rough and smooth) merge into just the one whilst the bigger Scottish dog was allowed to become two breeds in those two coats? In 1909 the Sheltie was expected to be 12in high; now its ideal height is put at 14½ins. Is that for the better of the *dogs*? Who let the Bearded Collie disappear under a mighty rug of coat? Who was supervising the wellbeing of dog breeds when all this change was being inflicted?

A judge of the Old English Sheepdog, in a post-show critique in September 2003 was moved to write: 'I last judged the breed at Windsor some three years ago, I thought then, the breed had deteriorated to such

an extent that this might be as bad as it gets…how wrong I was.' Then came a long depressing list of faults found, ranging from bad mouths and poor toplines to a lack of spring of rib and long weak loins, before he went on to state: 'I feel something must be done to the foundation of this breed… I always believed the Breed Clubs were the custodians of this lovely breed and their job was to promote and protect the breed and to encourage betterment within it…' If breed clubs are misguided and actually harm a breed, should not the KC step in? Hands-off distant overseeing may be democratic in spirit but when a breed is being harmed, strong decisive action is surely essential.

TOP: *Note the leg and back length of this 1934 Corgi.*

Welsh Corgi of today – is the leg and back length still typical for this breed?

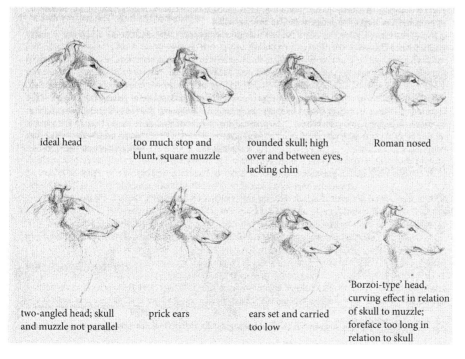

ideal head

too much stop and blunt, square muzzle

rounded skull; high over and between eyes, lacking chin

Roman nosed

two-angled head; skull and muzzle not parallel

prick ears

ears set and carried too low

'Borzoi-type' head, curving effect in relation of skull to muzzle; foreface too long in relation to skull

ABOVE LEFT: Is the 'rug of coat' in the Bearded Collie the correct one for this breed?

ABOVE RIGHT: Smooth Collie of 1904 – is this the true head shape for this breed?

Collie heads, correct and various faults.

Pointing the Finger

Who decides the narrowness of the Collie's skull? Who advises on the jaw length of a healthier Shetland Sheepdog? How high off the ground should the Corgi's torso be? What is unacceptably long in the leg length of a Corgi? Who will prevent the Collie's muzzle from becoming too snipy? Are the little differences between the Cardigan and Pembroke Corgis worth perpetuating or are they just breed vanity? Why does the Old English Sheepdog need to have a 'rather short body'? Has this led to its Standard under Gait/Movement to need the words: 'some dogs may need to pace'? This is *not* sound movement in any working dog. Who decides the weight of a Pyrenean Mountain Dog – a breed council or, one day, an animal rights group? There is a clear need for an 'Ofmorph' inspector, an official to monitor shape, an inspector of canine morphology! But who would they be, how would they operate and with whose authority? No one person could have all the skills involved – it would need a combination of canine historian, veterinary anatomist and functional advisor to work on the morphology of each subject breed for the betterment of that breed. More interference in breed business? Greater outside intrusion in breed matters? Even more bureaucracy for breeders and breeds to cope with?

Truly there are greater dangers in *not* having such a person; untraditional and harmful alterations have already been made to our precious breeds. Comparison between depictions of breeds when they were first developed and photographs of their descendants today are revealing and what they reveal is not always flattering to a breed's alleged 'improvement' in the show arena. Old depictions may lack pictorial quality and the subject dogs may lack 'glamour' but they illustrate breed type and a functional anatomy only too well.

A Comparison of the Early Breed Types with those of today

<table>
<tr><td align="center">**Early Type**</td><td align="center">**Today's Type**</td></tr>
</table>

Miss May McTurk's Old English Sheepdog Ch. Night Raider, depicted in 1925.

RIGHT: *Old English Sheepdog today.*

Early Type

Today's Type

Miss M. Grey's Shetland Sheepdog Wishaw Myrtle, depicted in 1925.

RIGHT: *Sheltie of today.*

Rough Collie of 1893.

RIGHT: *Rough Collie of today.*

Early Type

Today's Type

Welsh Corgi of 1930.

Tailed Pembrokeshire Corgi of today.

Respecting the Past
The physical form or morphology of each pedigree breed really needs safeguarding, to preserve true type, restore functional type and achieve a healthier breed. A morphologist could ensure that a breed standard contributes to the health of that breed. Photography too has given us a simply marvellous tool in the conservation of true type in dogs. Of course each breed changes subtly as the years go by, but truly who wants a breed to change its appearance

Smooth Collie of 1893, by Arthur Wardle – note the head type.

Rough Collie *of 1896, by Arthur Wardle, a most accurate animal artist.*

fundamentally – surely only those not skilful enough to breed to the standard or more wallet-led than honest. Historic photographs can show you what you don't want in a breed – if you respect its past and the pioneer breeders who devoted their lives to the best interests of such breeds.

The Bateson Inquiry into pedigree dog breeding in Britain considered such an aspect, recording in its recommendations the need 'to avoid extremes of conformation that create welfare problems'. An informed morphologist would soon spot an Old English Sheepdog handicapped by sheer weight of coat or see a grossly over-bulked Pyrenean Mountain Dog as just a warm-blooded obstacle. A Corgi with its keel on the ground is no longer a cattle dog, just an animated draught-excluder. These are ancient, quite admirable breeds deserving of both our compassion and our best endeavours, not grumpy opposition based on contemporary lazy thinking.

The Kennel Club may actually be better placed to monitor design flaws than the Department for the Environment, Food and Rural Affairs or Defra, as Bateson recommended. The KC appoints judges and publishes Breed Standards. Making them responsible for harmful breed design, *actionable in the courts*, could work wonders. When those in authority create welfare problems, the first resort should always be the firm insistence that it is *they* who must remedy their neglect and accept responsibility for repairing the sad situation created in fact by *them*. New bodies take time to achieve results but the design of quite a number of our dog breeds urgently requires reshaping – make the KC right their wrongs! Pressure them into accepting *responsibility*!

Loss of Type

What is the *correct type* for each of our native pastoral breeds? Is the less refined head illustrated in the trials dogs of, say, the 1930s the true type for the Border Collie breeders to exemplify? Is it the type shown of several of our native breeds, say, in the accurate depictions by the artist Arthur Wardle in his sketches of the late 1800s? He was extraordinarily gifted in capturing breed type in his work on dogs and for this was favoured by many late Victorian and then Edwardian writers and publishers. Sometimes loss of type is easier to spot than the preservation of genuine type. But what exactly is type? The KC defines it, in its *Glossary of Terms*, as 'The characteristic qualities distinguishing a breed'. But are those qualities physical, mental or in temperament? Baker, in *The Collie – Its Show Points* (1900), wrote that: 'It is extremely difficult to define in words the general outline and symmetry of a Collie, but it may be summed up in one word "type"'. Again, not conclusive, precise or particularly instructive. My definition would be on these lines: type is the manifestation in a breed of those particular innate physical and mental characteristics that, without exaggeration, distinguish the traditional form that a breed should take. In using these words I am seeking to preserve and perpetuate the character and conformation that was stabilized and then established when

The first show type – the Pyrenean Mountain Dog in Paris in the 1860s.

BOTTOM: The rustic dogs.

distinct breeds evolved – nearly always in pursuit of a specific function. Every breed needs type to define its identity.

In 2011, the fanciers of the Pyrenean Mountain Dog produced a brief but quite excellent, well-illustrated brochure on their breed, valuable because of its remarkable honesty and as an admirable example to other breed fanciers whose breed has temporarily gone 'off the rails'. In it they argue that true type and the essence of the Pyrenean is being lost in the British show ring. They stress that the show ring must not promote selection on the grounds of fashion

and exaggeration. They considered that fashion was winning over true type, mainly through judges who have never learned or who have lost sight of the breed's original purpose. They point out that over the years, the handsome, working, 'rustique' dog has been steadily replaced by a glamorous over-coated and back-combed dog. They remind fellow fanciers that any dog able to work on high, exposed mountainsides must have a lean and muscular build and a weatherproof coat, and they end with a plea for them to respect the 'dog of the mountains'. I salute them for this publication and applaud their criticism of judges who resort, in their after-show critiques, to words such as 'cobby' and 'upstanding' that simply do not reflect the Breed Standard for the breed.

Over the years, however, the critiques written by judges at conformation shows have revealed the state of the pastoral breeds all too starkly, indicating not

just unsound breeding but also a sad loss of basic type in so many breeds. It's worth looking at the wording of some of these, past and present:

William Arkwright (a highly experienced and very knowledgeable sporting dog expert) in his judge's critique on Collies in *The Kennel Gazette* of November 1890:

SHEEPDOGS

I thought these were wretchedly bad. I had not looked at these dogs for about eighteen months, and I was shocked at their deterioration in type, in character, and in structural formation. I fear the unfortunate sheepdog has fallen into bad hands, and very soon the true animal will be a thing of the past.

TOP LEFT:*The World Dog Show type, 1998.*

TOP RIGHT: *The 'Suburban' type, 2013.*

Rough-coated Collie, Carlyle, of Dr W.A.G. James, the lost type.

From the annual report on Collies, written by Trefoil in *The Kennel Gazette*, January 1891:

> During the past year, the premier honours of the show bench have again and again gone to dogs of this greyhound type whose faces bore an inane expressionless look, whose coats were soft and woolly, their bodies weedy and supported on stilt-like legs. These creatures tell their own tale of humiliation as they gazed into one's face with their miserable look: 'We are being *improved* off the face of the earth.' That is exactly what is going on, and breeders and judges, with a few exceptions, are joining hand in hand in the work of destruction.

By the judge of Collies at the Manchester Dog Show, J.J. Steward, in *The Kennel Gazette*, June 1888:

> The collie classes were all well filled, and there was an absence of 'the mongrel', only one St Bernard (or a relative) being exhibited, but many of the exhibits looked as if they had been brought up in town.

By S.E. Shirley, writing the critique on Collies at the Kennel Club's 35th Show in *The Kennel Gazette* of April 1891:

TOP: *Darnley II, Queen Victoria's dog – broad-skulled and not over-coated.*

ABOVE: *Old English Sheepdogs depicted by Arthur Wardle in 1896, with the coat of that time.*

Smooth Collie Young Trim in 1891, much more Border Collie-like.

Writing generally, I may be allowed to express a sincere hope that Collie breeders will pause before they commit themselves to so dangerous an innovation as a weak, narrow-headed, brainless Collie, the animal that of all others should excel in intelligence and capacity of intellect.

By the judge of Bearded Collies at a Championship (Ch) Show in 2012: 'I penalized wide fronts,

One of the Tilley dogs; note the working type here.

coarse/heavy shoulders and short upper arms, these faults being commonplace in some that have been winning… Far too much emphasis is placed on looks and not on make-up.'

Priority Given to Type
Many breeders of pedigree dogs in Britain put 'type' at the top of their list when it comes to placing, in order of priority, their breeding desiderata. Despite that, it is disappointing to note just how many breeds have lost their essential 'typiness' over the years. Breeds like the Shetland Sheepdog, the Rough and Smooth Collies, the two Corgi breeds and the Bearded Collie get less and less like the early specimens of the breed with each generation. If you study depictions of Queen Victoria's Rough Collie Darnley II you can see at once how this breed has been changed by show-ring criteria. On the other hand, breeds like the Border Terrier, the Deerhound, the Curly-coated Retriever, the Dalmatian, the Schipperke and the Pug seem able to resist human whim and retain the truly traditional look of the breed. Exaggerations exaggerating themselves play a part, as the Collie's head

Old English Sheepdogs working in Hampshire in the late 1930s.

illustrates. Unwise blueprints play a role too, as the 100-plus words on the head and skull of the Collie demonstrate increasingly each year.

For me, there are two very simple criteria to be brought to bear here. Firstly, if you admire a breed and respect its ancestry, why make it look like something different? To do so is an entirely irrational act. Secondly, if you love dogs and one breed above all others, how can you possibly justify breeding dogs of that favoured breed with an anatomy which is not only quite unlike that of their ancestors but one which threatens their health and well-being? To do so lacks any real affection, merely indicates self-interest and the absence of any real empathy with subject creatures.

The great expert on the Old English Sheepdog, H.A. Tilley wrote, in his booklet on the breed (undated but Florence Tilley kindly gave me a copy in 1981) of the cramped outlook of those who maintain that this, that, or the other dog represents 'the best type':

> Such restricted opinions are usually based on personal fancy, or an obeisance to some current fashion which pays more attention to aesthetic considerations than to utility value… If someone asked me to select for him a well-bred and trained OES, my first question would be: 'What kind of work do you want him for?' If the reply were, 'General work about the farm, but more particularly for sheep', I should then ask, 'Is your farm dry or hilly, or low-lying and on the 'wet side' from late autumn to spring-time?' If he answered, 'Mainly high and dry', one would advise a dog of rather less than medium height, i.e. not more than 20 inches in height, whereas for heavier conditions a bigger and stronger one would be desirable. In either case each would be 'true to type', but the final choice would be determined by the nature of the surroundings in which the dog would be required to work.

Such wisdom is not common in today's show-biased world, in which breeds are so often shaped by 'prominent breeder's whim'.

Poor Conformation
Type can manifest itself in movement and stance; it is unwise to try to 'stack' every breed identically in

ABOVE: *Heavily coated Sheltie at Crufts.*

Shetland Sheepdog; note position of the rear feet – under the croup.

the ring or to expect a common gait between breeds. I have seen judges try to correct a Border Collie in the ring for proceeding in a stealthy crouch, a style totally in keeping with the breed. The Greater Swiss Mountain Dog has to have a 10:9 body length to height ratio; if not 'stacked' naturally this ratio is disturbed. The Shetland Sheepdog has all but lost its forechest, lying in front of the point of shoulder, but crafty 'stacking' can conceal this fault. I see Shelties too with their legs too short but made to stand 'tall'. I expect to see a 'show of pads' when the Corgi is being moved in the ring; when it is not displayed I strive to look closer. I see GSDs over-reaching when 'gaited' and sometimes they even win a ticket. This is a serious fault in a working breed. But unless the dog moves crab-wise or not straight ahead, few judges penalize it. The flying trot in this breed so often conceals a multitude of flaws. The heavily coated breeds all too often get away with poor conformation when clever 'stacking' before the judge conceals the position of the hind feet relative to the torso, but the effortless classic Collie movement cannot take place with hyper-extension at the back. Type isn't just about coat colour, head shape, ear carriage or set of tail.

Satisfying the Breed Standard

A number of breeds strive, through their Breed Standard's words, to make a breed unique or 'racially special', as my vet put it rather cruelly recently. If you read the Standard of, say, the Old English Sheepdog, you can soon pick up such a tendency. Under Gait/Movement, these words appear: 'When walking, exhibits a bear-like roll from the rear.' Some breed fanciers put a value on this when claiming it

ABOVE: *The Sheltie of the 1930s showing plenty of leg length and much shorter coat.*

Old English Sheepdog about to show its 'bear-like roll'.

as Bobtail-type. But let another vet, R.H. Smythe, in his informative *The Dog – Structure and Movement* (1970), comment on this: 'In the case of the O.E. Sheepdog the reason for the roll is rather different {from that of the Bulldog]. In this breed exaggerated hock flexion causes the body to descend slightly on the side which carries the weight, while the opposite hock is being lifted.' This Breed Standard, under the same heading, states that: 'At slow speed, some dogs may tend to pace.' Pacing, that is the hind and forelimbs on each side advancing together, is tiring, unnatural and wearing to the locomotive muscles. It is not an acceptable feature in a breed once famous for its long-distance walking feats. Type must never conflict with soundness.

Unrealistic Expectation
It is foolish to regard any dog registered with the KC as a purebred product with true type just because it is a registered pedigree dog. Type in any breed of dog is far more subtle and a lot more elusive than that. For me dogs with the genuine look of their breed are always to be preferred to untypical specimens with 'papers'. Is a German Shepherd Dog with a roach back, hyper-angulation in its hindquarters and a lack of substance, with two show-ring wins and KC registration, to be preferred to an upstanding, well-boned and symmetrically built dog with a level topline but no papers? Contemporary GSD breeders seem to

have lost their way and it is going to take decades to restore true type to this quite outstanding breed. I wholeheartedly agree with Lady Malpas, who wrote a few years ago to one of the dog papers: 'There can be no justification for any attempt, accidental or intentional, to produce different types of German shepherd.' I also support the view of a GSD breed correspondent who asked:

What has happened to this noble breed? I was brought up in the school that had as a pattern dogs like Ch Fenton of Kentwood, Ch Sergeant of Rozavel and dogs of similar type. My mentors told me that a good Alsatian could carry a glass of water on its back without spilling when moving…

ABOVE: *The 1946 version of the Alsatian.*

The 2007 version of the German Shepherd Dog (Alsatian).

Whatever makes a breed clique alter a breed to its disadvantage? The first show Alsatians I ever saw, as a young teenager, were from the celebrated 'of Movem' kennel and had a topline for any breeder to die for!

In Germany, the 'breed wardens' for the GSD wield enormous power. It was therefore good to read that a new (2013) breed warden has taken a long, hard look at the breed and outlined his main priorities: health and agility, return to the Standard, a broadening of the bloodline basis or gene pool and reduction of inbreeding, the promotion of working ability and, significantly, opposition to the trend of breeding look-alike 'clones', wherein every dog in the breed resembles the next one – the dreaded 'cookie-cutter' dogs. The last point is of interest; how do you breed to the Standard without producing dogs of almost exact appearance? It could lead to a temporary loss of breed type but it might also result in the best working dog physique being favoured over rows of extremely handsome identical dogs – all with the same faults.

The service to man of the German Shepherd Dog is difficult for any other breed to match. I have seen them at work and witnessed their versatility in nearly twenty different countries. I had always considered their breed type to be fixed. Unlike manufactured breeds like the Dobermann and the Leonberger, there is no risk of a strong prototypal ancestor breed like the Greyhound or the Bulldog manifesting itself. *Any* breeder who tampers with a breed type long established, long accepted and long proven able to produce an intelligent, healthy, biddable dog is a dangerous, misguided maverick who should be halted in his tracks. In any breed of pedigree dog it only takes one determined breeder with more money than sense to promote his concept or a dominant clique to gain ascendancy for true type to be threatened. Breeds don't just lose type; breeders lose their way. But who lets them? The KC really must appoint breed councils as the guardians of each breed – it is truly a high priority.

Restoration of Type

Breed type distinguishes breeds; it can provide the essential difference between, say, a black and tan Hovawart and a black and tan Tibetan Mastiff of similar size. If breed type, real breed type, not 'flavour of the month' or false phenotypes compounded over recent years by show-ring whim or temporary fashion, *actually* matters, and I do believe it does, an argument could be made for starting again. By that I mean the drawing-up of the correct historical type for each native pastoral breed from the earliest depictions, principally from very old photographs, then by a programme of planned breeding, re-creating or restoring that type in each of our native pastoral breeds. When you look at the KC acceptance of a created breed such as the Eurasier and that by the FCI of the Kromfohrlander, a far stronger case could be made for the restoration of our lost native breeds, mentioned in the Preface. I see unintentionally bred-look-alikes as well as some deliberate re-creations of the Welsh Hillman, the Old Welsh Grey, the Black and Tan Sheepdog and the Irish breeds – the Galway Sheepdog and the Glenwherry Collie – remarkably often; the type is clearly strongly perpetuated. It

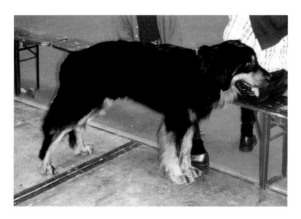

A black and tan Hovawart.

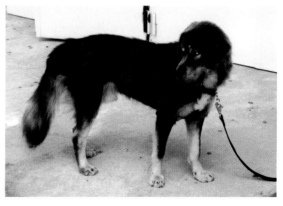

A black and tan Tibetan Mastiff.

A re-created red-coated Welsh Hillman.

A re-created Black and Tan Sheepdog puppy.

would be a fascinating project too to reproduce the lost Smooth Shetland Sheepdog; those who admire the breed but not its contemporary coat would certainly find such a scheme of interest. Perpetuating sickly or overdone pedigree breeds, *just because they are pedigree*, makes no sense at all in today's more compassionate society.

Feet First – Putting Dog's Best Foot Forward

'No hoof, no horse' is a time-honoured saying in equestrian circles but I've never heard a cry of 'No foot, no dog' in canine circles. And when I see judging at dog shows, I find it rare indeed to see a judge check a dog's feet. But which is more important, sound feet or set of tail? I suppose in an arena where dogs are valued solely for what they look like rather than what they can do, this oversight is not surprising. Ignoring the soundness of your dog's feet is, however, a recipe for disaster in breeding programmes. Unless sound feet are produced in every breed of dog from toy breeds to giant ones, then the future of the domestic pedigree dog as an active animal is threatened.

It is enlightening to look at the various Breed Standards and see what the different breeds are expected to walk on. Taking the pedigree pastoral breeds, we come across some widely differing expectations: for example the Shetland Sheepdog is required to have oval feet, as are the Swedish and Finnish Lapphunds, Swedish Vallhund, Pyrenean Sheepdog, Polish Lowland Sheepdog and the Pembroke Corgi – but not the Cardigan variety, whose feet have to be round. The Norwegian Buhund is expected to have rather small feet; the Old English Sheepdog, surprisingly, has to have small, round feet, the Maremma Sheepdog large, almost round feet. Does that mean small for the size of the dog or small when compared to a bigger breed? In these breeds, if judges look out for feet smaller in proportion to the size of dog than is sensible, is that right or wrong according to the breed standard? It is surely essential for each breed of dog to have feet of a size appropriate to its weight. It is even more damaging if a dog's feet are bred to a harmful design. Being able to walk is fairly important to dogs!

Indifference of Judges

How many judges look at the relative size of fore and hind feet? This is an important feature of balance in a dog. No working sheepdog would last a day without good feet. The Border Collie has to possess oval feet, as does the Bearded Collie, the Rough and Smooth Collies, the Shetland Sheepdog and the Polish Lowland Sheepdog. But the Old English Sheepdog is expected to have small, round feet and the Belgian Shepherd Dog forefeet that are round and hind feet slightly oval. The Australian Cattle Dog and the Australian Kelpie should have round feet but the Australian Shepherd is expected to have oval feet. Does it matter whether a herding dog's feet are round or oval?

In her valuable book *Foxhounds* (1981), Daphne Moore wrote:

> The foot of the foxhound is of the most vital importance. The terms 'cat-foot' and 'hare-foot' are frequently used, but the best type of forefoot is that which more resembles that of a wolf; a nice natural foot, on which the hound stands firmly, with the weight on all four toes *and* the heel.

I would support that but I do see, especially in the smooth-haired breeds where it is more easily picked out, dogs in the ring with their heel-pad not touching the ground when standing. Feet therefore need to be judged from the side as well as being examined individually. An examination of the wear on the pads themselves will reveal a balanced or unbalanced stance or gait.

The appearance of a dog's feet has more to do with exercise than Breed Standards. Dogs with soundly constructed feet will still develop splay feet and slack pasterns if exercised on pastureland that is lush and soft. Road work is essential and is usually recommended to 'tighten up' the feet, but rough cinder tracks are probably best. Shape of foot can usually be linked to function. I see coursing Greyhounds with long hare feet and show Greyhounds with cat-like feet and toes compactly bunched. But both those descriptions are flawed. How many dog owners have seen the underside of a hare's foot? 'Cat-like' originally meant like the round, compact feet of the cat family, rather than like the ginger tom next door.

Importance of Balance

It is important to keep in mind too the origin of the breed when considering feet, that is, what the breed was designed to do. Galloping breeds like the sight-hounds have great freedom of the upper arm and elbows that are separated from the chest wall. The Greyhound's weight falls mainly on the toe pads. The German Shepherd Dog's weight falls on to the heel pad of the forefoot. The Greyhound is therefore usually seen comparatively more 'up on the feet' in its stance. The soundness or otherwise of the foot can affect the balance of a dog. If the heel pad is not sharing the body weight of the dog with the toe pads, then the latter are bearing extra weight and this will in time weaken the toes. The dog's knee will absorb what the toes haven't the strength to do. This is why at the turn of the century, when Foxhounds with massively timbered forelegs and fleshy, contracted, bunched-up feet were favoured, so many stood over at the knee to reduce the jarring. Such hounds had their weight all on the forehand, which in turn led to their shoulders becoming more upright. There is a danger in the pursuit of round, over-compact, knuckled-over, bunched-toed feet.

Lack of Scrutiny

From time to time, a committee of the Kennel Club looks at the wording of Breed Standards, in an attempt to avoid harmful end-effects on dogs from unwise written anatomical designs. The words on feet should receive their urgent attention. I am

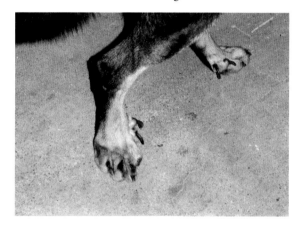

The double hind dew claws of the Beauceron.

A flat-footed Spanish Mastiff.

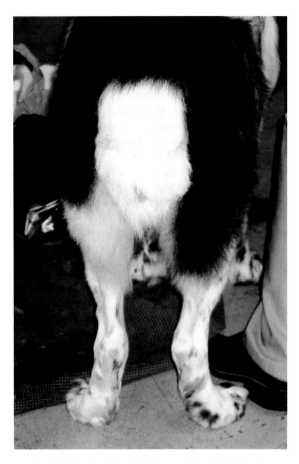

Cow-hocked, flat-footed Owtcharka entered for World Dog Show in Helsinki.

Dog-show judges should murmur to themselves 'No foot, no dog' before they begin their duties, advancing 'feet first' in every ring. Before writing 'movement disappointing' in the critique, a judge should ask, 'did I examine the feet?' The feet may not exactly be the mirror of the soul but the soles of the feet can so often reveal the quality of the dog. For me the quality of judges starts at the feet of the exhibits. At least the dogs judged by them can actually walk off with a prize!

Much is made by breed enthusiasts of the importance to their breed of, say, double dew claws, or dew claws on the rear hind leg as well as the front, as in the Beauceron and the Pyrenean Mountain Dog, with their respective Breed Standards emphasizing this feature. But I have seen judges at World Dog Shows check this 'asset' yet omit any check on flat or splay feet, which are not good for the dog. I have seen Spanish Mastiffs, Owtcharkas and our Rough Collies with quite appalling feet at shows – and the judges have never checked such a vital feature in the ring. Tight feet come from exercise; I have seen sheepdogs that operate entirely in soft pasture having well-spread toes, but never flat feet. There is an important difference.

The soundness of the feet does of course affect the quality of the dog's movement, just as the set of shoulders, the transmission from the hindquarters and the co-ordination between the front action and that of the rear is revealed to a watchful judge. Whilst it is disappointing to see a Sheltie with too short a tail, the dentition of a Pom and a frail bone structure, it is deeply depressing to observe at Crufts, a Shetland Sheepdog win not just its breed ticket but the group one too when it displays a Hackney action, forbidden in its Breed Standard. It is tiresome to see yet another Old English Sheepdog get its breed ticket at Crufts while demonstrating extremely poor hind movement. It is even sadder to see the Best in Show there clearly afflicted by a luxating patella in its right hind leg. If this is 'the best of the very best' as the 1998 Crufts slogan assured us, God help the mongrels of England! There would be enormous merit in dogs at KC-licensed shows being judged on movement alone for a few years, especially in the so-called 'head' or 'coat' breeds. The shortcomings, indeed the deceit, of Crufts is covered later.

The Importance of Movement

It's impossible to overrate the importance of movement – how the dog moves – in judging show dogs,

against a dog's feet being described in its breed blueprint as large, small, a different size fore and aft (as in the Hungarian Kuvasz's standard) or being unhelpfully worded, as in the Estrela Mountain Dog, whose feet have to be 'well made, neither very round nor excessively long' and in the Old English Sheepdog: 'Small, round and tight'. How small? I've never seen a specimen in this breed with small feet! Who is not confused by the Pyrenean Sheepdog having to possess feet that are 'lean, rather flat, oval shape'. Who *wants* to own a flat-footed dog? Nearly every breed in the Pastoral Group has to have well-padded feet; when was the last time *you* saw a judge examine the soles of an exhibit's feet?

Feet are a vital part of the dog's anatomy, more important than 'bite', colour of coat, length of coat, set of tail, length and carriage of ears and pigmentation.

especially as so many are bred from. Overall soundness is always best assessed when the dog is on the move; unsoundness is unlikely to be concealed from the judge once he or she has studied the dog's gait. It was therefore so pleasing to note that the National Association of Veterinary Physiotherapists (NAVP) chose gait analysis as the subject of its 2013 annual conference. This conference discussed the different aspects of the application of gait analysis to diagnosis, treatment and rehabilitation. Poor gait reveals poor conformation; poor conformation can lead to all manner of anatomical and locomotive problems in the dog. Future judges will be able to benefit from the findings and recommendations coming down from this NAVP conference. For over half a century I have watched judges considering the movement of the entry before deciding relative merit; one particular judge, the late Tom Horner, took infinite pains to study the movement of each and every exhibit, from different angles and at different speeds, and was wise enough to know its importance. I was so pleased to see, in 2013, an Australian Shepherd, Ch Allmark Fifth Avenue, handled by Angie Allan, owned by Neil Allan and Robert Harlow, display excellent extension, front and back, on the move; it is such a joy to see a good dog moving soundly.

Concealing Unsoundness

Writing in her informative *Showing & Judging Dogs* (1977), Hilary Harmar provided some valuable words on the effect on movement of anatomical unsoundness and abnormalities of the joint in show dogs:

> Certain forms of unsoundness are not very noticeable when the dog is moving, and unsoundness may, for example, be detected by the way in which a dog with severe hip dysplasia stands. Similarly, a dog with weak stifles will from time to time stand with straight hocks and stifles, other dogs when standing may knuckle-over at the pastern joint. A straight stifle may alter the normally level top-line and give a tilted one. For example, over-angulation in one joint will automatically have to be compensated for in one or more of the joints nearest to the fault. Unsoundness is more often revealed when the dog gaits.

Despite such insight from a distinguished judge, it is not unusual to see poor judgement of movement in show rings today. If judges shape the breed of the future there is cause for worry.

Prizing the Pedigree Ahead of the Dog

Which is riskier: breeding on the pedigree or on the *dog you can see*? In his valuable two-volume *The Dog Book* (1906), the underrated Scottish writer James Watson describes quite scathingly those in the world of purebred dogs who fail to realize that a pedigree is only a piece of paper. He records a conversation with the great Irish Terrier breeder of one hundred years ago, William Graham, who cast his eye over a show entry of his time and declared: 'Some men show pedigrees; I show dogs and take the prizes.' Vero Shaw, the distinguished canine authority of that time, gave the view in a show report that, all too often, the pedigree was worth more than the dog. And to this day, you still hear an indifferent animal excused on the grounds that it 'has a good pedigree'. As James Watson observed: 'No one with any knowledge of the subject will breed to a dog merely on pedigree…a good dog makes a pedigree good, and not the other way.'

There used to be a saying in dog-breeding circles: *no animal is well-bred unless it is good in itself.* I haven't heard it spoken of as a received wisdom for some years. Much more important than the names on the written pedigree is the ability to 'read' it, that is, translate the names into physical content. As the great Scottish Terrier breeder W.L. McCandlish wrote in his book on the breed: 'The names in a pedigree form are merely cyphers, designating certain groupings of features and certain sources of blood, and pedigree is of no value unless the breeder can translate what these cyphers mean.' Yet even some quite experienced dog breeders get dazzled by names on forms, rather than by dogs, supported by blood from distinct ancestors. The eminent canine geneticist Malcolm Willis has written: 'Never does pedigree information become more important than information on the dog itself.' We must always value dogs that are good in themselves. The pedigree form can be used to effect, but it can never herd sheep!

Of course there are some good dogs in the ring, but pastoral breeds really have to be far sounder than dogs from the other non-sporting Groups. I have long admired Alison Grainger's Samhaven kennel of Rough Collies; the best test of any breeder is to produce top quality dogs *consistently*. I have been impressed from the ringside by multi-Ch Smooth Collie Cligstone Sounds Good NV 12, owned by Laila Sehlin of Norway, a far sounder dog than many in this breed. Imports are coming in but bringing back old British blood in fact; perhaps the use of more distant (in time and number of generations) American blood would improve some lines. The Americans are ahead in terms of soundness and temperament, if not in head shape. It's good to see newcomers matching the old hands in the registration figures for this breed, but, for me, poor angulation is spoiling the breed, with the wrong slope of shoulder and short upper arms (as in the Australian Shepherd too) all too prevalent. Showiness can never be a better attribute than soundness; a sound dog leads a far better life.

Limitations of Show Success

In the pedigree dog world, much is made of the stud dog of the year competition, which is entirely based on the show success of the progeny of often over-used sires. The progeny of such successful sires could have bitten children, savaged other dogs or died young of some inheritable disease. Is this truly the best we can do? Does this, as the leitmotiv of the KC puts it, improve dogs? When I was working in Germany nearly half a century ago, I learned of the work, in the German Democratic Republic, of Dr F.K. Dorn, in a book entitled *Hund und Umwelt* or *Dog and the World around him*, that is, his environment. Dorn devised a system of four categories: A = Type, B = Appearance, C = Conformation and D = Temperament. Within each category, Dorn devised a numerical scoring system, in which, for example, A1 = shelly, A8 = too heavy and clumsy; B0 = lack of pigmentation, B5 = excellent appearance, outline and symmetry; D0 = nervous or timid, D3 = cautious, not self-assured and D 8= unafraid but not aggressive. Such details could then be written on a dog's pedigree for use when breeding plans were being formulated.

This became known as the Merseberg scoring system, after the GSD breed club there. Dorn was seeking to establish a clear picture of the hereditary qualities of the whole bloodline of a dog. But now, half a century later, our pedigrees merely list the ancestors for five generations, without any checks on their accuracy or the slightest whiff of real information about the dog. Is this progress? Is this in the best interests of good breeding? Prizes for

phenotype and beauty are given sole weight and to hell with such basic information as health, intelligence and working ability. In livestock breeding, a stud has no value until the performance of its progeny has been established. But in the pedigree dog world, a stud is valued not on the performance of its offspring but on their imposing stance in the ring. Does that produce the best companion animals? The KC's self-imposed mandate is the improvement of dogs, not the improvement of show dogs. Is their remit being met? Have we truly progressed in the last century or so?

When are we going to stop valuing our precious breeds of dog on their appearance alone, when it's their temperament that makes them a successful companion animal? Breeding for the pedigree and show-ring success is not the activity of either a real dog-lover or a true breed-lover; it can become a hobby for the mindless pursuit of winning for winning's sake, and it ruins distinguished breeds. In one half-century the Alsatian is renowned for its level topline, in the next it is desired to feature a 'banana-back' with its tail dragging along the floor. Such specimens may have great pedigrees, but they are not great dogs. Genuine dog-lovers know the difference! A Shetland Sheepdog lacking a full set of teeth and unable to chew a bone competently may have an impressive pedigree but will never be an impressive, or even a contented, dog. Sound dogs impress; unsound ones just suffer – in silence. Their pedigree never speaks!

Breeding a Working Dog – Respecting Function

In his excellent *Sheepdogs at Work* (1979), Tony Iley opened his text with:

One of the wonders of the world is to see a good Border Collie working in harmony with his master. Science and art are so closely combined as to make them inseparable. Each purposeful movement of the dog stems from instinctive knowledge and skilful training. The control of the sheep by the dog and the close knit partnership between dog and man cannot fail to move even the casual observer. The enthusiast, however, will not be content merely to observe. He

The Foster Mother *by Walter Hunt, 1887; Collie bitches can muti-task!*

BELOW: The Proud Father *by Basil Bradley, 1885; Collie sires do show affection.*

will want to probe deeper into the phenomenon of the working dog.

Many pastoral breed dog owners have a desire to know much more about the origin and motivation of their dogs; some may just want a 'pedigree dog', but a dog only good on paper is less of a companion and its health, both physical and genetic, may not be robust. The public are slowly coming to realize that having a pedigree does not automatically bestow quality. Recognition of this fact and the knowledge that a dog exercising its breed's function is a far more contented pet can lead to enhanced pet-ownership.

Breeding a Sounder Dog – the Limitations of Pedigree

In Canada it's a federal offence to sell an unregistered purebred dog. Every purebred dog, if it is to be legally sold there, has to be registered with the Canadian Kennel Club. In Britain anyone can sell a dog as a 'pedigree' animal; it doesn't need to be registered with anyone. In the United States, several states have enacted what are called 'Lemon Laws for Pets', which are designed to protect the purchaser of a dog but they are not there to protect the dog. Such laws give the purchaser the right to return a sick or dead puppy for a refund or replacement, with some going even further and allowing the purchaser to retain the puppy, have it treated and get some form of reimbursement from the purchaser for veterinary expenses. For the pedigree dog to flourish it's important for both the dog and the purchasing public to be protected.

There is a misunderstanding amongst the general public over the use of the word 'pedigree' when used to describe a dog's breeding. Strictly speaking it

Mountain Dog with Litter *by Beno Adam, 1862; all-round protectors.*

A Kuvasz and litter.

means having a recorded line of descent, especially one showing purebreeding. But the possession of a pedigree (a piece of paper) has come to mean, for many people, a sign of excellence, a mark of quality. This is undeserved and the public is being misled. First of all, the pedigree form or registration certificate that comes from the dog being registered with the KC, is, when it is correct, just a birth certificate. I write 'when it is correct' because its compilation relies on just one factor: the honesty of the breeder.

In the middle of the last century, a Danish geneticist, Ojvind Winge, found on examining the Danish studbook that 15 per cent of the pedigrees he checked could not be correct, on coat-colour inheritance grounds alone. The American Kennel Club has introduced random DNA testing, after being shocked to discover the level of falsified pedigrees on their register. I know of cases in more than one breed here where the breeder, when requested to supply a particular stud dog, has not used this dog but a kennel mate to service the bitch. Yet the subsequent pedigree has shown that the requested stud dog performed the service, not the real sire. The pedigree or record of breeding was knowingly and intentionally falsified. It is not wise to rely entirely on breeder honesty.

Genetic Health

In 1913, it was understandable for the pedigree form to be merely a certified record of breeding. But in 2013, surely we have progressed in our information technology? Yet the pedigree form still only contains lists of ancestors. We know, however, that certain dogs in certain breeds are carriers of inheritable conditions. Disreputable breeders conceal this, but how is the general public seeking a purebred pup to discover such a risk?

In a letter to the weekly publication *Dog World* in July 2013, Alan Wood made a number of points for me, in stating that few people he had met could discuss the meaning and implications of a breeding programme based on the pedigrees of the prospective parents. Being involved in horse breeding, he had found the data on the thoroughbred (horse) to be far more comprehensive and available than that for pedigree dogs. Having observed how the horse-breeding world works he felt that the whole subject of the KC's position in the world of dogs needs a serious review, considering that the 'laissez faire' attitude of the Assured Breeder Scheme is just not strong enough and will never achieve the improvement in dog health and type required to separate the elite breeder from the puppy farmer. He has made a case; why can anyone, however ill-advised or misguided, be allowed to breed a litter of pedigree pups and automatically have them registered as purebred just by paying a sum to the KC? The desire for quality in a future litter shouldn't just rest with a breeder; a system for better assuring excellence is essential. You could make a case for every breeder of purebred dogs to need a licence from the KC *before* a litter is created.

Overseas, show dogs are routinely graded in order of merit, from 'excellent' downwards and their grading can be easily seen on a fuller registration certificate. Why not here? There are some deeply flawed dogs being exhibited and the after-show critiques reveal their seriousness. Here are some of the words used by judges in such critiques in the last few years: Estrela Mountain Dogs – 'I was horrified when I looked in the mouths of many of the dogs present'; Old English Sheepdogs – 'the quality in the males is still poor'; Bernese Mountain Dogs – 'sadly lacking in overall soundness and carrying too much weight'; Rough Collies – 'I was very sad to have so much bad movement.' These are comments on dogs being proudly exhibited by owners, some of them breeders, at championship shows, not village fete dog shows. All of these faulty dogs in the ring had what is so often conceived as a distinction – a pedigree. One exhibitor at such a show once described his latest litter to me as 'only pet-market quality'! If the comments of judges set out above are on the 'show-quality' dogs, God help future pet owners.

Even sadder, at the same show, was being told that one of the dogs in the ring had a litter mate with Wobbler Syndrome, but that the line was still being bred from. This means that a future dog from this line could have hind legs that collapse. Should vets, breed clubs, welfare organizations and the KC not be striving to get such concealment exposed? Until genetic pedigrees are issued, the public is not just being misled, but being cheated. Our KC is now working closer with the veterinary profession than ever before and that has to be good for the breeding of sounder pedigree dogs. Purchasers of a registered pedigree pup really do need

to know if their dog is sound – not just to obtain value for money but to obtain a truly healthy pet.

Breeders Need Data
The KC does deserve praise for facing up to some of the problems of health and breeding in the dogs registered with them. They have established the Dog Health Group, aiming to tackle all health issues affecting dogs, with particular emphasis understandably on those that may affect pedigree dogs. This group has four separate sub-groups that address: Genetics and Health Screening; Breed Standards and Conformation; the Assured Breeder Scheme; and Activities Health and Welfare. Also involved in this work are co-opted geneticists, vets and behaviourists. The launch of the Mate Select scheme for use by breeders to access coefficients for inbreeding in hypothetical matings between two dogs on the breed registers is a major step forward. Over 750,000 searches a year are now being carried out. The health data on prospective breeding stock is of particular value.

The Risks of Inbreeding
Inbreeding – both consanguineous marriage in some societies, and in pedigree dog circles – has attracted a great deal of attention recently. However, it's not exactly a fresh topic. In his valuable book of 1905, *The Kennel Handbook*, the knowledgeable C.J. Davies wrote:

> We will turn to a matter which is indirectly touched upon in Mendel's principles of heredity, that of the value of inbreeding. Perhaps no point in breeding is more subject to controversy than this one. From one breeder we may receive an alarming list of evils which will result from inbreeding; from the next we may receive nothing but praise of its virtues. Certainly the appearance and behaviour of some of our notoriously inbred animals is not a very favourable advertisement of its beneficiality; on the other hand we know that certain plants habitually fertilise themselves for apparently any number of generations, and no closer form of breeding can be imagined. Loss of size, sterility, loss of constitutional vigour, and, predisposition to disease are among the evils laid at its door. What we have to consider is, Are these caused by inbreeding? We should be inclined to answer: Indirectly, Yes; Directly, No.

He could have been writing yesterday; scientists and dog-breeders might answer quite differently.

In the last year or so in Britain a number of extremely important inquiries have been conducted into dog breeding, and considering that very question one hundred years on. Each one has expressed concerns about breeding to close relatives in pedigree breeds. The Bateson Report recommended the establishment of an Advisory Council (now set up under Professor Sheila Crispin) to address the issue. The cross-party Parliamentary Group's findings also recommended greater scrutiny of such dog-breeding practices. But for a century or so, close breeding to certain lines or sires has been accepted practice amongst pedigree dog breeders. In her informative book *Advanced Labrador Breeding* (1988), Mary Roslin Williams, herself a successful breeder of both show and FT champions, wrote: 'To produce a strain of good ones, you *must* carry out a degree of line-breeding, possibly even using the dangerous practice of mild inbreeding in special cases. Top breeders hate the moment they have to use a complete outcross.'

She defined line-breeding as 'a gathering of lines leading back in three or four generations to a known good dog or bitch or very often to one or two good dogs and bitches, with the rest of the pedigree filled with outcross names'. The famous Golden Retriever breeder Mrs W.M. Charlesworth warned against brother-sister matings but liked bitch to grandfather unions and favoured bitch to nephew matings. In the lurcher and terrier world, close matings can of course occur too. But when dogs are rated by their performance rather than their type or handsomeness, there are built-in safeguards. 'Master-race' thinking has long been discredited in the human race!

Inbreeding Ratios

Inbreeding amongst purebred dogs is very much in the limelight in the early part of the twenty-first century and rightly so. Pastoral and working breeds originating in a small genetic base need monitoring. The inbreeding coefficients (a low one is better – the higher the percentage, the closer the breeding) in pedigree breeds have been identified and published. The KC's Mate Select system allows checks to be made on the genetic desirability of a proposed mating, merit apart. The coefficients of inbreeding (COIs, expressed as percentages) assessed for

pastoral breeds in 2010 gave some revealing (and some reassuring) figures: Anatolian Shepherd Dog 6.6 per cent; Australian Shepherd Dog and Cattle Dog 2.4; Bearded Collie 14.6; Beauceron 1.4; Belgian Shepherd Dogs 2.5 (Groenendael), 7.5 (Laekenois), 2.2 (Malinois), 4.3 (Tervueren); Bernese Mountain Dog 5.1; Border Collie 14.6; Bouvier des Flandres 8.1; Briard 3.3; Collie (Rough) 13.7; Collie (Smooth) 5.8; Entlebucher 0.1; Estrela Mountain Dog 1.5; Finnish Lapphund 1.3; GSD 3.2; Greater Swiss Mountain Dog 0.5; Hovawart 0.5; Hungarian Puli 7.5; Komondor 0.2; Lancashire Heeler 11.6; Leonberger 4.1; Maremma Sheepdog 1.2; Norwegian Buhund 9; Old English Sheepdog 9.5; Polish Lowland Sheepdog 7.2; Pyrenean Mastiff 0.8; Pyrenean Mountain Dog 8.9; Pyrenean Sheepdog 1.8; Shetland Sheepdog 5.8; Swedish Vallhund 3.7; Welsh Corgi (Cardigan) 5.2 and (Pembroke) 8.

These are *breed averages* and it would be wrong to apply these ratings to an individual in a breed; the KC website can make more precise measurements, based on pedigree names. It's worth noting that the

Shetland Sheepdogs of the 1950s; much less heavily coated.

A Collie *by E.J. Alexander, 1904; a noticeably broader-skulled dog.*

breeds with the bigger numbers aren't always the ones with the lowest percentage. In 2012, the new puppy contract launched by the British Veterinary Association's Animal Welfare Foundation, supported by the RSPCA and endorsed by the Advisory Council for the Welfare Issues of Dog Breeding, advised that puppies with an inbreeding coefficient of more than 12.5 per cent should be avoided. David Balding, Professor of Statistical Genetics at Imperial College, London, has advised:

> Inbreeding is not the only cause of canine health problems, and perhaps not even the worst, but it is the easiest problem to fix… Find out the coefficient of inbreeding for a puppy before buying it… at least make sure that the puppy has four different grandparents, not one of them directly related to another.

Penalties of Close Breeding

Inbreeding Depression is an acknowledged cause of small litter sizes, shorter lives and a reduced immune system in pedigree dogs, as Davies was noting a century ago. Dr Ian Ramsey of the University of Glasgow has stated:

> Inbreeding leads to certain genes being concentrated in particular breeds, or even lines within breeds, and a lack of variation follows… However, dogs' genes also determine how good their immune systems are at recognising their own bodies. If the 'bad' genes that stop a dog's immune system recognising its own body are, accidentally, concentrated along with the 'good' genes for a certain coat colour, physical size, etc., then the dog will have an inherited tendency to suffer from autoimmune disease. This dog may well pass this tendency on to its puppies.

He went on to point out the only way of avoiding this is to avoid inbreeding as much as possible – accepting that as you do so a greater variation in other things will be introduced. Breeders can choose, their dogs cannot. The admirable organization that oversees the breeding and registering of Border Collies that work – the International Sheep Dog Society (ISDS) has a database of over 355,000 dogs registered with them. Two sires, Wiston Cap and Wilson's Cap are immensely influential; Wiston Cap sired nearly 2,000 pups in 388 litters. It requires a knowledgeable breeder to make the best of such genes without such breeding being *too* close. The selection of breeding stock must never be done merely on appearance.

Inbreeding is coming under greater scientific scrutiny as inheritable defects in pedigree dogs increase. One researcher in America found that in dog breeds there is a decline in the average life span of around 7 per cent for every 10 per cent increase in inbreeding. Dwarfism has been found in Pointer litters at inbreeding coefficients of 13–37 per cent, whereas unaffected litters rated 0–24 per cent. In a Foxhound pack, the conception rate with sperm of inbred dogs was 73 per cent against 87 per cent with outbred ones; average litter size was seven against nine, and four against six at weaning. The sperm count was 70 against 367.

Swedish research shows that their pedigree dogs in sixty breeds had an average inbreeding coefficient of 14 per cent. Most dog breeds with good-sized populations have a coefficient of inbreeding of 4–5 per cent. Professional breeders of production animals such as cows, pigs, goats, sheep and horses consider that a coefficient of inbreeding of around 9 per cent is risky. Why do breeders of production animals seek healthier animals than dog-breeders? Is it not mainly based on market value related to beef and milk production? Show dogs have no performance rating, just breeder-whim appearance.

Uninformed out-crossing is not the answer; there has to be research as well as vision. Leading geneticist Professor Steve Jones has stated that for pedigree breeds of dog 'a universe of suffering' is ahead with continued inbreeding. Fellow geneticist Bruce Cattanach commented, '…inbreeding has been ingrained in dog breeder psyche from the beginning and is hard to break, even when it is possible to show that it is not the most successful way to breed'. He went on

to state that some pedigree breeds may well become extinct in our lifetimes without intervention, advising out-crossing to other related breeds. But who will listen to him; dogma will prevail and not just lurchermen will wonder at such folly – and such damage to long-established breeds. One of the weaknesses of the otherwise quite excellent Bateson Report into the state of pedigree dog-breeding in Britain was that it didn't gather any valuable evidence on the *genetic size* of each registered breed. The report uses the expression 'closely related breeding pair' when discussing the mating of dams with sires, but doesn't define what closely related actually means.

Relative Values
To put these figures into context, all dogs in a breed are related. A mother-son mating would produce a 25 per cent COI, first cousins will have a 6.25 per cent COI, and within breeds variations can be found: Standard Poodles have varied from 6.25 per cent to over 25 per cent, with the former living four years longer than the latter. If you bred with two totally unrelated Border Collies, then mated two of their offspring together, their pups' COI could theoretically be 25 per cent if they share the same grandparents. For many breeds, not just gundog ones, the average COI may be above 10 per cent, as common ancestors contribute.

Of course a COI of 1 per cent doesn't guarantee better health than a measurement of 30 per cent. Some low-scoring breeds have serious genetic defects as bad genes manifest themselves. The chances of inheriting a double dose of defective genes needs to be reduced. Without health checks the overuse of a defective sire can create long-term misery in any breed. Rushing to mate your bitch to the latest Crufts winner is not a rational act, nor always a compassionate one. It is important to note, however, that COIs are not all calculated from a common base; it would be more valuable, comparatively, if all were to be based on a five-generation survey. There would be greater clarity too if the advice to avoid breeding from stock with a COI of lower than 12.5 were altered to read *not more* than 12.5 per cent. The genetic health of pedigree pastoral dogs rests with breeders but others contribute hugely too.

The Germans have a word for reckless breeding leading to discomfort, disease and a shorter life for the pedigree dog. It is *qualzucht*, cruelty breeding, or more literally, 'torture breeding'. When a geneticist, himself in Boxers, finds it necessary to pose the question, 'are there any Boxers that are truly free of heart murmurs?', we have much to think about. He himself was brave to outcross for the naturally docked tail – and why not? Uninformed outcrossing is not the answer; there has to be research as well as vision. He, with two other geneticists, opposed the recognition of two breeds from Anatolia, during the Kangal Dog/Anatolian Shepherd Dog debate, on the grounds that smaller gene pools resulting from split breeds can degrade genetic diversity. I can see why,

but genetic diversity doesn't just depend on breed population, more on the selection of breeding stock. I don't recall these geneticists arguing for the Rough and Smooth Collie breeds to merge in order to widen their respective gene pools.

It's worrying to note that in 1982, when 5,663 Rough Collies were newly registered with the KC, a breeding research project found that over 80 per cent of these dogs could be traced back to one dog called Old Cockie, who was a frequent winner around 1870. Later, in 1989, when 1,945 Bearded Collies were newly registered with the KC, a similar research pro-

RIGHT: Bobs – a Collie in a Landscape *by John Emms, 1901; canine beauty does have drawbacks.*

A Collie in a Landscape *by Maud Earl, 1899; sheer handsomeness can become a higher priority than soundness.*

ject found that they all came from just twelve dogs. Every British Smooth Collie descends, within five generations, from a single dog. This is fine when inheritable defects are not present, or litter sizes are not reduced and when breed virility is not causing alarm. Inbreeding will not cause inherited problems if the problems are not present, in the genes, in the first place. The genetic size of a breed is crucially important; some ancient breeds are inbred and some relatively newly created breeds are not. But breeding practices decide whether a breed founded a century ago is inbred or genetically diverse.

Need for Patience

Writing in *Dogs in Canada* magazine in 1988, Dr R.D. Crawford, a professor in animal genetics at the College of Agriculture of the University of Saskatchewan, gave this advice:

> A useful rule of thumb might be the following. If your breed is a very ancient one, that has undergone very high levels of inbreeding, and that has had very intensive selection for its breed characteristics, then it should be possible to inbreed very heavily to make rapid progress in establishing a unique and distinctive line or strain. But if your breed is a relatively new one, which has not thus far been inbred and which

exhibits a lot of variation, then development of lines and strains within the breed using inbreeding can only be done very slowly; it will take many generations to make much progress. If your breed lies somewhere between these extremes, it should be safe to proceed with moderate inbreeding to develop your own line or strain. Regardless of the category of your breed, you should be emotionally prepared for genetic 'junk' to be uncovered and you should be prepared to eliminate it as part of your long-term breeding program.

But how many breeders of pedigree dogs have the patience for the 'long haul' or the resolve to eliminate genetic 'junk'?

Much can depend for example on the over-use in purebred dogs of prize-winning sires. One working champion Springer at the end of the last century sired over 210 litters without undergoing genetic health checks. In 2010 a magnificent Hungarian Vizsla won Best in Show at Crufts; he had been a highly successful prize-winner since arriving here in 2005. During his first four years in the UK, he produced 827 offspring, 517 being first generation from him. In that period just under 5,000 Vizslas were newly registered, which means that he sired more than 10 per cent of the newly registered Hungarian Vizslas in Britain. The over-use of a top dog can end up contributing

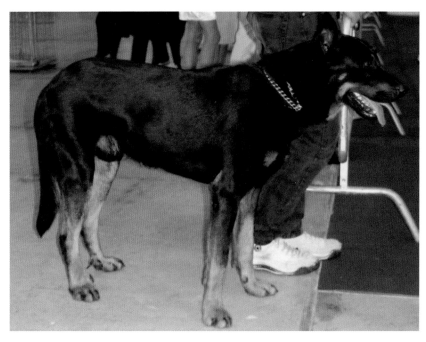

The Beauceron show and working dog.

The Border Collie: designed for work, not cosmetic appeal.

to a narrow genetic pool, which, without mandatory health clearances, can lead to an increased potential for inherited disease. It is good to learn that the Border Collie show breeders here have imported dogs of known quality from Australia and the USA, as well as importing frozen semen from Australia, in the search for a wider gene pool and a better dog.

> Not a few breeders who ought to know better have spoilt any breeding plans they may have made…by chasing after the latest champion dog as a mate for their bitches. If he really is the dog for them they should have been able to recognize this fact sooner; if he is not, the conferment of the title does not make him a better dog than he was before. Some people never seem able to make up their minds for themselves…
>
> Charles Lister-Kaye, *The Welsh Corgi* (1968)

Breeding Dogs that Work

In April 2013, Ch Littlethorn Colt at Tobermoray became the first Border Collie in over eighteen years to obtain full champion status, for both his sheep herding and showing abilities. That is worthy of praise but it indicates that for all that time no Border Collie, the show version of our principal working sheepdog, gained such dual recognition; that is worrying. I can understand why the judge of Border Collies at a championship show in 2012 reported:

The shepherd needs a dog that is very athletic, has tight feet, well sloped pasterns, correct shoulders and powerful hindquarters to drive the dog through a long day's work. Glamorous coats, perfect markings, straight pasterns and 10 to 12 pointy feet are all useless, even debilitating…I firmly believe we are breeding a show dog not a Border Collie.

A very enthusiastic young Danish dog breeder asked me a couple of decades ago how the planning of purebred dog breeding was conducted in this country. We were both employed in livestock breeding and were aware of how science has long been and is ever increasingly contributing to that activity. I am afraid that my description of our dog-breeding systems, apart from that conducted by one or two enlightened individuals and the Guide Dogs for the Blind Association, was full of regrets. By that I mean: little interest in the science of dog breeding from most breed societies, even less interest from the Kennel Club, at that time, and, seemingly, the lack of even one really determined individual to change the situation and prevailing attitudes. Compared to livestock breeders, far too many dog breeders are, in scientific breeding capability, ignorant, ill-informed and misguided. Oh, how tired I am of hearing *experienced* dog breeders use expressions like, 'Breed like to like, it's safer', or 'The pedigree goes in at the mouth', or 'Now that he's a champion, I'm going to use him on my bitch.'

Pedigree Limitations

I had to tell my keen young Danish colleague that we still only put numbers, names and coat colours on our pedigrees even in this advanced computer age; we still don't merit grade our dogs at shows, so that we never know relatively how good even the winners are; no one is appointed in each breed to act as a breeding adviser despite the existence of breed councils and there is no national scheme in dog breeding in the UK on the lines of the scientifically planned systems used in cattle and some other farm animals. If the Kennel Club exists for the improvement of dogs, as they themselves and they perhaps alone claim, what have they been doing whilst their opposite numbers in farm animals have been forging ahead with enterprise and vision?

These words will no doubt bring a response that 'we've managed to get along without scientists so far, why do we need them now?' I asked a livestock breeder who is also a pedigree dog breeder to comment on such a predictably negative response. Her reply was, 'In livestock breeding science is wanted and welcomed, in dog breeding no one wants to know.' What a commentary on attitudes five years before the next millennium! My own response is on these lines: selection is still the main element in dog breeding but with a closed gene pool in every registered breed, with so many inheritable conditions manifesting themselves, how can we progress without the help of scientists? We judge the phenotype (that is, what we see) but we should breed on the genotype (that is, the dog's genetic make-up).

Looking recently at the five-generation pedigree of a new champion Bullmastiff and noting that it had fifty-eight different ancestors out of a possible sixty-two, brought to my notice very starkly just how small the part that scientific knowledge plays in such an activity. A livestock breeder can take advantage of the internationally acclaimed BLUP (Best Linear Unbiased Prediction) technique; EBVs (Estimated Breeding Values) – an estimated measure of the animal's genetic merit; the BPA's Standards of Excellence for the pig; the grading-up procedure and Sire Ranking Lists. In the show ring, farm animals are still judged to a scale of points related directly to the wording of the breed description or standard. A well-known dog breeder recently asked me what I meant by the expression 'on the tail male side'! Where do we go from here?

Better-Planned Breeding

If the Kennel Club declined to register a dog unless the breeder was a member of a breed society for that breed and insisted on each breed council appointing an official geneticist to advise on breeding programmes, then a start could be made. Geneticists are not renowned for their skill *as breeders*, but as professionally qualified advisers they could contribute so much, especially as the science of DNA-testing advances. I understand that DNA analysis is already contributing to the better-planned breeding of Bernese Mountain Dogs in Switzerland. The KC was created to register the breeding of pedigree dogs; its best future surely lies in the *improvement* of pedigree dogs, whether through purebreeding or the best practice of breeding. The KC's shibboleth seems to be 'purebreeding – right or wrong'! But purebreeding should not conflict with *best-breeding*; if, for example, the mating of two Smooths produces a Rough Collie whelp in the litter, the KC will not accept its registration as purebred, yet it could grow into a quite outstanding dog. That is pure nonsense, not purebreeding!

The time-honoured KC response to pleas for national schemes for the improvement of dog breeding has been to say that it's a matter for individual breeders and breed councils. But the German Kennel Club has instructed judges not to reward dogs with harmful exaggerations. The latter were considered to range from size of eyes, length of hair and shortness of muzzles to the quest for giant and dwarf dogs. Dr Hellmuth Wachtel had a point when he wrote in *Dog World* (August 2006):

> Basically, neither breeders nor judges nor other dog specialists were to blame; it is inherent in human nature to compete in surpassing an existing achievement. In dogs, that means that typical traits tend to be replaced by the more typical. So long hair grew longer until down to the ground, small eyes crept into the skull, short muzzles disappeared altogether.

Who is going to address this problem? Vets, breed clubs alone and unaided, animal rights activists? But hasn't the KC set itself up as the ultimate authority in the UK for all matters affecting the purebred dog?

In *The Daily Telegraph* in August 1996 it was reported that an eighty-year-old breeder of champions, a judge for over fifty years, resigned, saying:

For many, winning is all that matters… Breeders use talcum powder and other cosmetics to make the animals look better… Some pluck whiskers with tweezers to conceal the fact that the colour has been changed… Now they breed genetic inventions that don't normally exist and give them a fancy name.

The report referred to a breeder of guinea pigs but its content supports Dr Wachtel's statement and dog fanciers will see some relevance in them. But if we acknowledge the strange whim in humans for selfish indulgence at the expense of living creatures, surely we can act in time to protect subject animals?

Dogmap and the Genome
In the absence of any moral leadership from our own Kennel Club, the responsibility for breeding out defects and harmful exaggerations is increasingly passing over to the scientist. The Animal Health Trust, for example, started gene-mapping in 1990 and participates in Dogmap, a worldwide effort to map the canine genome. Already the Department of Clinical Veterinary Medicine at Cambridge University, working with the Institute of Ophthalmology in London, has identified the gene responsible for PRA in Irish Setters. Potential carriers of the defect can now be omitted from breeding programmes. Work continues on locating the gene behind deafness in Dalmatians, a gene linked to the absence of coloured patches on the ears. Such work, and success, emphasizes the pressing need for every breed council to appoint a geneticist to advise the breed.

This *advisory* role needs to be just that; it is vital that breeders remain in charge of breeding decisions. For example, hip dysplasia is a genetically transmitted disease that can only be reduced in incidence through rigorous genetic selection. It would be unwise, however, to cull on the basis of one flaw in an otherwise excellent dog. In a breed with plenty of really outstanding dogs, the ruthless culling of dogs with defective genes makes sense. But in breeds struggling to produce quality in volume, we should look at the merit of a dog excellent in other ways and aim to reduce the likelihood of inherited defects through wise matings. Any dog with an inherited eye disease, epilepsy, a savage disposition or *bad* hips should definitely not be bred from but other defects must be balanced with the overall quality of the dog in question.

It is simply appalling to hear of a breeder continuing to breed from her stock knowing that she had primary glaucoma there. It is sad to hear breeders quoting pedigrees in their plans rather than the dogs themselves. It is depressing to hear breeders talking of using a certain stud dog because he has just been made a champion, or has recently been imported, or is just down the road or because there are lots of champions in his pedigree. It is foolish for dog breeders to stress one anatomical feature ahead of all others. Breeding for 'great bone' tells you at once that there is a surfeit of it between the ears of that particular breeder. Foxhound breeders learned the hard way a century ago that heavy, club-like legs are actually less capable of endurance than the lighter ones. The forearm of the dog corresponds with the ankle in man; how many of us want heavy ankles? Why breed for something the dog doesn't need? Why breed dogs to a size their own ancestors never needed?

What Does the *Dog* Need?
There is evidence that height at withers and body weight are quite highly inherited and tend to be related. Data in the breed of GSD shows that sixty-day weight in the breed is around 45 per cent heritable and therefore weights at other ages would be connected, while the genes influencing weight will also tend to influence height. In a breed desiring to increase height, as in some LPD breeds, using some of the tallest animals in the breed could quickly raise heights in that breed. At the same time, not surprisingly, body weight would tend to increase too, whether desired or not. Increased size would bring with it a more rapid growth rate and possibly an increased rate of hip dysplasia. It would probably increase susceptibility of the long bones to diseases like panosteosis and it might lead also to reduced hind angulation. Straight stifles are almost a feature in some of our bigger, heavier breeds. What truly is the value of seeking great size in a breed for its own sake and not for a distinct purpose benefiting the breed?

If we continue to breed for features a dog does not need we will not only do a disservice to dog but provide a great deal of ammunition to the ever-vocal anti-dog lobby. If we breed from the pedigree alone we will never retain type, character and the breed or kennel signature. If we do not breed for temperament we will be ignoring the key commercial fact that most purebred dogs become pets. If we breed for heads, bone, coat or excessive angulation in the hind legs then we will get what we deserve: degeneration in the less valued areas. If we do not embrace the advice of geneticists, introduce scientifically designed breeding programmes or take every advantage of scientific progress then we might as well wear Victorian dress, for we will merely be perpetuating dated concepts. The requirement for planned breeding is now greater than ever. The capability of science to aid us is now greater than ever. We must not fail our dogs!

Breeding Companions

The potential stud dog must come of stock in which there is no known inherent tendency to any particular disease or constitutional weakness, quite apart from his merit on show points… The stud should also be a dog of excellent temperament, for the shy dog is the greatest detriment to any breed.

Margaret Osborne, *The Popular Collie* (1960)

What do most dog-owners want in their pet dogs? Surely companionability, backed by health, vigour and longevity. But how little both serious innovation and enlightened enterprise feature in the breeding programmes of our pedigree dogs. Purebreeding is fine when strong, healthy dogs result from it, but in so many of our pedigree breeds there is a small gene pool and in all of them there is a closed gene pool. Our ancestors bred for results on legs not on paper and most of our revered pedigree breeds have a very mixed ancestry. Many scientists consider there is a proven case for producing healthy hybrids for the pet market and retaining pure breeds for show and breeding stock. In his most informative book *If Dogs Could Talk – Exploring the Canine Mind* (2006), the Hungarian ethologist Vilmos Csanyi makes a compelling case for it.

Knowledgeable breeders will of course point out that these so-called 'healthy hybrids' could themselves produce any old stock and that there would be no assurance of type or quality beyond the F1 hybrid, or first generation. This I accept, but most dog owners don't breed from their dogs; they would just be strong, healthy, long-lived pets costing little at the vets. Artisan hunters, with their 'bobbery packs' of lurchers and terriers, don't care much which pure breeds their dogs come from but will not tolerate a dog that can't function or costs a fortune at the vets. Cross-breeding is no magic answer – there has to be quality behind both dam and sire as well as the skill in knowing how to blend the two.

The flock protectors make understanding companions.

A Highland Breakfast *by John Emms, 1900; the boy–dog empathy is clear.*

BELOW: The Drovers' Departure *by W.C.W. Fisher, after Landseer, 1879; the Collie gets closest.*

Riding with Grandfather *by Wright Barker, 1920; the Collie is very much part of the family outing.*

Roy Robinson, in his *Genetics for Dog Breeders* (1990) wrote: 'If the outcross is wisely undertaken, it ought to be possible to preserve most of the better qualities of the strain, or at least not to lose too many. The first-cross progeny are often remarkably hardy and vigorous.' But what is 'hybrid vigour'? Strictly speaking a hybrid is the result of a cross between different species, for example a sheep and a goat. But three types of crossing are possible: that between species, that between breeds and that between an animal pure for breed and one impure for that breed – a process known in farm animals as 'grading'. Livestock breeding always seems to be well ahead of dog breeding in utilizing new scientific techniques; the BLUP (Best Linear Unbiased Prediction) system is available for farm livestock improvement in the UK but I believe has only been used in dog breeding in Germany.

Using Outside Blood

In the world of the purebred dog, the use of greyhound blood could improve the hips of many breeds. The racing greyhound has the most perfect canine hips and could be used to improve the hips of other breeds so that the pet market doesn't have the agony of hip dysplasia manifesting itself in precious companion dogs. Such a cross could also be used with a Rottweiler to counter the predisposition of young Rottweilers to cranial cruciate ligament rupture.

Other pedigree breeds could of course also benefit from such an outcross, but despite the clear benefits to dogs they claim to love, no pedigree dog breeder would consider such a step. If we want to breed healthier dogs for people who don't want to show a purebred dog, then F1 hybrids from crossing two different pedigree breeds are a definite option.

Bloodhound breeders revere the name of Brough, but ignore his advice to seek an outcross in every fifth generation. Setter breeders revere the name of Laverack, but never use his advice that 'a change of colour is as good as a change of blood'. If today's breeders of a pedigree setter breed won't themselves resort to this, then someone seeking a healthy setter as a country companion would be well advised to buy an inter-bred one. Pet owners want healthy pets that live a long time and don't need costly veterinary attention. This would be the great benefit of hybrid vigour in dog breeding. The skill required by a show breeder to utilize outside blood is something else. Perhaps the best-ever Smooth Collie was Ch Eastwood Extra of a century ago; he was the result of Rough Collie-Smooth Collie mating. Could that happen today? Purity has replaced the pursuit of excellence. The KC now permits the planned use of Dual Sires, the dual matings to a bitch by two sires instead of one during one conceptual season. Far better genetic diversity could be obtained by mating two similar breeds together, but sadly purebreeding is still worshipped despite the genetic limitations it inevitably brings with it. Pedigree dog breeding has long been over-rated.

The late Malcolm Willis, the eminent geneticist, in his *Practical Genetics for Dog Breeders* (1992), wrote:

> …it is just as dangerous to overestimate pedigrees. Ancestors a long way back in the pedigree are not normally likely to be very influential even if those ancestors were outstanding specimens…a breeder who 'gets excited' about famous names in generation 20 would be deluding himself because most of them would be there in name only.

But show-dog breeders are conformists, often buried in their personal interests. The great historian Friedrich Meinecke had a theory that man soon became blinded by his narrow 'specialisms', whatever the field of interest.

Recycling Old Genes

Most pedigree dog breeders practise inbreeding, often unthinkingly. C.J. Davies, in his valuable book, *The Theory and Practice of Breeding for Type and its Application to the Breeding of Dogs* (*c*.1930), wrote that:

> Inbreeding creates nothing new. It merely ensures the perpetuation of qualities already present. Therefore it is as fatal a policy to inbreed indifferent specimens in the hope of improving the race as it is folly to cross a good race which shows no sign of deterioration… A common fallacy of the present day is to assume that inbreeding will to some extent do away with the need for selection…the exact opposite is the case… If eye and judgement be lacking no amount of theoretical knowledge can make the successful breeder.

I have never come across a professional geneticist who was also an outstanding breeder of livestock of any kind. Outstanding parents don't always produce outstanding offspring; selection is the key skill.

Recycling genes within a breed is not always the best answer in attempting to improve the health and vigour of that breed. In their *Genetics of the Dog – the Basis of Successful Breeding* (1966), Burns and Fraser make my point for me:

> This suggestion of crossing with another breed will of course rather shock the pedigree purist. It was however used during the formative period of almost every breed and it is entirely unscientific to refuse to utilise the simplest method of attaining what is required. The important thing is to know exactly what is wanted from the crossing and to make only such matings as are necessary to attain that end.

You can relate these words to the experience of the breeding manager to the Guide Dogs for the Blind Association. For several years the highest pass rate (86 per cent in 1994) has been from Labrador cross Golden Retrievers. Against that evidence the forward plan of any commercial dog registry *must* embrace the registration of such crossbred dogs, as they are the future. A club like the Kennel Club, created in different times, reluctant to change with the times and reliant on the sluggish attitudes generated by committees, is going to look increasingly primitive as the next millennium unfolds. As more scientific evidence is presented to us in each decade we must have the vision to make good use of it – or waste it.

Genetic 'Junk'

I have already referred to the words, in *Dogs in Canada* magazine in May 1994, of a professor in genetics, Dr R.D. Crawford, who also pointed out some other valuable facts to breeders:

Swedish Vallhund; this breed could reinvigorate the Corgi.

…the older the breed, the smaller will be the amount of genetic 'junk' that it contains; the younger the breed, the more defects will be present. For instance, very old breeds such as the Saluki, Pekingese and Basenji will only rarely express a severe genetic abnormality…the Standard Poodle has become the classic example of a dog breed that is highly inbred and as a result it now possesses a relatively 'clean' genotype.

But those breeders inbreeding new breeds are going to have to demonstrate great skill if sound stock is to be produced. Most dog breeders breed on the phenotype (what the animal looks like), rather than the genotype (what genes the dog is carrying).

Without the breeding of one breed to another, we would not have most of the pedigree breeds of today. Why did skilled breeders like Dobermann and Korthals need to fuse the blood of different breeds? What was the purpose of Southern African hunters in producing the Rhodesian Ridgeback? The answer

The Canaan Dog could be used to reinvigorate the two Scottish Collie breeds.

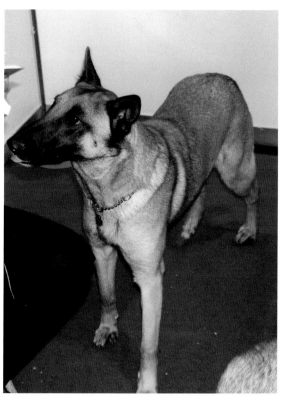

The Malinois could be used to reinvigorate the Smooth Collie.

The blood of the Polish Lowland Sheepdog could benefit that of the Bearded Collie.

BELOW LEFT: *The blue merle Border Collie could benefit the Aussie Shepherd.*

is functional excellence, supported by robustness and virility. Would our Welsh Corgi not benefit from an infusion of genes from look-alike breed the Swedish Vallhund? Could our Smooth Collie become more virile with added Malinois, or even Canaan Dog, blood? If our Bearded Collie has a small gene pool would the genes of the Polish Lowland Sheepdog or the Catalan Sheepdog help? If the Aussie Shepherd needs a bigger gene pool, we have plenty of native merle working collies to help the cause! For those screaming 'What about precious breed type?', I would point them towards the Corgi outcross used in the Boxer by geneticist Bruce Cattanach to install a naturally bobtailed dog; after just three generations even breed specialists could not detect the outcross progeny from the pure version.

The Need for Hybrid Vigour

A decade ago, there was a series of articles either advocating crossbreeding or disparaging it, in one of the national dog papers. The advocacy argument was convincing; the disparaging response very disappointing and intellectually quite lightweight. This is a debate worth conducting and of more value to the domestic dog than any wordy show report. It is a rather sad fact that the words of the few scientists I have read who support and defend purebreeding are themselves involved in the showing and breeding of purebred dogs. It is all too apparent where they are coming from and why their case is disappointingly tendentious. For a scientist not to have an open mind is worrying. The eminent British scientist Sir James Jeans wrote, a century ago: 'Science should leave off making pronouncements; the river of knowledge has too often turned back on itself.' The wish to improve dogs has to be heartfelt.

Consumers generally have higher expectations and an increased tendency to go to litigation in these times. Pet insurance is becoming very big business. Veterinary bills are rising steeply. A more sophisticated dog-owning public is just not going to tolerate sickly pets that die young even if they look roughly like their ancestors. If you add to this the strong moral voice being increasingly heard in Western Europe nowadays then the intentional breeding from flawed stock is going to receive a more hostile response than in previous times. The general public is gradually getting to understand the emotional and financial penalties of short-lived, medically expensive, physically fragile dogs as pets. It is time for hybrid vigour to play a part in planned dog breeding. Who wouldn't welcome healthier dogs?

In his enlightening book, Vilmos Csanyi produces such phrases as: 'It is high time for breeders and their organizations to introduce, in their own self-interest, breeding criteria based on behaviour'; 'Homozygous stocks pay a stiff price for genetic order. Whatever the species, its variability, resistance and performance are generally below that of heterozygous stocks'; 'It is hardly possible to create a homozygous dog breed without damaging side effects.' He recommends the creation of uniform hybrids, by crossbreeding different existing breeds. But, as a scientist, he does point out that such hybrids should not be bred further. Their merit is not as breeding material, but as healthy, stable companion dogs. This is after all the main market for dogs.

Unverified Parentage

Having been a harsh critic of the KC at the end of the last century, I am heartened by some of the measures introduced by this body in the first part of the new century. They introduced in 2011 a pilot scheme that could enhance genetic diversity by allowing purebred unregistered dogs to be registered on the breed register on a case-by-case basis. I seem to recall a similar scheme forty years ago. The KC statement read: 'The move will if used enhance genetic diversity by widening breed gene pools and allowing new bloodlines to be introduced within breeds.' Allowance involves the owner certifying how the dog was obtained, and its source, then the application being supported by DNA profiling, health clearances and its phenotype being verified as representative of the breed claimed by two championship-level judges approved by the KC. One huge drawback could be inflexibility by breed judges, more interested in breed type than the breed's future. I sometimes see working collies that simply take your breath away with their soundness and especially their movement. Their blood is important to the Border Collie's future. Open-minded breeders are often the very best ones.

Importance of Disposition

Shepherds have long understood how inheritance affects their dogs and their innate working ability. Scientists have long dismissed Lamarck's theories on 'acquired characteristics', stressing the inheritance of physical traits. But epigenetics is slowly revealing the fact that the genetic legacy can be subtly altered, with temperament, experience and talent likely to be inherited too. Breeding for temperament demands a study of temperament in the chosen parents. In his enlightening book *How To Breed Dogs* (1947), the highly experienced dog breeder Leon Whitney wrote:

> Now, as every breeder knows most dogs are bought on the basis of what cute puppies they are. The buyer hardly stops to ask, 'Will it have a calm even disposition when it is grown?' Nor does the breeder usually stress disposition. Instead he brags about the wonderful champion show dogs in the pedigree – anything to sell the pup. Why can't breeders all realize that what makes dogs lastingly popular is first, disposition?

If the general public buy puppies without any regard to their likely temperament, is it at all surprising that children get bitten, breeds can get a bad name as a result and fewer sales in that breed ensue. Most 'returned' puppies are returned because of behavioural defects. Were their parents well selected? The improvement in the quality of bone and tails in the Smooth Collie is claimed to result from the importation from

Canada in 1974 of Kelbonnie Chan-El-Gina; but for me, her best effect was on temperament.

Surely the very first question any responsible parent should ask when selecting a future family pet is, 'What is the *temperament* of the parents and previous litters from this mating?' Every breeder of purebred dogs needs sales to pet homes to sell litters; who is going to recommend breeders of dogs likely to have undesirable temperaments? The biggest *single* cause of each and every breed going into rescue is their temperament. What possible solace is there in saying later, in sorrow, that it was such a cute puppy! What comfort is it to be told that the dog that bit your child had ancestors that won Crufts? Even accredited breeders are not obliged to put temperament high on their list of desired qualities. Is this the best way to promote the breeding of companion animals? Is this the best way to promote the breed you love? Is this the best way to improve the man-dog relationship? Selectivity really does matter; selecting the breeder really does matter. Selecting the right genes is the key not just to breeding but successful ownership too.

Breeders aspire to breed the perfect 'specimen' as laid down in the breed standard, but few Bernese are kept as rural farm-working dogs nowadays. The vast majority are in demand as family companions, and most live in urban, highly populated communities. Breeders must regard good temperament as the primary objective, and must ensure that biddable, predictable, and above all else, manageable temperaments abound. Bernese are indeed one of the most beautiful breeds, but without a good temperament that beauty is worthless – RELIABLE TEMPERAMENT IS EVERYTHING.

Jude Simonds, writing in *Our Dogs* (November, 1998)

Showing and Judging a Functional Dog

Judging Criteria

How should a working breed, brought in from the pastures, be exhibited and then judged? Should not the paramount desiderata be: soundness of anatomy, powerful movement, hard muscular development and alertness in the eyes. Or, bearing in mind that show dogs are unlikely to do a day's work, should judges be seeking out show points: the 'very abundant mane and frill' in the Rough Collie, the 'clean wedge of skull' in the Smooth Collie, the 'bear-like roll' in the Old English Sheepdog, the 'foxy head' in

Prize dogs in the National Dog Show at Islington, London.

The Collie Club's Show at the Westminster Aquarium, 1888.
HOLZSTICH

the Corgis and the 'great size' demanded of the Pyrenean Mountain Dog? These features may make the breed but do they make the dog? Who keeps a breed *honest*? The KC? The Breed Council? Or the judges, when awarding rosettes? The 'rosetted' dogs get bred from; that surely influences the breed more than any collection of words. Judges' decisions can have far-reaching consequences: in exhibitor expectation, in future breeding choices and in breed morphology.

Showing the Judges

Tapio Eerola, the PR officer of the World Dog Show held in Helsinki in 1998, and editor-in-chief of the Finnish Kennel Club magazine produced these enlightened words in the commemorative issue for that show:

> Dog breeders should pay careful attention to which direction they want their breed to go. If the exaggeration of specific features continues in winning dogs the heavy bone structure will get heavier and heavier, short body becomes even shorter, deep chest deeper, wide head wider and long hair longer... Although the World Dog Show is essentially a beauty competition, nothing prevents us from taking up the theme of healthy dog breeding here also.

This was highly responsible campaigning by perhaps the most impressive kennel club in the world. There should not and need not be a difference between enthusiastic dog show exhibitors and morally motivated dog owners; the pursuit of certificates need not preclude the pursuit of healthier-bred, sounder dogs. Nothing but we ourselves prevents *us* from taking up the theme of healthy dog breeding here in the UK as well.

But if you read the judges' reports on the pastoral breeds in recent years, you can soon see that all is far from well. Take the words on just one pastoral breed's showing, the Shetland Sheepdog classes, in just one year, 2011: 'I struggled to find any with the correct angle of upper arm and shoulder…the worry is that no one seems to be taking any notice and now the lack of angulation is becoming the norm. I found just seven dogs in the entry with anything like the correct conformation'; 'Construction still needs to be addressed, particularly steepness and shortness of upper arms…'; '…as always shoulder angulation still gives concern, being in some cases short and steep'; and, alarmingly, 'I would just like to say that the breeders/exhibitors seem to be concentrating more on head, expression and fullness of coat to the detriment of construction'; 'There is more to a Sheltie than a big coat and a pretty face, but there does seem to be a move towards this which is a great worry.'

Built-In Faults

In *The Shetland Sheepdog* (1958), Olwyn Gwynne-Jones recorded that: 'All too many Shelties have upright shoulders (insufficiently angulated with too short an upper arm) and straight stifles giving a characteristically wooden and stilted gait.' Half a century later the very same faults are commonplace. That alone is a commentary, first, on the breeders in this charming breed; second, on the breed elders; and third, on the system in which flawed dogs can be exhibited with the same faults, decade after decade. Is there no overseeing of breed quality in our pedigree breeds? We have breed councils, a level above the breed clubs, but do they ever take action when chronic persistent faults afflict a breed? Clearly, not in this one. There has to be, in any breed from the pastures, a sincere desire by its fanciers to keep the breed honest, to be committed out of affection for their chosen breed, to seek a working construction. Or have such faults become fashionable?!

> Sadly, the advent of dog shows has offered scope too to those who follow fashion, want to win so much that fad-favouring becomes the *'zeitgeist'* rather than type and soundness. Fads may be passing indulgences for fanciers but they so often do lasting harm to breeds.

Kennel Club's Mission

Encouraging the welfare of the recognized breeds *has* to be the underlying mission of not just the Kennel Club but every breeder, every breed club and every judge officiating at dog shows. Yet the disturbing post-show comments by judges of pastoral breeds continues each year:

Border Collies, Ch Show, 2011: 'I was disappointed to find such a large number of exhibits with obvious faults, including level bites, short upper arms, poor layback of shoulder, weak necks with no arch, short stepping and crabbing movement…'

Shetland Sheepdogs, Crufts, 2012: '…there were a number of exhibits which appeared too cobby in their appearance due to upright shoulder angulations and shortness in back, which became more apparent when asked to move…'

Bearded Collies, Ch Show, 2013: 'It's five years since I judged the breed and there hasn't been a great improvement… Short upper arms and forelegs seem to be quite common as well as over-angulated rears…'

The faults listed in each critique are serious ones for a pastoral breed, where anatomical soundness is all-important.

Of course, there are some top-quality dogs on the show scene; I was impressed in 2013, from the ringside, by exhibits such as Cardigan Welsh Corgi Ch Yasashiikuma Telltail Dbledare, a Canadian import, Australian Shepherd Ch Allmark Fifth Avenue and, in Ireland, the Bearded Collie Ch Firstprize-bears John FK, a Galway-based dog. But you have to judge a breed on its depth, not its top dogs. So often among show people there is a tendency to seek a regular winner as a sire for their bitch, regardless of her quality and the sire's record of throwing consistently sound progeny. Breeding good-quality dogs demands knowledge, research, informed planning and never pursuing the latest fad, fashion or over-used sire. Judges rate the exhibits in order of excellence in the ring; breeders bear all the responsibility for the exhibits that never win yet still get bred from.

In *The Complete Book of the Dog* (1922), Robert Leighton wrote:

> The Shetland Sheepdog is a sturdy, altogether admirable little dog, most attractive in appearance, and possessing all the wisdom and sagacity of his larger relative. He is in no sense a toy dog, but in all essentials a reduced replica of the big working Collie, even as the Shetland pony is a small copy of the shire horse, differing only in bulk and weight. In the south he is kept as a very engaging companion and is not expected to the work of a shepherd's dog; but he ought to be judged with an eye on his fitness for working among flocks and herds.

It's that last phrase, with its clear advice to judges, that is of the most value; this breed, just like all the others, can only survive in the Pastoral Group if it's bred to be a pastoral dog, not just casually as an urban pet – ignoring its original design, whatever the pressures of town-dwelling owners and judges following the 'fashion of the day'.

Lack of Condition

> Taking the dogs all through there was but little fault to be found in the matter of coat, though the tendency was perhaps to quantity at the expense of texture. There were also too many heads of the narrow greyhound type, with insufficient space for brains. Many of the bitches, too, were fat.
>
> J.A. Doyle in his critique on Collies at the Crystal Palace Dog Show, reported in *The Kennel Gazette* (February, 1884)

Border Collies, Ch Show, 2011:

> The founders of the BCC of GB [Border Collie Club of Great Britain] were among the group of dedicated people who worked very hard to devise a Standard that described a sound, fit, working dog and this is reflected in the fact that this Standard uses such phrases as 'impression of endurance', 'athletic body', and 'muscular hindquarters'. I struggled to find more than a handful of dogs who were in a reasonable working condition; most of them being considerably overweight and lacking in muscle tone.

Border Collies, Ch Show, 2013: 'It was noticeable that there appears to be less depth of quality in the breed than in the past… Some dogs were far too fat and this affected their movement and outline.'

Those three critiques, a century apart, indicate at once the immediate distaste for exhibitors sending unfit dogs into the show ring. Spending a day at the National Working Breeds Dog Society's 24th Group Championship Show at Malvern a decade ago left me quite shocked – by the physical condition of far too many of the exhibits. Is this not the show of the year for those breeds that were meant to *work*? I use the word 'shocked' quite deliberately because, if the breeders, the exhibitors and especially the judges are prepared to go along with this situation, there is something fundamentally wrong – with worrying possibilities for the future.

Of those who argue that such a show is just a beauty contest and the condition of the dogs an afterthought, let me ask these questions. First, when did you ever see a national beauty queen with a spare tyre and podgy limbs? Second, what is the point of having a serious hobby if you don't take it seriously,

especially if you want to win? And thirdly, if exhibits are expected to be in 'show condition', why are judges taking a different view? I was also disturbed to watch four successive classes of one breed being 'judged' without the exhibits' feet once being examined. The bite of each dog was checked and infinite care taken over the comparative assessment of the entry. But feet are *crucial* to working breeds, as stressed earlier, more important even than mouths. Why does the organization inviting the judge invite such an inadequate individual?

Importance of Definition

What is actually meant by the expression 'show condition'? The Kennel Club's *Glossary of Terms* defines condition as: 'Health as shown by the body, coat, general appearance and deportment. Denoting overall fitness.' Not brilliantly written but the last phrase is the key one. Frank Jackson, in his most useful *Dictionary of Canine Terms*, defines condition as 'quality of health evident in coat, muscle, vitality and general demeanour'. Harold Spira, in his *Canine Terminology*, describes it as: 'An animal's state of fitness or health as reflected by external appearance and behaviour. For example, muscular development…' The Breed Standards and Stud Book Sub-Committee at the KC inform me that show condition indicated an expectation of 'a dog in good health as indicated by good coat condition, good muscle tone, a bright eye and up on the feet', adding that any competent judge would know this. One thing is inescapable in the interpretation of these definitions: condition means fitness, as demonstrated in the dog's muscular state.

Why then, at the working breeds show of the year, were judges putting up dogs in poor muscular condition and quite clearly *not* fit? Is it ignorance, incompetence or indifference? Some of the judges I watched simply did not know soft muscle from hard and seemed incapable of detecting the absence of muscular development. I shudder to think where this will lead us! Judging livestock is essentially a subjective skill based on what *you* see in the entry, *not* what the exhibitor wants you to see. Rather than a reaction to the animal before you, it is more a conscious action to relate the animal presented to you in the ring to the *beau idéal* for that particular breed.

Undesirable Impression

If we are going to accept unfit exhibits lacking muscular development as challenge certificate material, then novice exhibitors are being given a wholly undesirable impression and standards have already become unacceptably low. We are in effect betraying the work of the skilful pioneer breeders who handed these fine breeds down to us. That apart, where is the pride of the breeders, owners and handlers concerned? Who admires a puny, unfit, under-developed dog or an obese, flabby one? These breeds were designed to work! What sort of encouragement is this to those admirable exhibitors who spent hours getting their dogs into real show condition?

In his book *All About the Bull Terrier* (1973), the much-missed Tom Horner (an excellent judge of pastoral and working breeds) recorded: 'A wise breeder puts on show only his best stock and presents them in the peak of condition, physically fit, clean and trained to show off their points.' Are we losing our way as we lose our most experienced, most knowledgeable, most informed judges? There were not many dogs at that show at Malvern in mid-July in the peak of condition. There were far too many demonstrably not physically fit. Some of these were actually favoured by the judges. If this is the case at a show of this standing, where will it all end – with prizes for fat dog of the day?

In his informative *The Practical Guide to Showing Dogs* (1956), Captain Portman-Graham wrote:

> The fact that a dog is structurally sound is not in itself sufficient to ensure that it will always win at shows. It is of paramount importance that it must be…at the highest standard of condition. Perhaps one of the biggest advantages which dog showing confers on the dog as an animal is the care which must be bestowed upon it.

If unfit dogs with poor muscular condition can win at dog shows, then the whole argument that such shows improve dogs is totally destroyed. Dogs that are inadequately exercised and merely wheeled out for the next show can be so easily identified by any competent judge and quickly thrown out of the ring that such an insidious practice, both for dogs and the dog game, can be ended. Are our current crop of judges up to this?

Rough Collies on parade: Bath Dog Show, 2013.

Aussie Shepherds in the ring: Bath Dog Show, 2013.

A line-up of Pyrenean Mountain Dogs.

Bearded Collies being prepared for the class judge.

Appreciating Appearance

The esteemed Portman-Graham went on to write:

> …exercise is a vital consideration in maintaining any breed of show dog in bloom, health and vigour… When one watches the beautiful muscles of a race-horse one sees a similarity between a dog's muscles which have been developed correctly and naturally, and ripple in movement. Yet there is evidence of lack of muscular tone and development in many show breeds today.

He would not have liked the rings at the championship dog shows nowadays. Surely such a show should be didactic not merely epideictic; in other words it has a role in teaching those wanting to learn, not just being conducted literally for show. A dog show, properly conducted, should attract exhibitors, not exhibitionists.

What are the reports from other shows producing on this theme? Here are extracts from some: Bearded Collie dogs: 'So many dogs were lacking in muscle tone – does no one exercise their dogs anymore?'; Rottweiler bitches: 'A Rottweiler is classed as a herding breed, they are supposed to herd cattle not look like them…'; Rough Collie bitches (at Crufts): 'But I was faced with many, very fat, cloddy shaped bitches, who because of the fatness…moved so badly'. I would go further than the last judge and state that surplus flesh can only do harm. Nowadays we are bombarded with verbal and written instructions from a host of nutritionists and crafty manufacturers at shows yet I see more fat dogs these days than ever before. We all know that an overweight dog is an unhealthy dog. If exhibitors produce unhealthy dogs in the ring then every judge has a duty to point this out and decline entry to such exhibits. If a judge does not take this course of action, then a complaint should be made to the KC. This wholly undesirable situation in which unfit, unhealthy dogs are allowed in show rings simply cannot be condoned.

Those who exhibit dogs in a show ring have a distinct role in demonstrating to the public what the pedigree breeds should look like when presented, in *show condition*, to the judge. Their dogs should be exemplars of cosmetic excellence. The public as spectators, and novices as students, should not only admire what they see in the ring but be guided by the standards there. If an exhibit needs a good bath, it should, in rugby league parlance, be sent for an 'early bath'. If its claws need cutting, its teeth need cleaning, its coat needs unmatting and its eyes and ears need a thorough wipe, then the exhibit is not ready for its class and should be banished until it is. Soft-muscled and overweight dogs, however, pose a much more important, more long-term problem.

Killing by Kindness
Writing in the summer 1995 number of *You and Your Vet*, Simon Wolfensohn, a vet worth heeding, recorded that three out of every ten pet animals are overweight and that more pets are killed by misplaced kindness than are starved. He identified the concomitant health problems: fatty deposits around the heart, fat damage to the liver, weakness of muscles caused by fat deposits, diabetes and even arthritis because of the increased burden on the joints. He cited the cases of a Bouvier des Flandres that weighed 132lb (the weight of two Bouviers on one set of legs) and of a German pointer of 95lb, roughly twice her desired weight.

If you purchase an expensive pedigree dog, why try to feed it to death? If you spend time and money breeding and exhibiting pedigree dogs, why frustrate yourself by putting dogs in the ring that cannot win? I should hastily add '*should* not win', for the judge makes this differentiation. Ninety years ago, Theo Marples, writing in his *Prize Dogs,* put the condition of a dog in the ring ahead of its ability to 'show'. He also wrote, 'It is always best not to show a dog in bad condition, even although he may be entered for a show. Many a good dog has met defeat and tarnished his reputation by being exhibited in indifferent condition.' I see dogs 'in indifferent condition' being presented to the judge at most of the shows I go to. What folly! Some of the owners of such dogs moan later about the standard of the judging when their dogs fail to gain a place. Winning is all about the pursuit of excellence, not just turning up on the day.

Are soft-muscled, overweight exhibits now actually becoming *acceptable* at shows? If so, then we have not only too many incompetent judges but a potential disaster on our hands. For, if, as is claimed, the improvement of dogs is the Kennel Club's mandate and dog shows are the vehicle for this, then permitting soft-muscled, overweight dogs even to enter the ring substantially undermines this claim. Pedigree dog shows, and Pastoral and Working Breed shows in particular, *must* demonstrate to the dog-owning public what each breed should look like in *peak* condition. If this is not happening, then the whole credibility of pedigree dog breeding is put at risk. There is now an urgent need for us to exercise our minds as well as our dogs.

Damned by Judges
At the 2005 Crufts, this judge's comment was made on Pyrenean Mountain Dogs: 'There was a total lack of condition in some dogs, many were grossly overweight, so obvious when moving and they paid the penalty.' Those last four words are important. What really is the sense in exhibiting a good dog when its condition ensures that it can't win? Eight years later, the 2013 Crufts judge reported on Rough Collies (dogs): '...there is still problems [sic] with movement and weak pasterns but I do believe this is environmental not hereditary'. In other words the dogs were insufficiently exercised and out of condition. At Crufts in 2011, the Collie judges found, in Smooths, a 'lack of muscle-tone and conditioning on quite a number of exhibits', and in Roughs: 'I found bad movement in a few of the classes. A Rough Collie should be able to move with drive...' If the judge knows that basic fact, why don't the exhibitors? At this same show, the Old English Sheepdog judge observed that:

> Movement is a concern as many cannot move soundly and with drive; cow-hocked can also be seen on the move and standing. We are getting quite a few dogs that have little or no muscle on the rear thighs. This breed should be able to work all day; many would not last for long free running.

What a damning comment at our premier show where dogs have to qualify to compete there.

For comments like this to be passed by top judges on top exhibits is alarming. The Kennel Club tell us that this canine showcase displays 'the best of the very best'. How can the flab be fought when our top show is for unfit dogs and our leading animal charity has it in for fit dogs? The Kennel Club could lead the way by advising judges to omit from their deliberations any exhibit not in show condition, with obesity a disqualifying fault. In his admirable *The Practical Guide to Showing Dogs* (1956), Captain Portman-Graham wrote: 'I am convinced that in pre-war days any favourable comments passed on my dogs' fronts could be attributed to the systematic special exercises they were given in order to develop their muscles naturally…!'

The writer was clearly dedicated to the improvement of his dogs; his past work should now be overtly supported by the Kennel Club with a clear statement on overweight exhibits at shows licensed by them. It is not good enough to hide behind judges, the top body in the world of purebred dogs should set out its stall. Under-exercised, overweight dogs should not even be considered by show-ring judges. This would have an enormous effect on exhibitors and do an enormous amount of good for the healthier dog movement. With fat dogs appearing at Crufts, how do we campaign against the most widespread threat to dogs – obesity? Appeal to the dog food manufacturers? I don't think so. Appeal to the owners? Unrewarding, in my experience. Killing by kindness is not an emotive issue; it is probably condoned by the morally vain. Involve the veterinary profession? Not if the food being sold in so many surgeries these days is anything to go by. Educate the future generations? They are struggling with obesity themselves if the high street is any indicator.

In our allegedly more compassionate society, when, in the distant future, any dog capable of heeling, herding or guarding has become redundant and working dogs are unemployed, how will anyone know what a fit dog actually looks like? At the moment few judges, and even fewer exhibitors, at shows seem to know what hard condition, muscular development and sound movement really is. The link between the three escapes them. I once thought that shamelessness was the reason behind unfit dogs in the ring; now it is probably more due to ignorance. One day soon it will due to innocence; no one will know what a really fit dog looks like. This is very bad news for the domestic dog.

Obesity Campaign

One of my great joys in life is to see a working dog in action, coat gleaming, muscles rippling, eyes bright and feet tight. For me a beautiful dog is not one standing but one moving. A supremely fit, soundly constructed dog puts little stress on its joints, expends energy economically and performs highly efficiently in its locomotion. It makes less demand on its heart and lungs. It enjoys a higher quality of life and a longer life. A well-exercised dog usually means a well-exercised owner, an additional benefit. Overuse of the car may account for packed doctors' waiting rooms; it is becoming a cause of crowded vets' waiting rooms too.

But we all have apart to play in any campaign against canine obesity. Writers can extol fitness and condemn fatness. Vets can advise on diet, whatever the loss in turnover. Food manufacturers can be lobbied by the dog press to promote healthier eating. The Kennel Club could give the highest priority to show condition and make obesity a disqualifying fault. Judges could throw overweight exhibits out of the ring. Any self-respecting sheepdog trial judge would react strongly if a fat collie was offered for his consideration. Conformation dog shows sprang from hound judging at Agricultural Livestock Shows and should honour that heritage.

A more affluent society should mean better cared for pets, not under-exercised, overfed, shorter-lived ones. Just as the sporting dog is under unprecedented threat from the morally vain, so is the domestic pet from unenlightened owners who need waking up.

Callous, selfish, thoughtless dog owners like that don't deserve the loyalty and selfless companionship of a dog. It is that kind of unfeeling, indirect cruelty that has to be countered. If hard-muscled, super-fit Border Collies are not admired, if the entry at the showcase of Crufts happily displays obesity and the owners of fat pets are not condemned, we are undermining all the work of our predecessors in handing on superlative animals for our care. We should be eternally grateful, in this mean and nasty world, that we have the well-being of such admirable creatures as dogs available to us at all. It is perhaps a matter of honour. In times when the old expression 'as fat as a butcher's dog' has been craftily recast as 'as fit as a butcher's dog', we should ensure that we at least know the difference. Fit must *never* be replaced by fat!

The Task of the Judges

Competition should bring out the best dog at a dog show but can often bring out the worst in people. Since the first conformation dog show the task of the dog show judge has not always been straightforward; their comments have sometimes been deservedly hard-hitting but this can have enhanced value for the breed as a whole, even if some exhibitors prefer anodyne critiques, damning with faint praise. The range of judges' comments are indicated in these quotes:

> However beautiful we may breed our Collies, let us always bear in mind that they are Sheepdogs, a working breed, and let us resist the efforts of the lucre-led crew who seek to reduce the Collie to the level of a fancy breed.
>
> George R. Krehl reporting on the 1893 Kennel Club
> Show in *The Kennel Gazette* (November 1893)

> Much more dangerous than the deliberately dishonest judge, because much more numerous, is the judge who lacks complete confidence in his own opinion, who is afraid of offending somebody, who hesitates to put a big winner down, or an unknown up, for fear his placings will incur hostile criticism, who gets 'cold feet' as soon as he enters the ring, who goes home and lies awake half the night pondering over all the mistakes he thinks he may have made.
>
> Charles Lister-Kaye, *The Welsh Corgi* (1968)

> From their institution at Newcastle in 1858 there has been a growing feeling of dissatisfaction with the awards of the judges. Animals which have been successful under one set of judges in obtaining a first prize, have been altogether overlooked by another, not even obtaining a commendation, though in equally good condition at both places, and often with the same or nearly the same competitors.

No, these last words were not written this year by a disappointed exhibitor at Crufts. They were written by the esteemed 'Stonehenge' in his *Dogs of the British Isles* in 1878. He went on to state that single

judging requires 'some length of education' and to recommend a scale of points for each breed being judged.

> Not many shows can afford the expense of engaging a sufficient number of judges to enable each class to be judged by a gentleman who is qualified to do so, and there are very few judges who are able to deal fairly by all breeds. The unfortunate result of this is that many varieties are unsatisfactorily placed time after time…

The view of a disgruntled Bloodhound breeder at Crufts last year? No, the words of Vero Shaw in *The Illustrated Book of the Dog* (1879). He went on to disparage judging to a scale of points, stating that 'when dogs are judged by points, one notoriously defective in one portion of its anatomy can be awarded a prize…' He overlooked, of course, the ability then for 'negative' points to be awarded.

Too Loose a System

Writing in his *British Dogs* (1888), Hugh Dalziel recalls being told by S.E. Shirley, when president of the Kennel Club, that 'life's too short for the practice of judging by points'. This surprised Dalziel as it came from a man who had 'most precisely laid down the absolute numerical value of each point in the breed of Collie' in an article. Dalziel himself argued that each judge was an instructor, with every award he makes acting as a lesson. I think that that is very apt. He supported judging to a scale of points, describing any other system as 'too loose'. There is probably some truth in that. In his valuable three-volume work, *British Dogs*, Dalziel perceptively noted: 'What should be indelibly fixed on the minds of all concerned is that the judge's influence does not end, but really begins, with the distribution of prizes…' We have all seen the produce of unworthy champions and the long-term harm done in breeds by newcomers chasing prize-winning but poor-quality stock.

Henry Webb, in his quaintly titled *Dogs: their points, whims, instincts and peculiarities* (1882), made a key point on judges when he wrote that exhibitors should remember 'that by entering their dogs for competition they tacitly approve the appointment of the judges'. He is right – what really is the point of showing your dog under a judge you don't respect? If he places your dog, do you withdraw?

In his *Prize Dogs*, written a century ago, Theo Marples commented that 'the prevailing mistake which exhibitors make is thinking that their geese are swans, or, in other words, thinking their dogs better than they really are.' It is this fundamental flaw which not only brings dogs into the ring that have no right to be there but also leads to the quite shocking unsporting behaviour which we have all witnessed at shows.

This collection of quotes and comments from the early days of dog shows brings our contemporary talking points into perspective. So often over the years we seek remedy in systems and procedures when again and again it is human frailty causing the difficulty. We must acknowledge that the desire to win brings out the darker side of human nature, that corruption is always lurking when making

money is an aim but that human fallibility is proportionately more likely to lead to miscalculation than misdeed. There will always be more incompetent judges than corrupt ones. Removing the corrupt ones depends on the moral standards of those who become aware of it; reducing incompetence is the bigger problem.

Training Value
In *The Practical Guide to Showing Dogs* (1956), Captain Portman-Graham wrote:

> It has for some time been advocated that a training system would be beneficial, whereby a new judge

Winning Tervueren.

Winning Groenendael.

Winning Malinois.

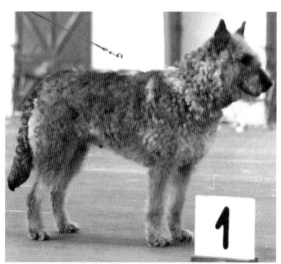

Winning Laekenois.

could officiate with a senior one, making his own unofficial awards for comparison later with the official ones, with discussion on his placings and advice given by the responsible judge. The time has come for this sound plan to be put into operation.

More than fifty years on, this 'sound plan' might find some supporters. In his book *The Dog Business* (1960), Douglas Appleton wrote that, 'There are dishonest judges; there are incompetent judges. Actually both are dishonest, for there is no honour in accepting a job you are unfit to do.' I don't think I can improve on that!

In the September 2013 issue of *Dog World*, the Letter of the Week award went to reader Carol Ogborn, and rightly so, for it made some salient points. Carol, dismayed by a KC Breed Watch Update, wrote:

> The reason for this is the inadequacy of more than 50 per cent of judges to correctly identify the breed in front of them, to recognize a lame dog when they see it and to withhold placings from dogs with serious faults… Until judges can meet a recognized, tested minimum standard of judging, stop placing lame dogs and can be relied on to recognize all breeds in front of them, giving them the right to make comments on breed health is tantamount to encouraging a breed's demise.

She threatened to give up showing if judges were given increased power from such an ignorant knowledge base. Strong comments such as these and from such a source really do deserve being listened to.

I have been attending dog shows since 1947, when I worked as a teenaged kennel-boy for my local vet. I have watched the most famous British dog show judges of the last fifty years in action. At various times I have been surprised to see a whole series of classes completed at championship shows without the judge once examining the feet of any exhibit. Is that not incompetence? I have watched judges 'go over', with their hands the anatomies of pastoral and sporting dogs and then put up a dog with soft muscles. A sheepdog, gundog, hound or terrier *must* have hard muscles to be in show condition. There is little point in placing hands on dogs if you don't know soft muscle from hard. Hard muscle apart, judges face a whole range of other dilemmas; the four varieties of the Belgian Shepherd Dog, once considered as four separate breeds, but sharing the same Standard apart from coat texture and colour, could each produce a winner: best dog, best bitch, best puppy and best veteran, in a class for Best of Breed. Soft muscle is exposed in the shorter-haired varieties but concealed in the longer-haired varieties without a competent hands-on examination – is this always given?

Show-Ring Discipline
I have observed dogs being strung up on nylon cord collars to mask faulty movement. We all see the wholly undesirable habit in the ring of stuffing food in the dog's mouth so that it looks expectant and therefore alert. I saw a Tibetan Mastiff (a breed I admire) being fed constantly to deter it from attacking the other exhibits or snapping at the judge.

Three versions of the Collie head.

Such a dog should have been thrown out of the ring. But the 'highly rated' judge elected not just to ignore this deceit but refrained from inspecting the dog's mouth too. Dogs must *never* be fed in the show ring and should always be shown on a loose lead so that they reveal themselves as they are. These are far more important matters than double handling will ever be.

Writing in *Dog World* in December 1994, Audrey Dallison, a highly experienced exhibitor, was advocating the appointment of 'neutral official observers to watch judges as a whole, and new judges in particular'. I rather like that idea. I have seen judges of high repute award prizes to a Pointer with a Hackney action, a cow-hocked Irish Wolfhound, a Bloodhound quite shockingly out at elbow, a Mastiff so unsound in construction it could get no power from its rear end and an endless number of dogs placed that were in clear breach of their own Breed Standard. Such faults are scarcely a matter of opinion or subjective judgement. There are far too many incompetent judges; why should they not be judged? There are judges too who I know disapprove of, say, the head bestowed on the Collie by the show-ring fraternity but feel they have to judge what is before them; what truly is the *classic* head type of the Scottish Collie?

Minimum Standard

Hound-show judging at shows such as Peterborough and Honiton is conducted with *two* judges in the ring, who discuss the entry before them. This must increase competence, reduce corruption and encourage confidence. Conformation and movement are judged, just as in KC-licensed shows. Masters of Foxhounds *do* care what their hounds look like. Newton Rycroft, a greatly respected authority on working scenthounds has written:

> Conformation will always be important, but perhaps we look at this importance from the wrong angle. What we need I think is not so much fantastic physical beauty, which may or may not have nose and voice, but a certain standard of working conformation BELOW which hounds must not fall.

At KC dog shows we regularly see exhibits that fall below a certain standard or breach their own Breed Standard. How often are such entries thrown out of the ring? The judge out of misguided kindness goes through the motions with such dogs and surprise, surprise, the dog is entered for another show. The pursuit of excellence is a ruthless business, not a game show in which everyone has to win something to go home happy. It is unwise to judge on faults; it is cruel to a breed to overlook blatant faults. Breed Standards often state 'the seriousness with which the fault should be regarded should be in exact proportion to its degree', but how can that be applied in particular? What are the *disqualifying* faults?

There would be sense in each Breed Standard stipulating a minimum standard of 'working conformation' and listing faults which disqualify. This may be more valuable in sporting and working breeds, where functional capability must always be kept in mind. The old system of 'negative' points might have relevance in this context. Standards of judging have deteriorated and it is foolish to press on regardless. Winning at dog shows so often determines the quality of future stock and is therefore vital for the good of pedigree breeds. Hugh Dalziel was right a hundred years ago when he wrote that the judge's influence really begins – not ends – with the awarding of prizes and that each judge is an instructor. Having two judges in the ring would undoubtedly go a long way in countering allegations of bias or corruption. Having random anonymous monitoring of judges in addition could prevent Breed Standards from being overlooked, ignored or defied. If judges are not themselves judged, they are being given free licence to indulge their personal whims. Judging to a scale of points, as one element – not the only one – in placing dogs, would bring a more *objective* dimension to decision-making. The awarding of negative points would punish faults without encouraging judging on faults.

Avoiding Smugness

I agree with 'Stonehenge' that single judging requires some 'length of education'. Unless we introduce training and examinations for judges then frankly we have not progressed in the last hundred years. Judging entirely by eye and experience alone would not be acceptable in other walks of life and I do not see why judges at dog shows should be a special case. Judging standards and well-worded Breed Standards represent two of the most important aspects of the

Kennel Club's work. That body has a job on its hands now if dog shows are to withstand scrutiny and retain exhibitor confidence. There is an unhealthy, unjustified and wholly undesirable smugness about judging at dog shows in the United Kingdom. It is time for change. It is time for judges to be judged too.

It was good to read in the KC's Annual Report of 2011/12 that the KC believes that dog show judges have a crucial role to play in improving the health and welfare of dogs. Judges are required to reward only healthy dogs in the show ring and have been given the authority to remove any dog from the ring on visible health grounds, as they see fit. For some breeds, official observers are appointed to assess judging to ensure that judges comply with these requirements. Judges also play an essential part in the KC's online Breed Watch scheme, under which they are asked to highlight any topical issues of concern within breeds for the attention of other judges due to judge that breed. Concerns voiced have to be discussed with the breed clubs and councils by way of the breed health co-ordinators before being placed on Breed Watch.

Having served on a breed committee for some years, I know that this whole scheme will rely for its success on the calibre of the people on the relevant committee. Committees are never dynamic and rarely inspired by fresh initiatives. They normally favour the status quo and a cosy life; showing dogs is their top priority, not health issues. If breeds, listed as 'vulnerable' by the KC because of their anatomical exaggerations/deficiencies, are to be better bred, remedial action starts in the ring with alert and honest judges discarding unsound exhibits but beyond that relies on breeders in each breed listed to put the breed's house in order, with the breed club and the breed council taking a pro-active interest not a casual passing glance, as so often the case in the past. I have argued for some years for each breed council to co-opt a geneticist into their ranks; all exaggerations have to be *bred out*, not talked out!

Judge's Dilemma

I have every sympathy, however, for an all-rounder judge, not a breed specialist, when faced with a GSD in the ring displaying a curvature of the spine, a noticeable falling-away at the croup and one rear pastern resting wholly on the ground, as weirdly accepted as desirable in this once-impressive breed. Does this judge dispatch the exhibit from the ring as 'unsound' (as it clearly is) or condone misguided fashion at the expense of the breed's future? The dog could be a champion! It would have been bred and trained to 'stand' in the ring in this entirely unnatural posture, one not normal for any other breed and not part of this breed's past, as every archive image reveals. It is surely doubly regrettable when a breed is handicapped by its own fanciers. When such a dog appears at Crufts, the general public see on TV

The GSD (Alsatian) of the 1990s.

The Alsatian (Deutsche Schäferhund) in Holland, 1922.

a handicapped dog, with the handicaps approved indirectly by the KC. Situations such as this simply *have to be stopped*!

The Value of Crufts – and its False Reputation

At the end of the second week in March, the canine clans come together, eager to compete for cups at Crufts, regarded across the nation as *the* dog show for the exhibition of pedigree dogs. Television cameras will dwell on the grave and protracted deliberations of the appointed judges. Fawning commentators will speculate enthusiastically on the judges' putative thought processes, overlooking their contrived self-importance. Breed fanciers will wait impatiently for their weighty decisions – so vital in future breeding programmes, dog trading and dog food advertising. Nearby, row upon row of benched dogs, bored out of their minds, will be waiting even more impatiently, too loyal to question the wisdom of man in conducting such a bizarre activity. Sadly the word bizarre might also be applied to many of the judges' placements! For these judges, at the most prestigious dog show in Europe, have no measurable qualifications to carry out their appointed task and make their decisions wholly subjectively.

I believe that it is entirely fair to say that the officially appointed judges at Kennel Club-licensed dog shows are chosen by their chums, never comprehensively trained or closely monitored, never required to justify their selections – and are placing dogs, with worrying regularity, that actually breach the blueprint for that breed. They quite often judge dogs bred by them; the weaker of them put up well-known winners for fear of being criticized. Judges have also long been accused of favouring entries by members of the committee behind that particular show. As long ago as 1871, at the major show of that year, adverse comment was made on the fact that committee members won nearly a quarter of the prize money. Satirists may lampoon ice-skating judges who raise scoreboards illustrating their marking, but dog show judges are not even required to award marks; they have become all but unchallengeable.

Precision by Points

In the early part of the last century, however, the word picture for each breed of dog or breed standard was accompanied by a scale of points. This allowed physical features to be judged against an allocated number of points. In this way, the Rough Collie could be awarded up to 10 points for the neck and shoulders but as many as 20 points for the coat, whilst other points could vary (for example, up to 10 points for the hindquarters and 15 for the head and expression). The Old English Sheepdog could be awarded up to

20 points for body, loins and hindquarters and only 15 for coat and 5 for head. The Alsatian Wolfdog could get up to 20 points for 'nature and expression', but only 7 for each of hind and forequarters. Every dog could therefore be rated out of 100 points against the same scale of points as rival entries in that breed. Some breeds could not be 'commended' unless the exhibit scored over 60. Some could have points deducted for undesirable features such as white nails, toes and feet (minus 10 points). Some could attract up to 95 'negative' points, at least one 100! Theoretically such a breed could score zero. The allocation of points to physical features can be questioned, but at least a judge had to be precise in the decisions taken on the day.

'Wouldn't work at Crufts!' today's pedigree dog fanciers might claim. But what do the judges at that most prestigious of shows think of the dogs arrayed before them, dogs that have had to qualify under other KC-approved judges if they are to appear there? Here are some of the judges' comments from Crufts shows: Cardigan Corgis (1995) – '…too many lack the drive and follow through that are a must in the working dog. They would not last on the hill pastures which they used to work and the old farmers would give them short shrift'; Norwegian Buhunds (1995) – 'It saddens me to see this happen to a breed I have owned and loved for the last twenty years.'

Such comments are not unusual. These are some judges' remarks from the year before: Bearded Collies – 'I was deeply disappointed with the quality in the lower classes'; Old English Sheepdogs – 'Overall the quality was poor.' In 2008, the Pembroke Corgi judge wrote: '…I feel the breed is at a low point. Twenty years ago, one could easily end up with a line-up of even type, classically headed Pembrokes… Heads now vary enormously.' The Smooth Collie judge wrote: 'Movement in general was not as I would have wished. There were very few with the correct bend of stifle, thus inhibiting their hind action. A couple exhibited a high-stepping front action, and very few produced the graceful flowing action required…' The Bouvier des Flandres judge wrote: 'Main fault was poor movement, caused often by upright shoulders and some were moving too close behind.'

Lack of Quality in Depth
The next year, 2009, the Australian Shepherd judge wrote: 'Many dogs were out of condition with little muscle tone and rather overweight.' A year later, in 2010, the Bernese Mountain Dog judge wrote: 'Placements were lost due to poor movement, incorrect set and carriage of the tail, too much length in the loin region and confusion between substance and carrying too much weight.' The Border Collie judge warned: '…breeders should address movement as in quite a number of exhibits movement was not good'. The Rough Collie judge reported that: 'Unfortunately the quality in depth was sadly lacking in some classes… I was sad to see one or two that looked completely alien and totally lacking in breed type.' Crufts is the only dog show in which the entry has first to qualify! The judge of Old English Sheepdogs at this show commented: '…quite a few had light eyes, poor underjaws, poorer constructed rears to the point of very little deviation from thigh to hocks… Toplines in many I found totally wrong.' Even sadder was this judge's closing comment in this critique: 'I am led to believe that some exhibitors were complaining that I moved the dogs too much; surely this can't be right, after all, this breed was bred to drive sheep to the market many miles away…'

A Beardie of today being prepared for the Crufts ring.

Australian Cattle Dogs – understandably bored at Crufts.

In 2011, the Briards judge wrote: 'Unfortunately, such movement is not often seen these days, with short stepping strides and shuffling rear action prevailing. This is a result of poorer construction than desired.' The Old English Sheepdog judge commented: 'Movement is a concern as many cannot move soundly and with drive, cow-hocked can also be seen on the move and standing. We are getting quite a few dogs that have little or no muscle on the rear thighs. This breed should be able to work all day, many would not last for long free running.' The Shetland Sheepdog judge noted: '…there were very few dogs who pushed from their hocks…' The Pyrenean Mountain Dog judge wrote: '…the general impression from a lot of the entry was of dogs moving too close behind and despite standing straight at the front, many seemed to move too wide or cross their front legs when coming towards me…let's hope we can improve movement in the coming years.' The Bernese Mountain Dog judge wrote: 'Upper arms are a source of concern, several could have been longer and some better angulated and some fore-chests lacked development while some toplines could have been straighter and firmer.' All these exhibits had to qualify for Crufts under KC-appointed judges. Is the system producing sound dogs?

Crufts Dogs Bred From
In 2012 the Australian Shepherd judge noted: 'A couple of numerically large classes did lack depth of quality and the real type that gives this breed its very definite identity.' One of the German Shepherd Dog entry tried to bite the judge and was banished from the ring. The Finnish Lapphund judge wrote: 'Mouths in some dogs were a major issue, with overshot, undershot and uneven bites – and these were not youngsters whose mouths may improve as they get older. I feel that breeders must look more deeply into the background of their breeding stock…' The Shetland Sheepdog judge stated: '…there were a number of exhibits which appeared too cobby due to upright shoulder angulations and shortness in back, which was made more apparent when asked to move…' Then in 2013, the judge of the Rough Collies (dogs) reported: '…there are still problems with movement and weak pasterns but I do believe this is environmental not hereditary'. So that's all right then! The dogs that qualify for Crufts get bred from. Owners boast when their dog appears at Crufts.

Of course there are plenty of judges' critiques full of praise for all breeds. But if there are doubts about the quality of the judges as assessors, can such praise withstand scrutiny? The sooner the Kennel Club introduces truly comprehensive training for dog show judges, with really testing examinations to confirm this training, the better for quality control at our dog shows and, more importantly, for quality assurance in our future pedigree stock. Would a marking system based on a scale of points produce a more accountable, much more precise measurement of an exhibit's worth – or just slow down the judging? If the present mark-less routine is not producing sound dogs, in the correct order of merit, should it not be rethought?

Qualifying the Judges
I understand that in Japan, in order to judge one breed, the Shiba Inu, it is necessary to be a member of the breed chapter for five years, a judge's assistant for at least two years, a judge's trainee for at least three years, to attend the judge's course at least twice *and* pass an examination. Even then an indefinite further period has to be served as an Associate Judge before fully qualifying. Small wonder that the specimens of this breed that I see at shows seem to be a great credit to their breeders, their breed and to their country of origin.

Dissatisfaction with the ability of dog show judges is not new, as these words illustrate: 'The general public, those who take any interest in dogs, are confident that the actual judging for Best in Show may be a farce. They feel, in the first place, that the person appointed is quite often not qualified to make the decision…' No, these are not the words of an anti-dog show journalist or a bitter exhibitor with an unplaced entry. They are the words of R.H. Smythe, a veterinary surgeon who bred, reared and exhibited dogs of almost every known breed, from his much-respected book *Judging Dogs*. The fact that it was written forty years ago gives it even more validity, for few would disagree that dog show judges were far better then.

As a counter to this, it could be argued that this is but one comment on the imprecise art of judging dogs on their appearance, made some time ago. However, for years there has been sustained discontent over how judges at dog shows are appointed and whether they should be formally trained and pass examinations for such a task. There are formal qualifications for judges on offer, but the Kennel Club has so far declined to develop them to the highest level justified by their role in the pedigree dog world – and their effect on dog breeding. In the United States, there is a Senior Conformation Judges Association Education Institute that runs very comprehensive courses even for senior American Kennel Club judges. Our own Kennel Club heard over thirty complaints against judges approved by them in just one year; seventeen of them alleged lack of knowledge or, worse, disregard of the written breed blueprint or standard.

In 1951, in *Our Dogs*, Harry Underwood, who showed his first dog in 1926, responding to a piece in an earlier issue that had labelled the Rough Collies in the ring at that time 'fluffy-stuffies' because of their profuse coats and short necks, wrote:

What are they doing to our lovely breed?… I spoke to a couple with a young dog recently; 'he's never been out of the cards' [ie unplaced in the ring], they said. Head-on, he didn't look too bad. But, side-elevation, what a bag of faults! His under-jaw was appalling, deep through the skull and as if his neck had been cut out and the head stuck on the body… Those hindquarters! A short time on the Fells and he

would have needed a mountain rescue team to get him home!

This is more a comment on the judges who had rewarded this dog than on the dog itself. Half a century later, are we any better at judging?

Breadth of Knowledge
Considerable concern was expressed in 1993 when a judge was approved by the Kennel Club to judge every single breed for which KC challenge certificates were then on offer, that is, 137 different breeds. A number of distinguished breed specialists have expressed worries over whether one person could, with the competence needed, judge across such a wide variety of size, shape, texture of coat, colour, head, gait and breed idiosyncrasies. How many hound-show judges would be happy to judge Toy breeds? How many lurcher and terrier judges would feel competent to judge Bulldogs and Bloodhounds? Would a gundog field trial judge be approved to officiate at a sheepdog trial? This is not the way to bolster confidence in dog show judges.

In the October 1994 issue of *The Kennel Gazette*, an executive of the Kennel Club, rather strangely, wrote:

Why do the adherents of our sport [sic] want to judge?… Perhaps those seeking these positions should examine their motives… But surely the whole show scene is basically dedicated to the improvement of dogs, the best stock for the future of breeds being identified by competent, adequately trained and selected judges. Is their motivation linked to the improvement of dogs? That is the question that must be asked.

Surely that is a question the Kennel Club must ask itself! Do they not realize that *they* are in charge? What are *their* plans for producing 'competent and adequately trained judges'? The Kennel Club once approved 738 new judges in one year, solely on recommendation. Is this really the best way to improve dogs and ensure that the best stock is identified for future breeding programmes?

It is abundantly clear from the critiques of the Crufts judges themselves that poor-quality dogs are qualifying for that top event. It is equally clear that behind the glitz and glamour of Crufts itself lies a sham: unqualified judges pompously deliberating over unimpressive exhibits. How on earth can such a situation possibly contribute to the improvement of pedigree dogs? The man in the street is being misled and television journalists are promoting that deceit.

Bishop William Stubbs, writing in the nineteenth century, gave us these apt lines: 'What cause for judgments so malign? A brief reflection solves the mystery...' A very brief reflection reveals the cause of malign judgments in the rings at pedigree dog shows: untrained, unqualified, unsupervised judges acting out a charade with far too many unworthy entries. Further reflection suggests obvious remedies: a marking system is called for – as our knowledgeable ancestors decreed; examinations for judges are urgently needed and basic training simply must be introduced before any tyro judge is let loose. It is

not unknown for a Crufts winner to sire 100 litters, perhaps 500 pups. If the comments of last decade of Crufts judges are anything to go by, don't touch one with a barge pole. At least the quality of the dog food goes up every year!

Judgemental Decisions

I have known men, some of them long departed, who could judge anything on four legs; they possessed a flair. If one of them, who had never judged dogs in his lifetime, were to be wafted back and put into the Corgi ring he would know nothing at all of the breed points, but I guarantee he would know unsoundness when he saw it – which is more than can be said for many of today's aspirants. He would be quick to recognize 'quality' and 'style'... How many exhibits in the ring today can really be said to boast these two indefinable attributes?

Charles Lister-Kaye, *The Welsh Corgi* (1968)

Where the pastoral dogs want to be – in the pastures: Guarding the Flock *by John Barker, 1871.*

I have written of the concern expressed in 1993 when a judge was approved by the Kennel Club to judge every single one of the breeds for which KC championship certificates were then on offer, 137 different breeds. A number of distinguished breed specialists have expressed worries over whether one person could, with the competence needed, judge across such a wide variety of size, shape, texture of coat, colour, head, gait, function and breed idiosyncrasies. But what do the judges themselves think of other judges? Here are two critiques by judges at Crufts, our premier show-dog event. Firstly: 'I was VERY disappointed in the quality... How do they qualify?'; and secondly, on a different breed: 'I did frankly wonder how some of the dogs there had even managed to win a 1st prize!... the lowering of the general quality of the hounds coming into the ring is only a long continuation of the process that respected senior all-rounders and our own experienced breed specialists have been warning us about for years...'

Head study of Beauceron; this is the classic 'herder-head' found wherever herding dogs are used.

Judging is Subjective

In a discussion document published by the Kennel Club in 1993 entitled 'The Exhibition of Dogs', it is stated that: 'Everyone is aware that judging of dogs is subjective and opinions regarding merit of a particular animal vary... It is necessary therefore to consider whether... a system of formal testing prior to a judge being passed for Championship Show Status awarding Challenge Certificates should be instituted.' Our championship shows attract 100,000 entries a year, although numbers are now falling. Crufts attracts around 20,000 'top' dogs, as well as over 80,000 visitors from some fifty countries. Its global appeal is gratifying. But behind the glitter is a clear need for a review of standards, both in dogs and judges. Clearly the association in the public mind between quality, dog show wins and Crufts itself is not justified. If you believe the dog show judges themselves there is a lack of quality in our pedigree breeds of dog, together with suspect temperament. Successful show dogs are likely to be bred from the most. The most prolific winners are extensively bred from – without any mandatory health checks being imposed on them. If the best of these is earning the kind of comments quoted above, what must the worst be like? And they are ending up in the pet market. Be careful when you are buying your next pedigree sheepdog!

CHAPTER 4
VALUING THE DOGS

Pricing Value

In *The Twentieth Century Dog* (1904), Herbert Compton quoted a contributor who wrote:

> The sheepdog trials cater for the working dog, which, by the way, is generally a nondescript cross between the Old English sheepdog, the lurcher and the collie. I myself cannot fancy a £1,000 dog working sheep! Although Ormskirk Charlie, a pure-bred rough collie, was a champion sheep-dog trialler, and Emerald Mystery, by Ormskirk Emerald, is also a first rate one; and there are others. I believe I am correct in stating that the highest price ever paid for a working field-trial sheep-dog is under £200.

Granddaughter of Alex Miller, famous Border Collie breeder, with three superlative working dogs – note the wide divergence of type.

In 2013, a Border Collie went into the record books after being sold for nearly £10,000 at auction. The previous record was £8,400 in 2012. The dog's owner, John Bell, bought him as a thirteen-week-old pup for £315; this dog was Mr Bell's third record-breaking sale in three years. Sheep farmers in the United States, where this dog was destined to work – and be bred from, no doubt – clearly realize the value of the working sheepdog to their profession.

Assessing Worth

There are just under 20,000 pastoral breed registrations each year with our KC, if you include the few breeds they choose to group as Working Group breeds despite their clear pastoral role. If each pup is worth around £500, that represents a substantial turnover, with the suddenly popular breeds vulnerable to exploitation by wallet-led breeders with little interest in quality or the welfare of the pups. The coats of Bearded Collies, Hungarian Pulis and

Two of the typical specimens of the breed that competed in the 1935 International Trials held in Scotland.

Old English Sheepdogs need regular and committed care. Border Collies can be so hyperactive and intense in attitude that they do not make good urban pets; those bred specifically for strong fly-ball energy can be too demanding for suburban families. Those bought from farms can end up with a massive work ethic but no outlet, not a good scenario for a family pet. The International Sheepdog Society (ISDS) registers several thousand dogs each year; whilst these are bred to be working dogs, many end up as pets. Their worth as a pet may be different from their value as a working dog. The good qualities in a working collie aren't exactly those expected of a companion dog and care is needed to ensure that the purchase of a pastoral dog is suitable for both owner and dog.

In her charming and beautifully illustrated *Rural Portraits – Scottish Native Farm Animals, Characters and Landscapes* of 2003, Polly Pullar wrote:

> Though I am filled with awe while watching the magnificent dogs and their handlers that win trials…it is the good old-fashioned farmyard collie that fascinates me the most. Many of these stalwarts of the farming community are often much-maligned… Many underworked dogs are far too keen…they end up rounding up everything within a mile radius of the homestead… A collie is only ever as good as its handler. But all too often this basic fact is overlooked, and the dog is shut away and tagged as useless, manic, stupid or impossible to train. Bad workmen always blame their tools.

A sheepdog with strong instinctive urges must have an outlet for such reined-in energy. The working ones have not always been wisely raised. Sheepdogs are generally seen as hardy and valued by shepherds, but a 1953 survey in Scotland revealed that at least 11 per cent were suffering from Black Tongue as a direct result of inadequate diet. These dogs were expected to run or walk 90 miles a day at lambing time and had to have protein, not just their diet of oats, if their health and stamina were to be maintained. Every 'employer' should value the 'staff'!

The relationship and the value both parties, shepherd and dog, placed on it is well summed up in this quote from W.L. Puxley's *Collies and Sheepdogs* of 1947:

> There is such an understanding between them and their masters that a shepherd will almost part with his life rather than part with his dog, while in the dog's eyes his master is probably a long dog which walks in a peculiar way. This explains the case of the shepherd who would not let his dog be taught any tricks and replied, when asked why, 'He is too fine to be made a fool of.' And though a shepherd lives what to many would be a most lonely and monotonous life, he get as much enjoyment out of it as many others obtain from a life passed in the bustle of some large town. Indeed, when such a man is prevented by age or illness from attending to his sheep he seems to lose all pleasure or interest in life, just as does his faithful dog.

Working dogs cannot always cope with idleness. Bred for work, hard work, their needs are basic but fundamental to their contentment.

The Value of Pastoral Dogs as Service Dogs

Despite being able to trace its ancestry back to the native sheep dogs of Thuringia and Wurtemberg, I believe it is fair to state that the GSD has ceased to be a pastoral dog and should now be regarded as a service dog. I believe it is also fair to state that for a century at least it was the most widely used service dog in the world. That is some tribute to the early breeders. It is not any solace to the breeders of today, however, to see that retrievers, purebred and crossbred, are replacing the GSD as guide dogs, the police in many European countries are turning towards the Belgian Malinois for their needs, with spaniels being preferred for drug, contraband and bomb-search work. The ubiquitous Border Collie, however, is emerging as the best-equipped, all-round, multi-purpose service dog, mainly because of its biddability and wide-ranging natural talent, but also through its physical robustness, which means lower maintenance costs for the user. The harm done to the GSD breed by misguided faddists is incalculable. In their important book on the breed, *The Complete German Shepherd Dog* (1983), Nem and Percy Elliott wrote:

> The breed definitely went wrong, of that there is no doubt. To get things back on an even keel, is what's

necessary, i.e: back to the balanced dog, of correct type. For some that is not enough. They wish to continue to exaggerate their breeding plans; but in the opposite direction! Consequently, there are those who wish their dogs to be shorter than normal, with sloping and raised backlines, half-starved during puppyhood so as not to be too heavy; and this is equally wrong. Those of us with the necessary experience, have to continue to try and guide the development of the breed on the right lines. I think we shall succeed, but time will tell.

This makes sad reading and I wish them and their enlightened colleagues eventual success. No farmer could afford to breed deformed dogs!

The Value of Pastoral Dog Blood

Most lurcher breeders have long accepted the value of the blood of the collie in their stock; it could be argued that to qualify as a genuine lurcher the involvement of collie blood is essential. Twenty years

TOP: *Messenger dogs billeted behind the front-line trenches in the First World War.*
SMITHFIELD SHEEPDOGS

Collie used as message-carrier in the First World War.

Two Smithfield Sheepdogs and a Smooth Collie on duty in the First World War.

BELOW LEFT: *First-aid dogs.* Petit Journal *pictorial paper, 18 April 1915.*

ago, I had two working sheepdogs, that is, unregistered Border Collies, with distinct sporting dog skills. The bitch was a natural setter; she never once gave a false point. The male dog was a remarkable marker and accomplished retriever, with a soft mouth and a willingness to go through any sort of cover. Their eagerness to work was commendable; their obedience constant; their astuteness remarkable. They did of course lack the sheer style of specialist gundogs but a more skilful trainer/handler than I could have developed them to a high standard. This combination of biddableness, cleverness and an unquenchable desire to work has led to the use of collies in a wide variety of ways in the sporting field. The renowned lurcher breeder, my namesake David Hancock, a West Midlands poultry farmer, has made the Bearded Collie × Greyhound lurcher world-famous.

Collie Blood for Deer Stalking

In his book *The Scottish Deerhound* (1892), Edwin Weston Bell summarized a report from the various deer-stalking estates of that time which covered the use of dogs on them. The extracts he prints are illuminating: Achanault Deer Forest – no deerhound ever used; Auchnashellach, collie breed – good-nosed tracker; Balmoral Deer Forest – very seldom do we

ABOVE: *Shepherd Dogs at work in the First World War.*

Fire safety Collie in the USA.

ABOVE: Deerhounds, and a collie, with a Gillie in a Highland Landscape, *1872, pencil and watercolour by James Hardy, Jnr.*

Collie × Deerhound used in the deer hunt, *late nineteenth century.*

use the staghounds – only keep them for breeding with the collie; Inverwick Forest – very few gentlemen use deerhounds nowadays in the forest – only the half-bred dogs, between the collie and retriever; Fairley Deer Forest – one collie in use now, one formerly. Deerhounds are not used in any deer forest that I know of in the north of Scotland. The best dog I ever saw for tracking a wounded stag was a cross between a retriever and a pure collie. Collie dogs, when trained young, turn out excellent trackers. Inchgrundle – Collie dogs have been chiefly used here for deer-stalking during the last twenty years. We generally find the collie more useful than the staghound.

The widespread use of the collie and the tributes paid to its prowess is astonishing, and many other estates stressed their value and sporting skills: Braemore Deer Forest – I consider a good collie as far superior to any other kind of dog for a wounded deer; Aviemore Deer Forest – three collies are at present in use… properly trained sheep dogs are the best; Mamore Forest – for tracking deer I think no dog so good as a good collie; Conaglen – we use sheepdogs here – they are more obedient and have more sense than the others; Rothiemurchus Deer Forest – good tracking collies are the best for deer-stalking; Glenartney – good collies are the best I ever saw. Twenty other estates used collies for deerstalking. Two artistic depictions of deer-stalking show the Collie in the hunting party: James Hardy's *Deerhounds with a Ghillie in a Highland Landscape* of 1872, and a hand-painted stalking scene on a Victorian cast iron centre table, after Landseer, of the third quarter of the nineteenth century. Both show how valued the Collie was in such an activity.

Extensive Tributes

Three estates used a collie-deerhound cross, one used a setter-collie cross and another chiefly used 'a collie of the grey shaggy breed', the beardie type. These extensive tributes to collie blood came from men who worked in the most testing country, in the most trying weather conditions and on a quarry never easy to stalk. The role demanded dogs that were hardy, had great stamina, immense perseverance and responded to commands often over some distance. There was not one mention in this wide-ranging estate survey of Bloodhounds, famous for their noses. The humble collie was the favoured dog. The retriever-collie cross came next. The collie-deerhound cross was clearly

used in Deerhound lines, before Deerhound to Deerhound breeding was restored.

The collie-setter cross was allegedly used by the Duke of Gordon in the development of his breed of setters. S.E. Shirley, the Flat-Coated Retriever pioneer, bred three of the most famous ancestors of the show collie – from an Irish Setter-collie cross. There is a distinct collie-look to many setters portrayed by artists in the nineteenth century. Iris Combe, in her book *Herding Dogs* (1987), relates how French sportsmen took their Brittanies to Scottish sporting estates and were so impressed by the cleverness of the local collies that they mated their dogs to them. They would have been seeking intelligence, trainability and responsiveness. Around 1826, the Marquis of Huntley angered the setter owners using Findhorn by utilizing the clever collie of a local gamekeeper/shepherd as a sire for his setters. He put brains before beauty and got much abuse for it. The Kurds, I believe, put brains before beauty when producing the

Collie × GSD.

Red Merle Kelpie × Whippet lurcher.

khilasi, a cross between their Saluqi and a Kurdish sheepdog, to improve scenting ability and response to training.

Lurcher with 25 per cent Briard blood.

Lurcher Breeding

In his *The Dog* (1887), the celebrated writer 'Stonehenge' observed:

> When the lurcher is bred from the rough Scotch greyhound and the collie, or even the English sheep-dog, he is a very handsome dog, and even more so than either of his progenitors when pure… A poacher possessing such an animal seldom keeps him long, every keeper being on the look-out, and putting a charge of shot into him on the first opportunity.

He went on to state that poachers made great efforts to avoid their lurchers *looking like* just that, to avoid being shot. But it has to be said that another reason, down the years, for antipathy towards collie cross lurchers in country areas, quite apart from poaching, is that the collie blood can contribute to an undesired canine criminal interest in mutton!

Ted Walsh, in his *Lurchers and Longdogs* (1977), states that to create his sort of lurcher, he would start with two collie bitches, mate one to a Greyhound and the other to a Deerhound. The resultant pups would be fully tested and then culled, the survivors being inter-bred. The progeny of this mating would then be put back to a coursing Greyhound. This would have given him a preponderance of Greyhound blood but a fair input of collie blood too. It is absurd to declare precise percentages in products of mixed blood – genes work at random, not mathematically. Old

Pyrenean Sheepdog × Whippet lurcher.

Deerhound × Collie lurcher.

Collie Blood Prized

Old lurcher breeders too prized the blood of the Smithfield collie, a type fast disappearing from the lurcher scene, in numbers at least. The leggy, hairy Smithfield sheepdog has never been conserved here as such, but in Tasmania Graham Rigby has some splendid specimens. Just as the Australian stumpy-tailed cattle dog is a descendant of the dogs once common in Cumberland, and still are so in the Black Mountain area near Hereford, these Tasmanian dogs originated here. Graham has had the breed for over twenty years. The first Smithfields to go to Australia were called black bobtails, big rough-coated, square-bodied dogs, with heads like wedges, a white frill round the neck and 'saddleflap' ears. Graham is not a lurcher man, but any lurcher breeder seeking this blood might find the expense of obtaining his stock worth every penny.

In his *Hunters All* of 1986, Brian Plummer paid tribute to the collie lurchers of the likes of my name-sake and Phil Lloyd. David's publication *Lambourn* of some thirty years ago contains the best collection of collie lurcher photos I have ever seen, well worth a study. What you will see there is not a type but a variety of types, depending on the mix. Once lurchers start looking like a *breed*, then there's a contradiction

lurcher breeders tended to put sagacity ahead of raw speed. The sighthound breeds are not renowned for their obedience or their brains; collies are.

Lurcher from a blend of Bearded Collie and Border Collie.

Beardie × Springer, specially bred by John and Mary Holmes, the canine film star Ben.

of his forefathers, who were horse-dealers. They obtained small coursing bitches from southern Ireland and mated them to the tricoloured cattle-herding collies found in the Highlands. These were, predictably, fearless, physically robust and immensely resolute dogs, used to working semi-wild cattle in every kind of weather, in testing terrain, and known to take hares and rabbits on the flatter fields. This blend of working collie skills and coursing dog prowess would has produced extremely competent pot-fillers.

Of course, you can get brainless collies, and long-backed, short-bodied ones, leading to weak loins, a bad feature in a lurcher, and sometimes a lack of lung room too – not good in a running dog. In addition, some collies are just too hyperactive to be valuable sporting dogs. Selection of breeding stock will always be the key to the successful production of lurchers, not the mix of ingredients. The dogs favoured for use in the Scottish deer forests were not valued because they were collies or collie crosses, but because they were outstanding dogs. If you want a dog with brains, biddability and a zeal for work, the collie offers all three. Every employer surely values a zeal for work! We have never truly valued our remarkable pastoral breeds. The Karst Shepherd or Illyrian Sheepdog is recognized in its homeland as a 'Slovene National Treasure' and regarded as part of the country's heritage; time perhaps for us to follow suit – we have more reason to celebrate our own pastoral breeds as they are world-class and worth every accolade.

in the making. The collie cross isn't meant to be the source of a distinct type, but evidence of an infusion of brains, biddability and a strong desire to work manifests itself in every hybrid carrying collie/sheepdog blood.

In an interesting letter to *Countryman's Weekly*, a Scottish reader, responding to an article of mine in that publication, outlined the lurcher-breeding policy

I think it is difficult to improve on the first cross Beardie/Border or Beardie/Border cross-bred. These I believe to be the best knock about, all round lurchers with ample speed, reasonable intelligence, excellent tractability and a really tough constitution. I am however open to comments about both half-bred and ¾ collie ¼ Greyhound hybrids.

Brian Plummer writing in *Sporting News* (1989)

THE FUTURE OF THE PASTORAL DOG

The townsman who knows the shepherd's dog only as he is to be seen, out of his true element, threading his confined way through crowded streets where sheep are not, can have small appreciation of his wisdom and his sterling worth. To know him properly, one needs to see him at work in a country where sheep abound, to watch him adroitly rounding up his scattered charges on a wide-stretching moorland, gathering the wandering wethers into close order and driving them before him in unbroken company to the fold; handling the stubborn flock in a narrow lane, or holding them in a corner of a field, immobile under the spell of his vigilant eye. He is at his best as a worker, conscious of the responsibility reposed in him; a marvel of generalship, gentle, judicious, slow to anger, quick to action; the priceless helpmeet of his master – the most useful member of all the tribe of dogs.

Robert Leighton, *The Complete Book of the Dog* (1922)

Remarkable Span

The dogs of the shepherds have profoundly influenced the use of dogs to support the activities of modern man, whether in the detection of banned substances or explosive devices, the support of disabled people who are deaf, blind or susceptible to illnesses such as diabetic comas, or in locating missing persons on remote hillsides. They provide companionship to lonely individuals across the developed world. They are quick to learn and eager to serve. They have influenced the companion dog scene right across the globe, with the beardie type perhaps providing the common dog of Europe from the Iberian Peninsula in the west to Hungary in the east, and the flock-guardian type protecting man's interests for centuries across the same span. Imposing breeds like the Tornjak of Croatia, the Central Asian Owtcharka, the Greek Sheepdog and the Transmontana Mastiff of Portugal must never be allowed to become extinct

The Tornjak of Croatia.

Central Asian Owtcharka.

BELOW: The Greek Sheepdog.

The Cao de Gado Transmontana of Portugal.

through our neglect. They may lack the glamour of the more fashionable breeds and the weight of words lavished on the sporting breeds, but they have supported man for longer and in more extreme conditions than any other type of dog. They have proved themselves as the ultimate in animal companions for man – and many of them still work with sheep! We owe them a secure future.

Surveying the Field

If you wish to have a quick 'snapshot' view of the state of the pastoral and working breeds of dog in Britain, then a visit to a championship dog show when these breeds are on display, is a good choice. The Bath Dog Show, held on a superb site, truly pastoral, for such dogs, on 'Pastoral and Working Breeds Day', in May 2013, gave me such an insight. The immediate impression was that the exotic breeds were there in greater numbers than our native ones. There were, not surprisingly, plenty of Rough Collies (128 entered), Bearded Collies (124), Shetland Sheepdogs (103) and Border Collies (82). But there were more

Belgian Shepherd Dogs (86 of all the breeds covered by this title) than Old English Sheepdogs (52), more Finnish Lapphunds (26) than our own Smooth Collies (18), and more Pyrenean Mountain Dogs (34), Briards (16), Estrela Mountain Dogs (18) and Hungarian Pulis (23) than our own Lancashire Heeler (9) and Cardiganshire Welsh Corgis (14).

Such a survey gives a much more immediate impression than say registration figures with the KC, and made a stark contrast with my memories of this show sixty years ago (as a teenage kennel-boy to the vet for this show, I was able to tour the annual shows with him, benefiting from his running commentary on the entry before us), when breeds from overseas were rare and our own breeds well supported. I welcome the foreign pastoral breeds but am concerned for our native ones. I was concerned too about the unsound physique of far too many of the entry. Over the years, I have attended seven World Dog Shows, innumerable championship shows, a wide variety of dog events, here and overseas; I see more unsound dogs now than ever before; in the show ring they look more glamorous and are more exhibitionist than the working dogs, but sound they are not.

Seeking Soundness

Studying this entry brought home to me how the general public regards the purebred dog as an emblem of good breeding, with the strange reverence for the pedigree prevailing. I expect to find truly functional dogs at a show with this collection of breeds; I am doubly disappointed to find unsound dogs on such a day. Taking time to study and then examine just a few of our native breeds gave a distinct impression of unsound front construction, poor movement, soft muscle and vision impaired by facial hair. These exhibits were mostly between one and seven years of age; when they were being bred the judges were already commenting on shortcomings in the breeds concerned. From 2008 to 2012, the critiques of championship show judges bemoaned the small eyes, weak jaws, thin muzzles, poor front movement, upright shoulders and short upper arms in Collies; short upper arms, lack of muscle tone, and exaggerated hind angulation in Beardies; dreadful and appalling movement, steep/straight upper arms, lack of muscle tone and a lack of drive on the move in Shelties; poor movement, weak hocks, being blindfolded by hair over the face, poor muscle tone and difficulty in locating the eyes in Bobtails. Old English Sheepdogs should be able to see – just as much as Corgis should have legs! Faults and flaws in these native breeds are simply not being addressed. This is very bad news for the breeds concerned, as well as future owners. It

ABOVE LEFT: Bobtails in the 1930s.

ABOVE RIGHT: Corgis in 1934.

Bobtails of the 1930s.

was good however to read in a 2013 (September) critique on the Rough Collie:

> I was positively surprised at the quality of the dogs. My wonderful breed has been too long a time in a very 'dark valley', so I was thrilled and happy to see the Standard has been read and understood. I want to thank you from the bottom of my heart for keeping the real Collie in your mind.

This judge acknowledged the lengthy period of low standards but recognized improvement. But without acknowledging the bad periods, no breed can move on.

Breeding for Quality

It is a sad fact that most dog breeders breed on the phenotype, that is, what the parents look like, rather than the genotype, that is, what genes are able to be passed on. Breeding living creatures can only ever be an exercise in genetics and breeders seeking to establish a line of consistent type must accept that every dog and bitch mating is a blending of two *families*, not just of a sire and a dam. The phrase that seems to lead to mistaken assumptions is the one that states that a puppy gets 50 per cent of its genes from the sire and 50 per cent from the dam. A better, more accurate, more valuable phrase is that a puppy gets 50 per cent of its genes *through* its sire and 50 per cent of its genes *through* its dam. That is why it is simply vital to know what stock is behind the parents of the puppy.

Breeding pedigree dogs is made more risky in Britain by the lack of reliable records. It is automatically assumed that the written pedigree is accurate whereas an alarming proportion of them are not. No dog has to be individually and irrevocably made identifiable by way of a tattoo or microchip. Judges in the show ring and owners of bitches only have someone's word that the dog before them in the ring or the sire being used for the service *is* the one named on the pedigree or put forward as such. It only needs one prolific breeder to be dishonest for the whole breeding record of a pedigree breed to be made unreliable. The written pedigree too is restricted to number, gender, colour and breed; there is no record of the strengths or faults of the dog on its pedigree despite

show critiques containing detailed comment being available after every major show.

Need for Health Checks

In Britain there are no unavoidable *mandatory* health checks on breeding stock, unlike the vast majority of other countries in which the pedigree dog is looked after by a kennel club. Health checks of course will never give a 100 per cent assurance of clear stock, a guarantee of faults being present or not, or be an indication of quality by themselves. There are bitches with worryingly high hip scores that regularly produce progeny with low hip scores. There is, however, no data on the hip health of the next generation from such dogs. No sensible breeder seeks dogs with perfect hips and eyes but lacking breed type or soundness of construction. Dog breeders should have access to sufficient data to enable them to make a balanced judgement. No humane person wants to produce dogs with a built-in likelihood of future lameness, blindness or deafness, but until quite recently no truly realistic attempts, on a proper scientific system, were being made nationally to seek a reduction in the chance of unhealthy or crippled dogs being bred. In 2013, the KC Genetics Centre at the Animal Health Trust began detailed studies into thirty-eight breeds, for the better understanding of the genetic structure and inherited diseases in all dogs. At last!

Beardie Initiative

I give praise to the Southern Counties Bearded Collie Club for their foresight and moral leadership in establishing their hip scoring scheme long before the KC/BVA Scheme switched entirely to hip scoring of all breeds. This visionary club set up a Special Open Class at their breed club shows for dogs certified clear of hip dysplasia or with a Breeders Letter under the old scheme or within a certain score range under the scoring scheme. This forward-looking action played a valuable role in getting owners to X-ray their dogs *and* publish the results. The wider scheme across the breed was also subsidized by the clubs in a praiseworthy campaign.

I would also like to see the Corgi breed clubs emulate the Dachshund and Basset Hound breed councils by responding to the research published by the Royal Veterinary College in 2013, that stated that dogs with longer backs relative to their legs are more in danger of suffering from intervertebral disc disease. If the ex-aggeration in the length of back and shortness of leg in Corgis continues unchecked, many dogs will suffer from painful and debilitating slipped discs. This is avoidable.

Healthy Breeding

A 2013 study at the University of California Veterinary Teaching Hospital used medical records from 27,000 dogs over fifteen years to study twenty-four known genetic disorders in dogs, such as cancer, dysplasia, cardiac problems, patellar luxation and epilepsy. Analysis indicated that 'genetic disorders were individual in their expression throughout the dog population' and that 'some genetic disorders were present with equal prevalence among all dogs in the study, regardless of purebred or mixed-breed status'. The show world immediately took this to prove that purebred dogs were no less healthy than crossbred ones; but which breeds contributed to the mix? This study actually found that ten of the disorders under scrutiny were more prominent in purebred dogs.

These were aortic stenosis, dilated cardiomyopathy, hypothyroidism, elbow dysplasia, intervertebral disc disease, atopy, dermatitis, bloat, cataracts, epilepsy and shunt. Fourth highest in intervertebral disc disease was the Pembroke Welsh Corgi; first in the elbow dysplasia category came the Bernese Mountain Dog, with the Anatolian Shepherd Dog in fifth highest. Mixed breeds showed the highest percentages affected by cruciate ligament ruptures, perhaps from the unwise crossing of two breeds with very different skeletal structures. The lesson from such a study is that breeding stock *must* be screened for those disorders where screening is possible.

Genetic Defects

If you consult authoritative books like Gough and Thomas's *Breed Predispositions to Disease in Dogs and Cats* (2004) and Clark and Stainer's *Medical and Genetic Aspects of Purebred Dogs* (1994), you can soon discern the worrying threat to the well-being of our pastoral and working breeds from faulty genes. In the Australian breeds, the cattle dog has recognized

Pembrokeshire Corgi of today.

Australian Shepherd of today.

ophthalmic problems such as cataracts, lens luxations and progressive retinal atrophy, with congenital portosystemic encephalopathy most common in this breed. Hereditary cerebellar abiotrophy has been diagnosed in Kelpies. A number of different eye problems have been reported in Australian Shepherds, together with hereditary deafness associated with the merle, piebald or extreme piebald genes. Rough Collies can suffer from dentition problems arising from too narrow a bottom jaw, micropthalmia from having small eyes and many veterinary dermatologists find the breed very susceptible to demodicosis, hydradivitis and nasal pyoderma, linking this with the heavy coat. The Bearded Collie has a low incidence of hereditary and congenital defects, although certain bloodlines produce dogs with a form of epilepsy. Breeders of Malinois have reported a high incidence of neoplasia; hypothyroid is of concern in the Tervueren and epilepsy has been reported but the breed is relatively free of hip dysplasia. The Shetland Sheepdog has the longest list of hereditary defects, with the breed having its own form of disproportionate dwarfism, often found when the parents themselves are unaffected. This list, across these breeds, sounds daunting, but the pastoral and working breeds suffer the least from such flawed genes.

One of the difficulties facing breeders of live animals, whether it's dogs or parakeets, is that professional scientists have made genetics a foreign language. The role of the expert surely is to make a complex subject more easily understood. Scientists are not good at this and yet display impatience when their work is misunderstood or not heeded. Dog breeders know too that there has never been a geneticist among the most successful of them. Geneticists are scientific advisors and breeding is an art as well as a science. They can advise us on how diseases that are inheritable are passed on. They can advise us on how physical and mental characteristics are likely to be passed on. But in the end the skill of the breeder lies in *selection* – the selection of breeding stock, the selection of parents and the selection of a breeding path to follow.

Selection of Breeding Stock

Selection based on the mere fact that the dam is a nice pet and ought to be bred from, or has won a couple of prizes and her pups will bring in income, or the future chosen sire is a current big winner, contributes little to a breed and even less to the reputation of the breeder concerned. No bitch should be bred from just because she is female and fertile. Puppies should, in the genuine dog-lover's world, never be produced to suit someone's bank balance; there are already too many unwanted and ill-kept dogs in Britain. For any breeder to mate his precious bitch to a dog just because the dog is currently winning well is sheer folly. It assumes that the judges rewarding the sire are knowledgeable and unbiased – but are they? And even if the sire-to-be is a worthy champion, what *family* does he come from? The genes of his ancestors will come *through* him.

Until we have better data from approved national schemes, selection of breeding stock will rely on the researching skills of each individual breeder. With the accuracy of the written pedigree never being checked by the Kennel Club, just the breeder's word accepted, with no mandatory health clearances, no national dog identification scheme and no information of breeding value on the written pedigree, coupled with untrained judges rewarding unworthy dogs, any breeder faces an uphill battle in the pursuit of breeding better dogs. The appointment of a geneticist for each breed and the appointment of a breed archivist to verify pedigrees, together with a grading system to establish just how good each dog is, would help enormously. Sire ranking lists are available to livestock breeders but not yet to dog breeders – how long can that continue? It is just not good enough to rate a sire by how many champions he has sired; who is testing his offspring for genetic quality?

Novice breeders may well despair of finding the essential data on which to base their breeding programme. Veteran breeders usually know that dogs bearing this particular affix display certain good qualities, whilst those bearing another one feature other complementary ones. Shrewd breeders usually utilize an older stud dog, his track record can at least be examined. There is financial sense in a small breeder not kennelling his own stud dog but using outside blood to a well-researched plan. Long-established kennels in every breed often develop their own kennel signature or kennel type. When this conforms precisely to the Breed Standard, it provides valuable stable genetic material. But when one influential breeder is producing untypical stock, however

attractive or successful, it is most important for the novice breeder to detect this. In the end, the Breed Standard is the breeding blueprint, a design for the future product. Knowledge of it and, more important still, an understanding of it, is essential for the successful breeding to type in a purebred breed of dog.

Morphological Changes

All over the world there are enthusiasts at work, pioneering their particular breed or type of dog. Most work with established breeds, ideally in pursuit of enhancement. Some work towards kennel club recognition for their favoured type; others are seeking variations on breeds already recognized, some are seeking to avoid the inbred or exaggerated features of accepted breeds and many just promote superlative heeling or herding dogs and don't give a damn about kennel clubs. They are mostly nonconformists and often deserve our admiration. As Ralph Waldo Emerson put it, in the mid-nineteenth century: 'Whoso would be a man must be a nonconformist.' The slavish adherence to a closed gene pool is not always wise and it takes a nonconformist, as Emerson hinted, to be prepared to stand alone. The recognition of a breed usually relies on vigorous promotion by a group of enthusiasts rather than vision from a kennel club. Such enthusiasts have to be careful to respect type in their chosen breed, not alter its appearance to suit *their* concept.

The fanciers of Shiloh Shepherds, white GSDs and Saarloos Wolfdogs are only doing what our distant ancestors did – seeking an unexaggerated, soundly constructed, virile breed and not just marching in step with the others. I mourn the loss of the impressive GSDs of my youth, displaying a level topline and a hindquarter that would not disgrace a Foxhound. Half a century ago, some GSD breeders decided to lengthen the back, despite the evidence from America and experience from service dog users. Breeding for excessive angulation in the breed too has combined to produce poor movement, cow hocks, spinal problems and disc-size difficulties. Once, when working in London thirty years ago, I walked behind a Met police-GSD and its handler for the best part of a mile. The hind movement of the dog was simply appalling. The dog reflected the faulty thinking in the breed at that time; time for a nonconformist, a kicker against consensus, to step forward!

Shiloh Shepherd.

BELOW: *GSD with the longer back.*

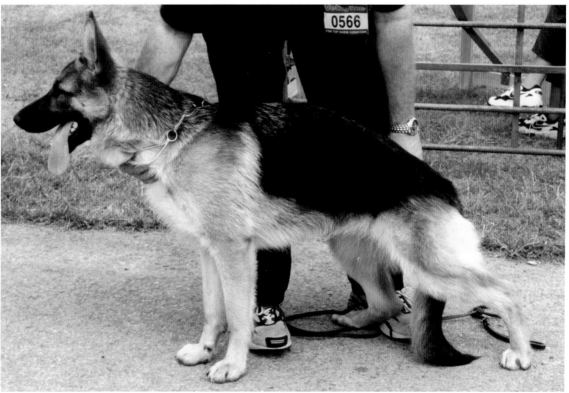

Perpetuation of Type

At a time when breed health, breed purity and instructions to show-ring judges are all receiving much merited attention, there is one extremely important aspect of pedigree dog breeding and showing which still needs emphasizing. It would be sad if we lost breeds to perpetual and prolonged inbreeding, more than regrettable if we lost breeds to rogue genes and monstrous if judges rewarded exhibits displaying harmful exaggerations. But sad, regrettable and monstrous too if our precious breeds are bred to the wrong template; the show ring has changed a number of breeds, not for the better; fashion, fad and pressure from influential kennels can impose a changed type on a breed. Gradual changes, viewed initially as slight exaggerations, develop into bigger ones, reactions to docking in breeds not previously docked and 'the fashion of the day' can all contribute to the classic fundamental type in a distinctive breed being reshaped. This reshaping can be whimsical in origin, untraditional in effect, even harmful in its manifestation, but as time passes, can become acceptable. Time to send for breed architects, experts on safe structures, canine morphologists. The shape of a breed, its physical form or morphology, should result from its functional design, be protected by its Breed Standard, guarded by its breed clubs and treasured across the generations of breed devotees as its unique identity. But all too often breed points become breed exaggerations as close breeding overplays its hand.

Responsibility of Judges

Exhibiting dogs can be a rewarding pastime, but the fashions involved should not provide an arena for self-promotion. Dogs should not be made uncomfortable in the ring and breed characteristics should be valued and exemplified, not subsumed into a common practice. The show ring has one huge, huge disadvantage, whatever the ruling fashion: it cannot reveal the dog's capability. We must be vigilant if we are not to lose character, determination, working prowess, instinctive behaviour, individuality, courage, intelligence and fortitude. A handsome dog without character has cosmetic appeal and is likely to win in the show ring but for me it has no breeding potential. I would place character ahead of any other virtues. Style is for showing off; fashion is blind copying.

It is worth remembering the extraordinary racehorse in America that triumphed over serious defects by sheer determination. Seabiscuit achieved thirty-three race wins, thirteen track records at eight tracks over six distances, including a world record over half a mile and a track record over twice that distance. But he was a stunted colt, with asymmetrical knees and permanently damaged legs. Even a ruptured suspensory ligament, spelling early euthanasia for other horses did not halt his career. Interestingly his jockey had been abandoned at a racecourse as a child and was blind in one eye. The genes for character and determination are those that provided us with the breeding stock from which we now plan to produce perfection of form.

Far too many breeds of pastoral and working dog are now fashioned by show criteria but we would be more than stupid if we bred solely for looks, especially the 'fashion of the day'. The working dog fraternity might claim that that's what's been happening for a century in the show dog world, a world in which a dog that is useless can still have high value. Commendably, the KC has a Show Border Collie Herding Test to test the natural herding qualities they were originally bred for; where is such a test for other native pastoral breeds? In the show ring appearance rules, understandably; but who wants, even as a companion dog, one that has no brains and no character? Not being an exhibitor I can choose my next pup on how I think its character might develop, though I must admit that I hope the pup I choose will become a handsome adult. But those purebred dog breeders who rely on the pet market for valuable income *need* characters, pups with substance. Fashions come and go; but favouring style over substance in companion dogs makes no sense at all and threatens the whole future of dogs, especially in our increasingly busy, evermore urban world.

Public Protection

For the pedigree dog to flourish it's important for both the dog and the purchasing public to be protected. There is a misunderstanding amongst the general public over the use of the word 'pedigree' when used to describe a dog's breeding. Strictly speaking it means having a recorded line of descent, especially one showing purebreeding. But the possession of a pedigree (a piece of paper) has come to mean, for many people, a sign of excellence, a guarantee of quality. This is undeserved and the public is being misled. First of all, the pedigree form or registration certificate, which comes from the dog being registered with the Kennel Club, is just a birth certificate, the information on it supplied by the breeder alone.

The American Kennel Club has introduced random DNA testing to try to deal with the problem of falsified pedigrees. There have been cases in the UK where kennels have supplied a different stud dog to one specifically requested to service a bitch, and have subsequently falsified the paperwork. It is not wise to rely entirely on breeder honesty. Significantly, there is nothing on the pedigree form but a list of ancestors, no indication of genetic health, no record of the quality of the ancestors listed and no legal accountability should the information on the form later prove to be inaccurate.

At the time the Kennel Club was formed it was understandable for the pedigree form to be merely a certified record of breeding, but nowadays we have the information technology available to do so much more. Yet the pedigree form still only contains lists of ancestors. We know that certain dogs in certain breeds are carriers of inheritable conditions. Disreputable breeders conceal this, but how is the general public seeking a purebred pup to discover such a risk? The pedigree form needs expanding – to cover genetic health, not just be a birth certificate. I do wish that our KC would stop posing as the first base for *all things canine*, and concentrate on setting an example to the whole dog-owning world through the exemplary stewardship of pedigree dogs and the show world. That is certainly the view too of the Canine Alliance, now questioning the effectiveness of the KC in attempting to speak for *all* canines and their welfare, so much better handled by the admirable Dogs' Trust. There are signs that the championship show world is beginning to crumble, with the KC declining to acknowledge these signs. They need to concentrate on what their founding fathers intended them to do – ensuring that merit in the show ring is rewarded. They need to assert supreme custodianship much more energetically.

Safeguarding the Breeds
In the very best interests of the pastoral breeds, our native breeds especially, it is vitally important for all

the agencies involved: breeders, breed clubs, breed councils, judges, and in particular, the governing body – the Kennel Club – to observe their remit, respect their basic function and *work together*. Writers too have a role to play as I have attempted in this book. The general public is unlikely ever to see the critical comments of dog show judges. They are only set out in specific 'dog papers' such as *Dog World* and *Our Dogs* that are only read by dog show devotees. This could conceal from the man in the street serious breed faults, some of them inbuilt, in a number of pedigree breeds, and from non-show-going dog owners seeking a companion dog from a pedigree pastoral breed. This I have striven to rectify. I could be accused of condemning certain popular breeds by stressing the adverse criticisms of them in the show ring. But these critiques are important, valid and have been made by breed experts, not writers. The dog-owning public can end up with high veterinary bills as well as needless heartache if they are not made

English shepherd with his Beardie, 1920.

aware of what the experts are reporting to the specialist dog press. The mantra of 'my breed – right or wrong' may represent breed loyalty and is fine when all's well, but is truly delusional when the welfare and long-term future of a breed is threatened. Honesty is not just the best policy but simply essential in this matter. We need the humility and honesty of the shepherds in our approach to the future of these precious breeds.

Honouring the Work of the Shepherds

Overseas, show dogs are routinely graded in order of merit, from 'excellent' downwards, and their grading can be easily seen on a fuller registration certificate. Why not here? If the merit of functional dogs is to be decided in the show ring, let's get it right. Winning dogs get bred from; unworthy winners produce reduced value in a breed. Once away from the pastures or their place of work, these dogs are especially vulnerable – to human greed, vanity and the ugly desire to win – often with the title of champion not truly earned and even if the breed as a whole is undermined. No humble shepherd is there any more to breed them honestly, for working value, for physical soundness and, perhaps most important of all, for their spiritual happiness when exercising a strong innate desire to work, to be useful, to feel valued.

All over the populated world there are still dogs used to assist farmers with cattle, sheep, goats and even yaks, with no breed title to distinguish them. Further afield, I have seen cattle dogs with the Masai in Kenya looking a little like Smooth Collies. The Bedouin use a sheepdog quite like a Border Collie to control their big flocks. When serving with Ghurkas I have picked their brains, especially the Gurungs, about pastoral dogs in Nepal. They referred to dogs by their employment, not by a title or size or coat colour, although certain regions clearly made use of dogs only found there. Their dogs were never prized for their looks alone. They had to earn their keep.

Have *breeds* become too important? In some breeds, breed type is valued more than soundness. Primitive shepherds never created breeds – they had to rely on performance. Breed purity is now a *handicap* for the domestic dog. We really must start to focus on *purpose* – what each breed was developed to *do* – not just what they have been bred to look like. We are ignoring what peasant-breeders learned the hard way. It is not a human right for us to use dogs in any way that we choose. They are subject creatures

OPPOSITE PAGE
TOP: Found *by Richard Ansdell, 1871.*

BOTTOM RIGHT: Waiting for Master *by Arthur Wardle, 1885.*

The Rescue, 1834, *by Landseer.*

vulnerable to our whims and fancies. This bestows a heavy responsibility on dog owners and especially on dog breeders in this more enlightened century. We would be failing each breed if we didn't respect its need to be healthy, sound and much more like its distant ancestors than some of the comparatively new moulds inflicted upon a number of famous old breeds and on some more recently developed ones. Favouring a breed simply *has* to mean favouring a better future for it.

We are at last beginning to see the importance of genetic health; we have finally accepted the need for better-informed, more knowledgeable judges so that the best breeding stock is identified. We are starting to accept that indirect cruelty is caused by the wilful exaggeration of physical points, often from the intentional misinterpretation of a Breed Standard by misguided faddists and, after over a century of breeding for appearance, we are learning to value physical and mental *soundness* in our precious breeds of dogs. Producing breeds of dog meets human desires; producing soundness in dogs meets their needs. Surely in the twenty-first century we can *at last* start thinking of their needs ahead of inflicting our selfish indulgences on them. There has to be a strong moral element to pedigree dog breeding and, where the pastoral and working breeds are concerned, enormous respect for the lowly shepherds who bequeathed

these quite remarkable animals to our committed care. These dogs have enriched our lives; now we must enrich theirs.

THE ANATOMY OF THE DOG

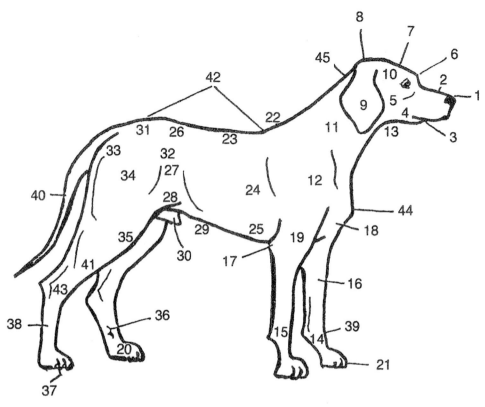

1. Nose	24. Ribs
2. Muzzle	25. Chest
3. Lips	26. Loin
4. Flews	27. Flank
5. Cheek	28. Groin
6. Stop	29. Belly or abdomen
7. Foreface	30. Sheath
8. Peak or occiput	31. Croup
9. Ear	32. Hip
10. Brow	33. Rump
11. Neck	34. Thigh (upper) (first)
12. Shoulder	35. Stifle or knee
13. Dewlap	36. Dewclaw
14. Pastern or metacarpus	37. Toenail
15. Wrist or carpus	38. Metatarsus or hind pastern
16. Forearm	39. Knee or manus
17. Elbow	40. Tail or stern
18. Brisket	41. Thigh (lower) (second)
19. Upper arm	42. Topline
20. Foot	43. Hock
21. Toes or digits	44. Sternum or breast bone
22. Withers	43. Crest
23. Back	

GLOSSARY OF TERMS

Action Movement; the way a dog moves

Angulation The degree of slope or angle of the shoulder blade in the forequarters and in the sharp angles of the inter-related bones in the hindquarters – thigh, hock and metacarsus

Back Area of the dog between the withers and the root of tail

Balanced Symmetrically proportioned

Banana-backed having a convex curve over the topline from withers to hocks

Barrel hocks Hocks turned outwards, resulting in feet with inward-pointing toes (similar to bandy legs)

Barrel-ribbed Well-rounded rib cage

Blanket The coat colour on the back from the withers to the rump

Blaze A white patch of hair in the centre of the face, usually between the eyes

Bloom The sheen of a coat in prime condition

Bodied-up Well developed in maturity

Borzoi head Skull without a stop and elongated, narrow jaw

Brace A pair, a couple

Breed points Characteristic physical features of a breed, often exaggerated by breed fanciers

Brisket The part of the body in front of the chest

Button ear The ear flap folding forward, usually towards the eye

Cat foot The rounded, shorter-toed, compact type of foot

Champion (Ch) A dog achieving this level of merit under KC-approved judges

Championship (Ch) Show KC-approved dog show where the best exhibits in each gender can win a Challenge Certificate (CC)

Chest The area from the brisket up to the belly, underneath the dog

Chiselled Clean cut, especially in the head

Chopping Exaggerated forward movement through abbreviated reach

Close-coupled Comparatively short from the last rib to the leading edge of the thigh

Coarse Lacking refinement

Cobby Short-bodied, compact in torso

Conformation The relationship between the physical appearance of a dog and the imagined perfect mould for that breed or type

Couples Connection of hindquarters to torso

Cow hocks Hocks turned towards each other (similar to knock-knees)

Crossbred Having parents from two different breeds

Croup (rump) Region of the pelvic girdle formed by the sacrum and the surrounding tissue

Dewlaps Loose, pendulous skin under the throat

Down at pastern Weak or faulty metacarpus set at an angle to the vertical

Drive A solid thrust from the hindquarters, denoting strength of locomotion

Drop ear The ends of the ear folded or falling forward

Elbows out Elbows positioned away from the body

Even bite Meeting of both sets of front teeth at edges with no overlap

Feathering Distinctly longer hair on rear line of legs, back of ears and along underside of tail

Flank The side of the body between the last rib and the hip

Flat-sided A noticeable lack of roundness in the rib cage

Forearm Part of foreleg extending from elbow to pastern

Forequarters Front part of dog excluding head and neck

Front Forepart of body viewed from the head-on position

Furnishings Long hair on ears, trailing edge of legs and under part of tail

Gait Pattern or rhythm of footsteps

Gallop The fastest gait; a four-beat rhythm, propelling the dog at great speed, with all four feet off the ground during the seeking of sheer pace

Hackney action High-stepping action in the front legs (named after the carriage horse)

Hare foot A longer, narrower foot, usually with an elongated third digit

Haunch Rump or buttock; bones of that area

Height Distance or measurement from the withers to ground contact in the standing dog

Hock Joint on the hind leg between the knee and the fetlock; the heel in humans

Hound or gay tail Tail carried on high, above the rump

Jacket Coat or pelage of the dog

Knee The joint attaching fore-pastern and forearm

Layback The angle of the shoulder compared to the vertical

Lay of shoulder Angled position of the shoulder

Leather The flap of the ear

Leggy A dog with legs noticeably longer than its breed mates

Level back The line of the back is horizontal, parallel to the ground

Level bite (pincer-bite) The front teeth of both jaws meeting exactly

Loaded shoulders When the shoulder blades are pushed outwards by over-muscled development (often confused in the show ring with well-muscled shoulders on a supremely fit dog)

Lumber Superfluous flesh and/or cumbersome movement arising from lack of condition or faulty construction

Mask Dark shading on the foreface, most usually on a tan or red-tan dog

Moving close When the hind limbs move too near each other

Occiput The peak of the skull

Out at elbow *See* elbows out

Over-reaching Faulty gait in which the hind feet pass the fore feet on the outside due to hyper-angulation in the hindquarters

Overshot jaw The front upper set of teeth overlapping the lower set

Oversprung ribs Exaggerated curvature of rib cage

Pace Rate of movement, usually speed

Padding A Hackney action due to lack of angulation in forequarters

Paddling A heavy, clumsy, threshing action in the forelegs with the feet too wide of the body on the move

Pastern Lowest section of the leg, below the knee or hock

Pedigree The dog's record of past breeding, usually five generations back; sometimes used as shorthand for purebreeding

Pelage Coat of hair or fur on a mammal

Pile Dense undercoat of softer hair

Pincer bite *See* level bite

Plaiting (or weaving or crossing) The movement of one front leg across the path of the other front leg on the move

Prick ear Ear carriage in which the ear is erect and usually pointed at tip

Racy Lightly built and leggier than normal in the breed

Ribbed-up Long last rib

Roach- or carp-backed A back arched convexly along the spine, especially in the hindmost section

Root of the tail Where the tail joins the dog's back

Rough-haired With a broken-coated, longer-haired but still close-fitting jacket

Saddle A solid area of colour extending over the shoulders and back

Saddle-backed A sagging back from extreme length or weak musculature

Scissor bite The outer side of the lower incisors touches the inner side of the upper incisors

Second thigh The (calf) muscle between the stifle and the hock in the hindquarters

Self-coloured A solid or single-coloured coat

Set on Where the root of the tail is positioned in the hindquarters

Shelly Weedy and narrow-boned, lacking substance

Short-coupled *See* close-coupled

Shoulder layback *See* layback

Sickle-hocked Lack of extension in the hock on the rear drive

Slab-sided Flat ribs, with too little spring from the spinal column

Snipiness Condition in which the muzzle is too pointed, weak and lacking strength right to the nose end

Soundness Correct physical conformation and movement

Splay feet Flat, open-toed, widely spread feet

Spring of rib The extent to which the ribs are well-rounded

Stacked Static posture in the ring before the judge, to show conformation

Stance Standing position, usually when formally presented

Standard The written word picture of a breed

Stifle The joint in the hind leg between the upper and lower thigh, equating to the knee in man, sadly weak in some breeds

Stop The depression at the junction of the nasal bone and the skull between the eyes

Straight-hocked Lacking in angulation of the hock joint

Straight-shouldered Straight up and down shoulder blades, lacking angulation or layback

Strain A family line throwing offspring of a set type

Strong-eyed A feature of a header/stalker sheepdog in which the dog fixes its intense stare at sheep to compel their obedience

Symmetry Balance and correct proportions of anatomy

Throatiness An excess of loose skin at the front of the neck

Tied at the elbows When the elbows are set too close under the body, thereby restricting freedom of movement

Topline The dog's outline from just behind the withers to the rump

Trot A rhythmical two-beat gait, with hind- and forequarters working in unison

Tuck-up Concave underline of torso, between last rib and hindquarters, lack of discernible belly

Type Characteristic attributes distinguishing a breed or strain of a breed

Undershot Malformation of the jaw, projecting the lower jaw and incisors beyond the upper (in puppies with this condition, they appear to be grinning)

Upper arm The foreleg bone between the shoulder blade and the elbow

Upright shoulders Too straight an angle in the shoulder joint, also called steep in shoulders, usually giving a shortened front stride and a short-necked appearance

Variety A subdivision of a breed

Well-angulated Well-defined angle in the thigh-hock-metatarsus area

Well-coupled Well made in the area from the withers to the hip bones

Well-knit Neat and compactly constructed and connected

Well-laid Soundly placed and correctly angled

Well-laid back shoulders Oblique shoulders ideally slanting at 45 degrees to the ground

Well let-down Hocks close to the ground; having low hocks as a result of long muscles in what in humans is the calf. (This is an often misunderstood term; in both racehorses

Sheep, their lambs and resting – but still watchful – dog by George W. Horlor, 1877.

and sporting dogs, the seeking of long cannon bones led to the use of this expression. It was never intended to promote short rear pasterns)

Well ribbed-up Ribs neither too long nor too wide apart; compact

Well-sprung With noticeably rounded ribs

Well tucked-up Absence of visible abdomen

Wheel back Excessive roaching, marked arching over the loins

Wire-haired A coat of bristly crispness to the touch, hard in texture

Withers The highest point on the body of a standing dog, immediately behind the neck, above the shoulders

Yawing (crabbing) Body moving at an angle to the legs' line of movement

North country cowherd of 1901– with old-type Beardie.

BIBLIOGRAPHY

Appleton, D., *The Dog Business* (1960)

Ash, E.C., *The Practical Dog Book* (1930)

Baker, T., *The Collie: its Show Points* (1899)

Barton, F. Townend, *Non-Sporting Dogs* (Everett & Co., 1905)

Burns, M., and Fraser, M.N., *Genetics of the Dog – the Basis of Successful Breeding* (Olive & Boyd, 1966)

Clark, N.R., *A Dog Called Blue, The Australian Cattle Dog and the Stumpy Tail Cattle Dog 1840–2000* (WriteLight Pty Ltd., 2003)

Clark, R. and Stainer, J. (eds), *Medical and Genetic Aspects of Purebred Dogs* (Forum, 1994)

Clutton-Brock, J., *Domesticated Animals from Early Times* (Heinemann, 1981)

Cole, R.W., *An Eye For A Dog* (Dogwise, USA, 2004)

Collis, Joyce, *All About the Bearded Collie* (Pelham Books, 1989)

Combe, I., *Herding Dogs, Their Origins & Development in Britain* (Faber, 1987)

Compton, H., *The Twentieth Century Dog (Non-Sporting)* (Grant Richards, 1904)

Coppinger, R. and L., *Dogs – a New Understanding of Canine Origin, Behavior, & Evolution* (Scribner, 2001)

Croxton Smith, A., *About Our Dogs* (Ward Lock, 1947)

Csanyi, V., *If Dogs Could Talk – Exploring the Canine Mind* (Sutton, 2006)

Cummins, B. and Lore, P., *Pyrenean Partners, Herding and Guarding Dogs in the French Pyrenees* (Detselig Enterprises Ltd, Calgary, 2006)

Dalziel, H., *British Dogs* (1888)

Davies, C.J., *The Kennel Handbook* (1905)

Davies, C.J., *The Theory and Practice of Breeding for Type and its Application to the Breeding of Dogs* (c.1930)

Dickie, J., *The Dog* (1933)

Dog World, Sep 2013

Drury, W.D., *British Dogs* (Upcott Gill, 1903)

Duconte, C.M. and Sabouraud, J.A., *Pyrenean Dogs* (Kaye & Ward, 1982)

Edwards, S., *Cynographia Britannica* (1800)

Ekvall, R., 'Role of the Dog in Tibetan Monastic Society', *Central Asiatic Journal*, Vol. 3 (1963)

Elliott, N. and P., *The Complete German Shepherd Dog* (Kaye & Ward, 1983)

Evans, T., *The Welsh Corgi* (Watmoughs, 1948)

Forder, J. and E., *Hill Shepherd* (Frank Peters Publishing, 1989)

Gardner, W., *About the Border Terrier* (1991)

Gough, A. and Thomas, A., *Breed Dispositions to Disease in Dogs and Cats* (Blackwell, 2004)

Gray, T., *The Corgi* (Chambers, 1952)

Gwynne-Jones, O., *The Shetland Sheepdog* (Nicholson & Watson, 1958)

Halsall, E., *Sheepdogs – My Faithful Friends* (Patrick Stephens, 1980)

Hamilton Smith, C., *The Naturalist's Library*, Vol. X (1840)

Hancock, D., *Old Farm Dogs* (Shire Publications, 1999)

Harding Cox, Major, *Dogs and I* (Hutchinson, 1928)

Harmar, H., *Showing & Judging Dogs* (John Gifford/Arco, 1977)

Holmes, J., *The Farmer's Dog* (Popular Dogs, 1975)

Horner, T., *All About the Bull Terrier* (1973)

Horowitz, G., *The Alsatian (German Shepherd Dog)* (Our Dogs, 1934)

Hubbard, C.L.B., *Working Dogs of the World* (Sidgwick & Jackson, 1947)

Hubbard, C.L.B., *The Observer's Book of Dogs* (Warne, 1947)

Hubbard, C.L.B., *The Pembrokeshire Corgi Handbook* (Nicholson & Watson, 1952)

Hubbard, C.L.B., *The Cardiganshire Corgi Handbook* (Nicholson & Watson, 1952)

Hutchinson, W. (ed.), *Hutchinson's Dog Encyclopaedia* (1934)

Iley, T., *Sheepdogs at Work* (Dalesman Books, 1979)

Jackson, F., *Dictionary of Canine Terms* (The Crowood Press, 1995)

Jesse, G., *Researches into the History of the British Dog* (1866)

Kaleski, R., *Australian Barkers & Biters* (Endeavor Press, Sydney, 1914)

Kennel Control Council, Victoria, Australia, *Dogs of Australia* (1973)

The Kennel Gazette, Feb 1884, Mar 1888, June 1888, July 1888, Feb 1889, June 1890, Nov 1890, Apr 1891, Jan 1891, June 1891, June 1892, Jan 1893, Nov 1893

Kohl, J.G., *Journeys in South Russia* (1841)

Lee, R., *Modern Dogs of Great Britain and Ireland (Non-Sporting Division)* (Horace Cox, 1894)

Leighton, R., *The Complete Book of the Dog* (Cassell, 1922).

Leighton, R., *The New Book of the Dog* (Cassell, 1912)

Lister-Kaye, C., *The Welsh Corgi* (Popular Dogs, 1968)

Marples, T., *Prize Dogs* (1908)

Martin, W.C.L., *The History of the Dog* (Charles Knight & Co., 1845)

Moore, D., *Foxhounds* (1981)

Moorhouse, S., *The British Sheepdog* (Witherby, 1950)

Murray, J.E., *A Summer in the Pyrenees* (1837)

Osborne, M., *The Popular Collie* (Popular Dogs, 1960)

Our Dogs magazine, Nov 1998

Pasco, L.J., *The Working Sheepdog* (*Sheep Breeder* magazine, Chicago, 1937)

Plummer, B., *Hunters All* (1986)

Portman-Graham, R., *The Practical Guide to Showing Dogs* (1956)

Pryor, F., *Farmers in Prehistoric Britain* (The History Press, 2011)

Pullar, P., *Rural Portraits – Scottish Native Farm Animals, Characters and Landscapes* (Langford, 2003)

Puxley, W.L., *Collies & Sheep-dogs* (Williams & Norgate, 1948)

Pyne, W.H., *The Costumes of Great Britain* (1808)

Robinson, R., *Genetics for Dog Breeders* (1990)

Rohrer, A., and Flamholtz, C., *The Tibetan Mastiff – Legendary Guardian of the Himalayas* (1989)

Ruddle, M., *Dogs Through History* (Denlinger, 1987)

Sarkany, P. and Ocsag, I., *Dogs of Hungary* (Corvina Press, 1977)

Schwabacher, Joseph, *The Popular Alsatian* (Popular Dogs, 1959)

Serpell, J. (ed.), *The Domestic Dog – its evolution, behaviour and interaction with people* (Cambridge University Press, 1995)

Shaw, V., *The Illustrated Book of the Dog* (Cassell, 1879)

Shelley, E.M., *Hunting Big Game with Dogs in Africa* (1924)

Smythe, R.H., *The Dog – Structure and Movement* (Foulsham, 1970)

Smythe, R.H., *Judging Dogs* (Gifford, 1972)

Smythe, R.H., *The Conformation of the Dog* (Popular Dogs, 1957)

Spira, H., *Canine Technology* (Harper Collins, 1983)

Stables, G., *Our Friend the Dog* (Dean & Son, 1907)

Stanley, A., *Search & Rescue Dogs* (Howell Book House, 2002)

'Stonehenge', *The Dogs of the British Isles* (1878)

'Stonehenge', *The Dog* (1887)

Strebel, R.H., *Die Deutschen Hunde* (1904)

Tahtakilic, L. and Mellor, M., *The Kangal Dog of Turkey* (Towcester, 2009)

Thurston, M., *The Lost History of the Canine Race* (Andrews and McMeel, 1996)

Tilley, H.A., *The Old English Sheepdog* (Shepton Mallet, 1972)

Toulson, S., *The Droves* (Shire Publications, 1980)

Waldron, J. (ed.), *The Millennium Book, The Southern Counties Bearded Collie Club* (2000)

Walsh, T., *Lurchers and Longdogs* (1977)

Watson, J., *The Dog Book* (1906)

Webb, H., *Dogs: their points, whims, instincts and peculiarities* (Dean & Son, 1883)

Wendt, L.M., *Dogs: A Historical Journey* (Howell Book House, 1996)

Weston Bell, E., *The Scottish Deerhound* (1892)

Whitney, L.F., *How to Breed Dogs* (Orange Judd, 1947)

Williams, C., *Dogs and their Ways* (1863)

Williams, M.R., *Advanced Labrador Breeding* (1988)

Willis, M., *Practical Genetics for Dog Breeding* (1992)

Wimhurst, C.G.E., *The Book of Working Dogs* (Muller, 1967)

Wynn, M.B., *The History of the Mastiff* (William Loxley, 1886)

Youath, W., *The Dog* (1854)

Zeuner, F., *A History of Domesticated Animals* (Hutchinson, 1963)

Hot sheepdog in water trough.

INDEX

RIGHT: *Cream GSD.* NICOLA FLYNN